Fi...

12 Va.

Kershaw

12 Va.

41 Va.

Va.

Mahone

To
Fredericksburg

HANCOCK

Brock Road

Brock Run

Scale in feet

0   1000

George Skoch

D0847915

A FIRE IN THE
Wilderness

A FIRE IN THE
Wilderness

THE FIRST BATTLE BETWEEN
ULYSSES S. GRANT
AND ROBERT E. LEE

JOHN REEVES

PEGASUS BOOKS
NEW YORK LONDON

A FIRE IN THE WILDERNESS

Pegasus Books, Ltd.
148 West 37th Street, 13th Floor
New York, NY 10018

ISBN: 978-1-64313-700-1

10 9 8 7 6 5 4 3 2 1

Printed in the United States of America
Distributed by Simon & Schuster
www.pegasusbooks.com

To Justine with gratitude

CONTENTS

Those hot, sad, wrenching times—the army of volunteers, all States,—or North or South—the wounded, suffering, dying—the exhausting, sweating summers, marches, battles, carnage—those trenches hurriedly heap'd by the corpse-thousands, mainly unknown—Will the America of the future—will this vast rich Union ever realize what itself cost, back there after all?—those hecatombs of battle-deaths—Those times of which, O far-off reader, this whole book is indeed finally but a reminiscent memorial from thence by me to you?

—Walt Whitman

Organization of Union forces under Lieutenant General Ulysses S. Grant on the morning of May 4, 1864.

ARMY OF THE POTOMAC

Major General George G. Meade

SECOND ARMY CORPS

Major General Winfield S. Hancock

FIRST DIVISION

Brigadier General Francis C. Barlow

SECOND DIVISION

Brigadier General John Gibbon

THIRD DIVISION

Major General David B. Birney

FOURTH DIVISION

Brigadier General Gershom Mott

Major General Gouverneur K. Warren

FIRST DIVISION
Brigadier General Charles Griffin

SECOND DIVISION
Brigadier General John C. Robinson

THIRD DIVISION
Brigadier General Samuel W. Crawford

FOURTH DIVISION
Brigadier General James Wadsworth

SIXTH ARMY CORPS
Major General John Sedgwick

FIRST DIVISION
Brigadier General Horatio G. Wright

SECOND DIVISION
Brigadier General George W. Getty

THIRD DIVISION
Brigadier General James B. Ricketts

NINTH ARMY CORPS (reporting directly to Gen. Grant)
Major General Ambrose E. Burnside

FIRST DIVISION
Brigadier General Thomas G. Stevenson

SECOND DIVISION
Brigadier General Robert B. Potter

THIRD DIVISION
Brigadier General Orlando B. Willcox

FOURTH DIVISION
Brigadier General Edward Ferrero

CAVALRY CORPS
Major General Philip H. Sheridan

FIRST DIVISION
Brigadier General Alfred T. A. Torbert

SECOND DIVISION
Brigadier General David McMurtrie Gregg

THIRD DIVISION
Brigadier General James H. Wilson

ONE

The Ghost of Stonewall Jackson

"It is an approved maxim in war, never to do what the enemy wishes you to do, for this reason alone, that he desires it. A field of battle, therefore, which he has previously studied and reconnoitered, should be avoided, and double care should be taken where he has had time to fortify or entrench."

—Napoleon Bonaparte

The Army of the Potomac began to move during the early morning hours of Wednesday, May 4, 1864. The general-in-chief of the Union Army, Lieutenant General Ulysses S. Grant, believed a head start under the cover of darkness might allow his troops to cross the Rapidan River quickly and then pass through the Wilderness—a tangled forest of underbrush and thickets—before a battle could take place with General Robert E. Lee's Army of Northern Virginia. The coming spring campaign would be the first contest between Grant and Lee, the two most successful military leaders of the war. Not since Napoleon fought the Duke of Wellington at Waterloo in 1815 had two such celebrated commanders faced one another in the field.

As the soldiers marched in long, blue columns during a pleasantly warm morning, they knew a murderous struggle was imminent. Before breaking camp, many of the men had notified their loved ones about what lay ahead. "In a few days you will probably hear of the greatest battle yet fought in America," Lieutenant Uberto Burnham of the 76th New York Infantry informed his mother. "If successful, Richmond and all Virginia will soon be ours. If we are defeated, Lee will probably again invade the northern states."[1] Union Brigadier General James Rice wrote similarly, "We are about to commence the campaign, the greatest in magnitude, strength and importance since the beginning of the war. God grant that victory may crown our arms; that this wicked rebellion be crushed, our Union preserved, and peace and prosperity again be restored to our beloved country."[2] The Massachusetts gentleman, Major Henry Livermore Abbott, told his family, "It makes me sad to look on this gallant regiment which I am instructing and disciplining for slaughter, to think that probably 250 or 300 of the 400 which go in will get bowled over."[3]

Private Charles Biddlecom, who served in Rice's brigade, tried to be philosophical in a letter to his wife, "Everything indicates an early move and when you will hear from me again I cannot tell. Perhaps never, but I will try and not expose myself to danger that can be avoided. Esther, if I am killed do not mourn, but try and think that everything is ordained for the best. Teach my children to believe that Charlie died a glorious death and above all things, teach them to hate and despise a slaveholder as the meanest of beings."[4]

Across the North and South, everyone wondered if this might be the last campaign of the war. General Lee, lacking in provisions and a sustainable supply of fresh troops, hoped to encourage the peace movement in the North by delivering a quick and decisive blow against Grant's army. In a letter to his son, Rooney, in late April, Lee wrote, "Our Country demands all our thoughts, all our energies. To resist the powerful Combination now forming against us, will require every man at his place. If victorious we have everything to hope for in the future. If defeated, nothing will be left us to live for." The Confederate general added, "This week will in all probability bring us active work & we must strike fast & strong. My whole trust is in God, & I am ready for whatever he may ordain."[5] The stakes for this battle were especially high for Lee personally. At that moment, Union troops occupied his beloved estate at Arlington, Virginia.

Unfortunately for Grant, only the complete destruction of the Army of Northern Virginia would be viewed as a success by his countrymen, who were tired of war. Failure would lead to cries for an armistice and might even result in the victory of a "peace candidate" in the fall presidential election. Quite simply, if the Rebels drove Grant back across the river, as they had Union Generals George McClellan, Ambrose Burnside, and Joseph Hooker before him, it could mean the end of the Union. Understandably, soldiers and citizens from all parts of America were apprehensive on the eve of the spring campaign. As Grant succinctly put it, "The two armies had been confronting each other so long, without any decisive result, that they hardly knew which could whip."[6]

On the day before crossing the Rapidan, Grant met with eight of his most senior staff officers to discuss the forthcoming campaign. Grant felt that northern armies had previously acted independently of one another "without concert, like a balky team, no two ever pulling together."[7] Going forward, Grant intended to coordinate all attacks against Confederate forces across the South. His goal would be "to hammer continuously at the Armed force of the enemy, and his resources, until by mere attrition, if in no other way, there should be nothing left to him but an equal submission with the loyal section of our common country to the universal law of the land."[8] In conjunction with the attack on Lee in the Wilderness, Grant announced that Major General William T. Sherman had been ordered to attack Confederate forces in northwest Georgia.

Grant then told his officers he had carefully studied whether to move against Lee's left or right, and had decided on the latter. By moving to Lee's right via the Wilderness, the Union Army would be better able to protect its supply lines as it moved farther south. As he concluded his remarks, Grant went over to the map on the wall and drew an imaginary circle around Richmond and Petersburg. He then declared, "When my troops are here, Richmond is mine. Lee must retreat or surrender."[9]

After the meeting, Grant retired to his tent to write a letter to his wife, Julia. He finally shared the news she knew was coming, "Before you receive this I will be away from Culpeper and the Army will be in motion. I know the greatest anxiety is now felt in the North for the success of this move, and the anxiety will increase when it is once known that the Army is in motion." Despite the high stakes of the campaign, Grant admitted, "I feel well myself. Do not know that this is any criterion to judge results because I have never felt otherwise. I believe it has never been my misfortune to be placed where I lost my presence of mind, unless indeed it has been when thrown in strange company, particularly of ladies."[10] Grant's sense of calm was extraordinary given that the nation's survival depended on the success of his Virginia Campaign. A few days earlier Grant received a letter from President Abraham Lincoln, who wrote, "And now with a brave army, and a just cause, may God sustain you."[11]

Hiram Ulysses Grant, who had turned forty-two years old on the eve of the campaign, was born in Ohio to laboring parents. His father, Jesse Grant, eventually built a successful tanning business. A classmate at West Point described young Ulysses "as a plain, common-sense straightforward youth; quiet, rather of the old-head-on-the-young-shoulder order; shunning notoriety; quite contented while others were grumbling . . . respected by all and very popular with his friends."[12] Uncle Sam Grant, as he was known by his fellow cadets, was also an outstanding horseman.

An aide-de-camp on Grant's staff, Lieutenant Colonel Horace Porter, described his chief as "a man of slim figure, slightly stooped, five feet eight inches in height, weighing only a hundred and thirty-five pounds."[13] He had chestnut-brown hair and his beard "was always kept closely and neatly trimmed."[14] The prominent lawyer, Richard Henry Dana, upon meeting Grant for the first time in March 1864, saw an "ordinary, scrubby-looking man, with a slightly seedy look, as if he was out of office and on half-pay with nothing to do but hang around the entry of Willard's, cigar in mouth." Dana was shocked that such a person was "the generalissimo of our armies, on whom the destiny of the empire seemed to hang!"[15] One observer of Grant in 1864 said, "Among men he is nowise noticeable. There is no glitter or parade about him. To me he seems but an earnest business man."[16]

Grant's ascent in the Union Army was one of the most remarkable stories of the war up to that point. Before Fort Sumter, Grant had been a clerk at a leather goods store in Galena, Illinois. Having been educated at West Point and having served in the Mexican War, Grant sought a suitable position in the army when the war broke out. Eventually, the governor of Illinois gave him a regiment. Quickly promoted to brigadier general, he began winning battles, among them Fort Donelson, Shiloh, Vicksburg, and Chattanooga. That last campaign resulted in Congress restoring the rank of lieutenant general specifically for Grant, who also became general-in-chief of all Union Armies in March 1864.

Northerners showered praise on Grant for his victories at Vicksburg and Chattanooga in 1863. His generalship during the Battle of Shiloh in April 1862 had been worryingly subpar, however. The enemy caught him by surprise and his army was almost swept into the Tennessee River during the first day of battle. "The neglect of pickets and out-posts approached criminality," the journalist Whitelaw Reid wrote. A soldier who survived the disaster said, "For the great loss of life in this battle, General Grant is in great degree responsible, as it cannot be denied that we were completely surprised, for which there was, nor is, the least explanation or excuse."[17] Reid added, "The fearful loss of life was charged directly to his negligence, and exaggerated stories of his habits were widely circulated. Even the gross slander, that explained the disasters of the first day's battle by the allegation of Grant's absence for hours in a state of intoxication at Savannah, found ready believers."[18] Years later, Grant defended his decision not to entrench in anticipation of an attack at Shiloh, stating, "the troops with me, officers and men, needed discipline and drill more than they did experience with the pick, shovel, and axe."[19] Grant was lucky he hadn't been cashiered by his superiors for the debacle—albeit a Union victory—at Shiloh.

The Union troops that crossed the Rapidan and entered the Wilderness on that lovely morning in May 1864 made up one of the largest invasion forces ever witnessed on the North American continent. The Army of the Potomac consisted of 99,438 soldiers "present for duty equipped."[20] Grant also had the Ninth Corps, commanded by Major General Ambrose Burnside, at his disposal, adding another 19,331 for a total force of about 120,000 soldiers. Among Burnside's men was a division of African American soldiers led by Brigadier General Edward Ferrero. They would be the first black troops to take the field against the Army of Northern Virginia. Colonel Charles Wainwright, a reliable observer serving with the Fifth Corps, believed that roughly one-third of the total number of Grant's force were green troops, yet he also felt "the army was never in better condition, take it altogether."[21] The troops were supported by 4,300 wagons, 835 ambulances, 34,981 horses, and 22,528 mules. General Lee would only be able to deploy around 65,000 men to somehow stop this perilous host.[22]

Numbers alone wouldn't achieve victory, as recent history demonstrated. Exactly one year ago in the same geographical area, the overconfident and unfortunate Major General Joseph Hooker directed 134,000 Union troops against 62,000 of Lee's veterans during the Chancellorsville Campaign. Hooker suffered a humiliating defeat, losing over 17,000 men. Upon learning of the debacle and Hooker's subsequent retreat across the Rappahannock River, President Lincoln muttered, "What will the country say? Oh, what will the country say?" A prominent journalist said of Lincoln at this time, "Never, as long as I knew him, did he seem to be so broken, so dispirited, so ghostlike."[23]

Merely one year after the Chancellorsville debacle, Grant's army came pouring down the roads toward the bridges around midnight. Lieutenant Morris Schaff, an aide to Major General Gouverneur Warren, experienced the beauty and joy of seeing the entire army on the move, and described it as a "magical pageant" with flags of various colors, representing brigades, divisions, and corps, whipping high above the heads of the soldiers.[24] One of Grant's staff officers wrote, "the roads resounded to the measured tread of the advancing columns, and the deep forests were lighted by the glitter of their steel."[25] Schaff thought the soldiers "were very lighthearted, almost as joyous as schoolboys" and believed "there was illumination in every soldier's face." He wondered if "it was the light from the altar of duty that was shining there."[26] Herman Melville commemorated the epic invasion in verse,

> The livelong night they ford the flood;
> With guns held high they silent press,
> Till shimmers the grass in their bayonets' sheen—
> On Morning's banks their ranks they dress;
> Then by the forests lightly wind,
> Whose waving boughs the pennons seem to bless,
> Borne by the cavalry scouting on—
> Sounding the Wilderness.[27]

To cross the Rapidan, army engineers laid down pontoon bridges at Germanna Ford and Ely's Ford. Major General Winfield Scott Hancock's Second Corps crossed at Ely's Ford, six miles to the east, and then moved on to Chancellorsville—the same ground where Stonewall Jackson's devastating flanking movement decimated the Union right almost a year ago to the day. Warren's Fifth Corps and Major General John Sedgwick's Sixth Corps crossed at Germanna Ford. Warren's men soon moved to Wilderness Tavern at the intersection of the Germanna Plank Road and the Orange Turnpike, while the Sixth Corps bivouacked several miles to the rear.

The four divisions of the Fifth Corps began marching at midnight from Culpeper, Virginia, and passed over the pontoons starting around 7:00 A.M. on the morning of May 4. The entire corps was across by 1:00 P.M., reaching the area around Wilderness Tavern by 4:00 P.M. Upon reaching their destination, after sixteen hours of intense excitement and activity, the weary soldiers washed their feet and prepared their supper. "The scene is sublime," a 76th New York infantryman recalled, "the red sun hangs just over the woods, the trees are brilliantly green and filled with happy birds. Men by the thousands are boiling coffee and frying pork and hard tack."[28]

For the thirty-four-year-old commander of the Fifth Corps, who had won everlasting fame at the Battle of Gettysburg, the Virginia Campaign represented his biggest challenge yet. With long, dark hair and jet-black eyes, Gouverneur Kemble Warren was a slightly built man, who always seemed to wear an extremely grave expression on his face. On the morning of the march, he rode a majestic white horse and wore a smart uniform with the yellow sash of a major general. Unlike most officers in the Union Army, Warren cared a great deal about the way he dressed while in the field. A rival once derisively referred to Warren as "young Napoleon." Many senior officers in the army jealously watched his rapid rise through the ranks.

Though prone to melancholia on occasion, Warren exuded energy and good humor on that lovely spring morning. Right before starting out, he wrote his wife, "I am feeling very well, and, though I have no easy task, feel light-hearted and confident. We are going to have a magnificent campaign; and I have a situation commensurate with it." He then acknowledged the danger ahead and attempted to offer reassurance, "Come what may, we shall not fail of our full duty. Do not fear, my sweetheart, for me. I am only too happy in the high place I fill, and if I am to die, I can never do so more gloriously than in the now opened campaign."[29] Despite these positive sentiments, Warren experienced some anxiety on the eve of the campaign.[30] As a young corps commander, he knew his actions would be scrutinized by his senior officers. Normally deliberative by temperament, Warren would be expected to be decisive when the fighting began.

◆

Grant and his staff followed closely behind Warren's troops as they marched toward Germanna Ford. The Union commander rode his large bay horse, Cincinnati, and wore top-boots that reached his knees. On his head, he had a black felt slouch hat with a simple gold cord around it. Unusually for Grant, he appeared in full-regulation attire and even wore a pair of elegant, yellow-brown thread gloves. Melville called him "the silent General." Elihu Washburne, a congressman from Illinois who had asked to witness the fighting, accompanied Grant. The soldiers nervously joked that Washburne, dressed in black civilian clothes, was Grant's personal undertaker.

The congressman slept in the same tent as Grant during the first week of the spring campaign.[31]

Around midday on May 4, shortly after crossing the river, Grant stopped at an old farmhouse. He sat down on the steps and lit one of many cigars that day. Watching the last of Sedgwick's troops passing over the bridge, he told his staff, "Well, the movement so far has been as satisfactory as could be desired. We have succeeded in seizing the fords and crossing the river without loss or delay. Lee must by this time know upon what roads we are advancing, but he may not yet realize the full extent of the movement. We shall probably soon get some indications as to what he intends to do."[32]

A journalist accompanying the army then asked, "General Grant, about how long will it take you to get to Richmond?" Grant replied, "I will agree to be there in about four days—that is, if General Lee becomes a party to the agreement; but if he objects, the trip will undoubtedly be prolonged."[33] Later that afternoon, Grant telegraphed Chief of Staff Henry Halleck in Washington, D.C., "The crossing of Rapidan effected. Forty-eight hours now will demonstrate whether the enemy intends giving battle this side of Richmond."[34]

Early in the afternoon of May 4, Grant received his first indication of what Lee might do. Signal officers deciphered a message from Lee to one of his corps commanders, Lieutenant General Richard Ewell, which read, "We are moving. Had I not better move D. and D. toward New Verdierville? (Signed) R."[35] Grant interpreted the message to mean Lee was leaving his entrenchments along the southern banks of the Rapidan, and was most likely moving some of his army toward his Mine Run works, approximately ten miles west of Wilderness Tavern. Grant then dispatched a message to General Burnside, "Make forced marches until you reach this place. Start your troops now in the rear the moment they can be got off, and require them to make a night march."[36] Grant hoped to have his entire force in line as he attempted to threaten Lee's right flank.

Before Grant's crossing of the Rapidan, Lee had been headquartered among the pines at the foot of Clark Mountain, near Orange Court House, Virginia, approximately seventy miles northwest of Richmond and twenty miles west of Wilderness Tavern along the Orange Turnpike. Over the previous few months, Lee worried about the condition of his army. In a letter to the secretary of war in January 1864, Lee wrote, "Short rations are having a bad effect upon the men, both morally and physically. Desertions to the enemy are becoming more frequent . . . Unless there is a change, I fear the army cannot be effective, and probably cannot be kept together."[37] By May 1864, the supply problem hadn't gotten much better, though the morale of the army remained remarkably good. One Confederate soldier, proudly declared in April, "There is hard Fighting to do and our Army is in fine spirits and anxious for a Fight—the fighting has to be done and they Say they don't care how quick it commences."[38]

In April 1864, as the Union Army prepared for its spring campaign, Grant and Major General George Gordon Meade questioned how Lee might respond to the gathering threat against his forces. Meade, who defeated Lee at Gettysburg, remained the titular commander of the Army of the Potomac, though Grant provided direction on strategic matters. Both generals wondered if Lee would retreat toward Richmond when the Union Army finally launched its invasion. Or would Lee move toward his heavily fortified position behind nearby Mine Run, a small, northeasterly flowing stream that was "as crooked as a snake track" according to one Confederate veteran? Grant and Meade expected this last movement to be the most likely one.

Lee might possibly decide on one other plan of action. He could choose to attack the Army of the Potomac as it snaked through the Wilderness, an especially inhospitable place to fight. This heavily forested area with impenetrable undergrowth appeared to favor the Confederates, who were more familiar with the region. Artillery would be less effective there and a lack of visibility would make it difficult for officers to manage their men. Union advantages in troops and matériel most likely would be neutralized by Lee.

Major General Andrew Humphreys, who organized the initial advance for Grant and Meade, was aware of the risks and intended for the army to move through the Wilderness as quickly as possible. Union troops were required to bivouac there during the evening of May 4, however, to stay close to the supply trains that continued to lumber across the Rapidan. Despite this unavoidable delay, Grant and Meade remained confident they had plenty of time to get the army out of the Wilderness. In November 1863, it took Lee almost thirty hours to deploy his army from the south bank of the Rapidan to his Mine Run line. It seemed unlikely Lee would be able to move his troops more quickly this time around.[39] Melville noted that the Confederates would have to "speed to the woods afar."

> The foe that held his guarded hills
> Must speed to woods afar;
> For the scheme that was nursed by the Culpepper hearth
> With the slowly-smoked cigar—
> The scheme that smouldered through winter long
> Now bursts into act—into war—
> The resolute scheme of a heart as calm
> As the Cyclone's core.

In May 1864, a newspaper correspondent described the Wilderness as "an exceedingly broken table land, irregular in its confirmation, and so densely covered with dwarf timber and undergrowth, as to render progress through it very difficult and laborious off the few roads and paths that penetrate it."[40] Morris Schaff wrote, "It is made up chiefly of scrubby, stubborn oaks, and low-limbed, disordered, haggard pines—for the soil is cold and thin—with here and there scattering clumps of alien cedars."[41] Since the early 1700s, the Wilderness region had been noted for the poor condition of its soil and the presence of rich deposits of iron ore. These "poison" lands, as they were known, likely resulted from the overly extensive cultivation of tobacco beginning in the early 18th century. In 1732, a planter wrote, "I rode 8 Miles together over a Stony Road and had on either side continual poisen'd Fields, with nothing but Saplins growing on them."[42] The development of ironmaking in the Wilderness, during the 18th and early 19th centuries, also had a distinct impact on the forest.

The Rapidan and Rappahannock rivers marked the northern boundary of the Wilderness, which extended south to the area around Spotsylvania Court House. In 1864, its western limit began near Mine Run with the eastern boundary extending to Chancellorsville. Two main roads traverse the region from east to west. The Orange Turnpike, a well-known road built during the War of 1812, ran from Fredericksburg to Orange Court House. In the 1840s, the Orange Plank Road was constructed, which passed through the Wilderness along the same route, running parallel with the Turnpike, just a few miles to the south. Brock Road, located one mile from Wilderness Tavern, ran north to south, connecting the Turnpike and the Plank Road. Various small roads and windy paths also connected the two main thoroughfares. The thickest part of the Wilderness was roughly twelve miles wide and six miles long.

Both armies became all too familiar with the Wilderness during the Battle of Chancellorsville in May 1863. The most searing memory of that event by far was Lieutenant General Thomas "Stonewall" Jackson's flanking maneuver on May 2, which wreaked havoc on the Union right and helped secure a Confederate victory. Toward the end of his bloody assault, Confederate troops in the Wilderness accidently shot Jackson, who soon had his left arm amputated at Wilderness Tavern. He died of his wounds eight days later.

In brilliantly outflanking the Army of the Potomac, Jackson used the Wilderness to his advantage. He obtained the assistance of a local resident in finding a road that allowed him to move three divisions of troops, totaling 29,000 men, through the densely forested region. The cover of the woods and the audacity of the plan resulted in one of the most successful military actions of the Civil War. The soldiers of the Army of the Potomac, who eventually retreated across the Rappahannock River, were left wondering why they didn't have bold leaders like Jackson or Lee, instead of the hesitant, morally inferior Joseph Hooker and his detestable chief of staff, Major General Daniel Butterfield. Speaking of the dissolute Hooker and some of his advisors shortly after the disaster, Gouverneur Warren wondered, "Can a cause be holy which is entrusted to such hands? Can

God smile upon them and bring defeat upon such Christians as Lee and Jackson fighting for their own Virginia?"[43] Even President Lincoln said of Jackson, "If we only had such a man to lead the armies of the North, the country would not be appalled with so many disasters."[44]

Throughout the day on Wednesday, May 4, Grant's soldiers headed to their assigned resting spots after having crossed the Rapidan. One of Hancock's divisions stopped at the Chancellorsville battlefield at precisely the same location where it had seen action one year before. "The field still showed signs of that desperate conflict," reported Captain Edwin Houghton of the 17th Maine, "Skeletons and skulls of men and horses, fragments of shell and cannon balls, with all the incidental debris of a fiercely contested battle lay strewn upon the ground. Many of the bodies of our brave union soldiers, with their knapsacks and clothing still clinging to their skeleton forms, lay where they fighting fell."[45] After witnessing this gruesome spectacle, groups of soldiers began talking about their experiences during those horrible days. Houghton pitched his tent near where his horse had been killed by a shell a year ago. He could see the skeleton of the horse that was located where the "noble animal" fell.

The skulls and skeletons and other grim reminders of the previous year's battle spooked the men who bivouacked in the Wilderness near Chancellorsville. Colonel Robert McAllister, a brigade commander under Hancock, captured the mood perfectly in a letter to his wife:

> My dear Ellen,
>
> Here I am, writing this letter on my lap on the battlefield of Chancellorsville. We have reached this far without fighting—an unexpected matter for us. I have been over the battlefield this evening and found the bones of our dead laying and bleaching on top of the ground. Some where my regiment fought so gallantly! They had had a light covering of earth, but the bones were washed out. The trees and timber was cut to pieces. I did not sleep any last night and but little the night before. I must

lay down and get some rest. You will excuse me from writing no particulars at this time.

Inclosed you will find two or three pretty violets and flowers that I picked up on the very ground where my regiment stood and fought so splendidly. The ground was made rich by the blood of our brave soldiers. I thought the flowers would be a relick prised by you. We will not be here long; we will be kept moving. [46]

The belief that the blood from the battle had made the spring flowers grow more vibrantly was commonly held among veterans. One soldier wrote of how they would include a tiny wild flower in letters to loved ones. "It was a very easy matter to discover just where pools of blood had been," he believed, "for those particular spots were marked by the greenest tufts of grass and brightest flowers to be found upon the field." [47]

A sergeant from a New Jersey regiment shared a particularly ghoulish story that exemplifies some of the eerie experiences of the troops on the eve of the coming battle. He remembered a conversation back in 1863 between two soldiers, Daniel Bender of Company H and A. B. Searing of Company E. Before the battle of Chancellorsville, Bender told Searing he had a premonition he wouldn't survive the coming fight. One year later, as the New Jersey division bivouacked on the same ground, Searing discovered a skull with a cap still on it. On the visor was written, "D. Bender, Co. H, 11th N.J. Vols." Searing kept the visor as a relic. [48]

As the soldiers of the Second Corps, along with a couple of regiments from the Fifth Corps, gathered around their campfires near Chancellorsville after having marched for most of the day of May 4, they could see that the surrounding ground "was strewn more or less with human bones and skeletons of horses." In just one small area, "fifty skulls with their cavernous eyes were counted, their foreheads doming in silence above the brown leaves that were gathering about them." From their campfires, the tired troops could also see many half-open graves that displayed "arms and legs with bits of paling and mildewed clothing still clinging to them."

Schaff reported that everywhere one could see "tokens of the battlefield: shriveling cartridge-boxes, battered and rickety canteens, rotting caps and hats, broken artillery-carriages, barked and splintered trees, dead, or half-dead, dangling limbs, and groves of saplings, with which the woods abound, topped by volleys as if sheared by a blast."[49]

The debris from the battlefield reminded veterans of their stunning defeat after Stonewall Jackson's flanking movement rolled up Hooker's right. Melville set the scene,

> In glades they meet skull after skull
> Where pine-cones lay—the rusted gun,
> Green shoes full of bones, the mouldering coat
> And cuddled-up skeleton;
> And scores of such. Some start as in dreams,
> And comrades lost bemoan:
> By the edge of those wilds Stonewall had charged—
> But the Year and the Man were gone.

Would the coming battle end the same way? All of the Union soldiers, veterans and new recruits alike, instinctively grasped that the Wilderness was a bad place for a fight. They hoped they'd get through the region without a battle. The Confederates would fight well here as Jackson's troops demonstrated.

Around one of the many campfires on the evening of May 4, a New York artilleryman told his comrades about those unfortunate wounded Union soldiers who burned as they lay helpless in the woods at the Battle of Chancellorsville. The dense underbrush made the Wilderness prone to fires that could quickly rage out of control. The veteran finished his tale by saying, "This region is an awful place to fight in. The utmost vision is about one hundred yards. Artillery cannot be used effectively. The wounded are liable to be burned to death. I am willing to take my chances of getting killed, but I dread to have a leg broken and then to be burned slowly; and these woods will surely be burned if we fight here." As he finished his story, a nearby infantryman rolled a skull across the ground with a bayonet after having poked at a shallow grave. He then told those who were sitting around the fire, "That is what you are all coming to, and some of you will start toward it tomorrow."[50]

The specter of Stonewall Jackson haunted the soldiers of the Army of the Potomac as they settled down for their first evening in the Wilderness. A year ago in those woods, the Union Army appeared to be in an enviable position. General Hooker improved the discipline and morale of the army after its catastrophic defeat at Fredericksburg in December 1862. Before the battle of Chancellorsville, Hooker possessed superior numbers of men and guns compared to Lee. Hooker boasted he had "the finest army the sun ever shone on," and declared, "My plans are perfect, and when I start to carry them out, may God have mercy on General Lee, for I will have none."[51]

Initially, Hooker's plan did seem like a good one. At the opening of the campaign, a large Union force crossed the Rapidan and then concentrated on Lee's left flank near a former tavern called Chancellorsville. In response to this movement, Lee asked Stonewall Jackson, who many contemporaries considered to be the finest corps commander of the age, "How can we get at those people?" Lee and Jackson then came up with the brilliant idea of sending almost 30,000 soldiers under Jackson's command around the Union right via the forbidding Wilderness. Lee boldly decided to divide his smaller army in front of a much larger opposing force. It was a daring gamble.

Around 5:30 P.M. on May 2, 1863, Jackson's men came yelling and running out of the woods, catching the Eleventh Corps completely by surprise. The commander of the Eleventh Corps, Major General Oliver Otis Howard, later wrote, "On last Saturday Stonewall Jackson attacked my right, with a solid column & with great fury. Col. Von Gilsa's Brigade occupied the point of attack and immediately gave way, broke up & ran upon the other troops with such momentum that they gave way too. Such a mass of fugitives I hav'nt seen since the first Battle of Bull Run."[52] Jackson's flanking maneuver lost momentum with the coming of darkness. After more days of fighting across the entire front, the Army of the Potomac eventually retreated across the river. Lee and Jackson had won their greatest triumph of the war.

The veterans, bivouacked in the Wilderness on May 4, 1864, would have remembered the horrific losses they suffered during the Chancellorsville campaign. The Union lost 1,694 dead, 9,672 wounded, and 5,938 missing. Making matters worse, many of the men suspected Hooker of being drunk during the battle. The rank and file soldiers knew Hooker "communed with John Barley-corn and was said to be a three-bottle man."[53] Responding to another rumor that Hooker may have been injured during the fighting, Captain George Custer said it must have been "a wound he received from a projectile which requires cork to be drawn before it is serviceable."[54] Even one of his staff members said Hooker "drank to excess to celebrate the unhindered crossing of the Rapidan and consequently slept in a deep stupor until almost 10:00 A.M. the next morning when orders for the day's march were finally issued."[55] One wonders, in light of Hooker's disastrous performance, if the soldiers under Grant had concerns about rumors relating to *his* drinking. General Lee, by comparison, tended not to drink anything stronger than buttermilk.

Shortly after the catastrophe, Hooker explained what happened, "I was not hurt by a shell, and I was not drunk. For once I lost confidence in Joe Hooker, and that is all there is to it."[56] In one of the gravest errors of the battle, Union reconnaissance reported Stonewall Jackson moving through the Wilderness, but Hooker and other officers misinterpreted this intelligence to mean that Lee's army was retreating. Underestimating Robert E. Lee's willingness to take extreme risks in the face of the enemy may have been the Union Army's biggest mistake of all. Would Grant repeat Hooker's error?

Despite Lee's historic victory at Chancellorsville, he suffered a series of troubling setbacks in the immediate aftermath of the battle. Stonewall Jackson, by far Lee's most valuable lieutenant, died shortly after having been shot in the Wilderness. Before his death, Jackson's amputated left arm had been given a proper Christian burial on the grounds of Lacy House, just west of Wilderness Tavern. Of Jackson's loss, Lee said, "I know not how to replace him."[57]

Nevertheless, flush with victory after the Chancellorsville campaign, Lee invaded the North where his Army of Northern Virginia experienced a rare defeat at Gettysburg in early July 1863. An exhausted and unwell Lee offered his resignation to Jefferson Davis after this failure, but Davis refused to accept it. Throughout late 1863 and early 1864, Lee's army camped on the southern banks of the Rapidan opposite the Army of the Potomac on the other side of the river. Limited by a lack of fresh troops and supplies, the instinctively aggressive Lee remained on the defensive. Another northern invasion wouldn't be possible.

By May 1864, "Marse Robert"—as his soldiers affectionately called him—was an old-looking fifty-seven. His health had been poor during the winter, but he began to feel better in the spring. He knew his men could still fight as well as any in the world at that time, though he had considerable doubts about his corps commanders, Lieutenant Generals James Longstreet, Richard Ewell, and Ambrose Powell Hill. All three performed well in the past, but had been disappointing at Gettysburg, where the absence of Jackson proved too much to overcome. Lee wondered if his army lacked the necessary leadership to withstand Grant's spring invasion.

Lee's men still had unflinching trust and confidence in their commander. "All seems to be in tolerably good spirits," one Virginian wrote that spring, "and to repose the utmost confidence in Gen. Lee. Although he has to contend against the ablest one of the Yankee Generals, all think he will be more than a match for him."[58] When Lee reviewed Longstreet's First Corps in late April 1864, the troops greeted him enthusiastically. As he moved by a group of South Carolinians, he received "a wild and prolonged cheer, fraught with a feeling that thrilled all hearts, ran along the lines and rose to the heavens. Hats were thrown high, and many persons became almost frantic with emotion."[59]

Unlike Grant, Lee came from one of America's most prominent families. His father was "Light Horse Harry" Lee, a mythic cavalry commander during the Revolutionary War. Young Robert attended West Point—where he didn't receive a single demerit—graduating second in his class. A fellow cadet said of Lee, "His limbs, beautiful and symmetrical, looked as though they had come from the turning lathe, his step was elastic as if he spurned the ground upon which he trod."[60] Lee married Mary Anna Custis, the daughter of George Washington's adopted son. Robert and Mary lived on a beautiful estate in Arlington, Virginia, overlooking Washington, D.C., from across the Potomac River.

Early in the war, critics unfairly called General Lee "Granny Lee" for his cautious approach in the mountains of western Virginia in 1861. The world soon learned that passivity was foreign to his nature, however. Upon assuming the command of the Army of Northern Virginia in June 1862, an officer said, "if there is one man in either army, Federal or Confederate, who is, head & shoulders, far above every other one in either army in audacity that man is Genl. Lee, and you will very soon have lived to see it. Lee is audacity personified. His name is audacity."[61]

Over the past year, Southerners witnessed both the benefits and costs of Lee's aggressive risk-taking. At Chancellorsville, Lee's audacious division of his army in the face of a numerically superior enemy achieved a shocking victory. That same instinct, alas, caused Lee to order the disastrous Pickett's Charge on the third day of Gettysburg. Despite his failures at Gettysburg and earlier at Antietam, Lee won strategic victories at the Seven Days' Battles, Second Manassas, Fredericksburg, and Chancellorsville. In May 1864, most Americans considered him the most talented general on either side.

While confident in the faith of his own men, Lee wondered if Grant underestimated him. Other than a brief meeting during the Mexican War, Grant and Lee didn't know one another personally—even though both attended West Point, the younger Grant graduated fourteen years after Lee. Volunteering as a colonel in 1861, Grant experienced a string of stunning victories out West and perhaps believed, Lee suspected, he'd achieve similar results against the Army of Northern Virginia. General Meade, who knew Lee and his men rather well, certainly respected their mettle, however. Of Lee's army, Meade said, "A more sinewy, tawny, formidable-looking set of men could not be . . . they handle their weapons with terrible effect. Their great characteristic is their stoical manliness; they . . . look you straight in the face, with as little animosity as if they had never heard a gun."[62]

While the Rebels loved Lee, the soldiers of the Army of the Potomac were still getting to know Grant. Upon meeting the new Union Army commander-in-chief for the first time, Wainwright dismissed him as "stumpy, unmilitary, slouchy, and Western-looking; very ordinary in fact."[63] Schaff thought, "There was nothing in his manner or his tone or his face that indicated that he had ever had anything to do with the victories of Fort Donelson, Vicksburg, and Missionary Ridge."[64] Yet, a staff officer for Meade felt encouraged by Grant's appearance, "He habitually wears an expression as if he had determined to drive his head through a brick wall, and was about to do it. I have much confidence in him."[65]

Grant's simple looks and manner could be deceiving. When a group of Confederate officers expressed doubts about his abilities on the eve of the Virginia Campaign in 1864, James Longstreet asked them if they knew Grant. They didn't. Longstreet replied, "Well, I do. I was in the corps of cadets with him at West Point for three years, I was present at his wedding, I served with him in Mexico, I have observed his methods of warfare in the West, and I believe I know him through and through; and I tell you that we cannot afford to underrate him and the army he now commands . . . for that man will fight us every day and every hour till the end of the war."[66]

◆

On Monday, May 2, 1864, two days before Grant put his army in motion, Lee asked his corps and division commanders to meet him at the signal station on Clark's Mountain. During the meeting, Lee raised his field glasses to look out at the Army of the Potomac on the other side of the Rapidan. He told his commanders he was convinced the enemy would cross at either Germanna Ford or Ely's Ford. Lee "believed that General Grant would cross the Rapidan on our right, and resolved to attack him whenever he presented himself."[67]

Lee ordered Ewell to put his Second Corps in motion toward the east along the Orange Turnpike on Tuesday, May 3. Despite his confidence that Grant would pass through the Wilderness, Lee delayed moving Hill and Longstreet's corps until he was absolutely certain. He still had to be prepared for the possibility Grant would try to turn his left. Delaying the movement of Hill and Longstreet was a risky, though necessary, decision. If Grant did eventually move to Lee's right as expected and got through the Wilderness without opposition, then the Army of the Potomac would stand between Lee and Richmond. Such a disaster might mean the end of the war.[68]

Shortly after 9:00 A.M. on May 4, the Confederates learned Grant's army was crossing the Rapidan on their right just as Lee expected. Upon hearing the news, Lee immediately ordered A. P. Hill to move east on the Orange Plank Road and notified Longstreet that he should be prepared to leave Gordonsville, Virginia, which would require his men to march a full day or more to reach the heart of the Wilderness. Lee rode with Hill all day until they camped for the night at New Verdiersville, roughly 12 miles from Grant's army. Lee went to sleep at midnight, not knowing if Grant would get his men through the Wilderness by morning.

❖

Grant and Meade were equally unaware of Lee's intentions for the following day as they sat together around a campfire on the property of an old farmhouse on the evening of May 4. As Union troops lay down to rest throughout the Wilderness, they could hear the disconcerting sounds of thousands of chirping whippoorwills, who made their homes in those woods. Among the soldiers of the Army of the Potomac was Private William Reeves of the 76th New York Volunteer Infantry, Company C, which formed part of Warren's Fifth Corps. Just nineteen years old, Reeves had been in the army for only eight months, and had not yet witnessed a major engagement like Chancellorsville or Gettysburg.

Reeves and his comrades hadn't slept the night before. On this night, they laid down early, without pitching tents. As Reeves tried to sleep on the hard ground of the Wilderness that evening, he wondered about his fate in the coming battle. Would he run? Would he be killed or wounded? Would he be taken prisoner? He'd heard the fate of prisoners was especially frightful. Thinking of the odds facing him at that moment made it extremely difficult for him to get much-needed rest. The veterans of Gettysburg told Reeves of how the 76th lost nearly half of its men in just thirty minutes on the first day of that fight. Perhaps it was just as well that Reeves, who tossed and turned in the woods all night, had no idea that Confederate soldiers from General Ewell's Second Corps were also bivouacking in the very same woods, a mere three miles to the west along the Orange Turnpike.

TWO

Private William Reeves

"The youth was in a little trance of astonishment. So they were at last going to fight. On the morrow, perhaps, there would be a battle, and he would be in it . . . he was about to mingle in one of the great affairs of the earth."

—Stephen Crane, *Red Badge of Courage*

Private William Reeves enlisted as a substitute at Canandaigua, New York, on August 25, 1863, and was mustered into the Army on the same day. He joined the 76th New York Volunteer Infantry Regiment, which was being restored to full strength after experiencing devastating losses at the Battle of Gettysburg. The soldiers of the 76th took pride in their numerical designation, which connected them to the "Spirit of 1776." They also claimed credit for firing the first shots at Gettysburg on July 1, 1863.[1] Despite its impressive record of service in 1862 and 1863, the 76th consisted overwhelmingly of raw recruits by May 1864. Reeves's Company C, in particular, was made up of mostly new men. The bloody fighting at Gettysburg—which cost the Union 23,049 men overall—had transformed this regiment of hardened veterans into a unit of "fresh fish."

Gettysburg was a traumatic, yet sacred event in the life of the regiment. On the morning of July 1, the 76th was on the extreme right of Major General John Reynolds's First Corps. During the early hours of the fighting, the courageous Reynolds was killed and his troops were severely cut up by the Rebels. Many of the 76th's best officers were killed, wounded, or taken prisoner during the fighting that day. Three weeks after the hellish carnage at Gettysburg, there were only 80 men still present for duty in the 76th down from 375 men before the battle. [2] It required vigorous recruiting efforts in Upstate New York during the summer of 1863 to replenish the regiment's strength to 525 men present for duty on May 4, 1864.

Reeves expected another epic battle upon joining the army eight weeks after Gettysburg, though he was soon disappointed. For most of the eight months between August 1863 and May 1864, there was very little fighting to speak of. According to his military file, Reeves served with a detached unit guarding the ammunition train during much of the time from October 1863 until March 1864. [3] This duty was uneventful and Reeves focused his energies on trying to stay warm and dry. Referring to the winter of 1863–64, one new recruit remarked, "How tired I got of camp, and drill, and guard duty! And how tired I got of the rain and mud!" The soldier also recorded that the enlisted men "were comfortably housed in canvas-covered log huts" and "were well fed, having plenty of bread, fresh beef, salted pork, beans, rice, sugar, and coffee." [4] On a strictly material basis, the Union soldiers had it much better than their Rebel counterparts.

Before entering the Wilderness in May 1864, the new recruits of the late summer and fall of 1863 came under sustained fire during the aborted Mine Run Campaign between November 7 and December 2, 1863. In the end, General Warren—who had been given the responsibility of leading the main assault—decided against attacking Lee's well-fortified entrenchments at Mine Run, saying "I would sooner sacrifice my commission than my men." [5] General Meade supported Warren's decision, even though Meade would eventually be criticized in Washington for his apparent lack of aggression.

On November 27 at Mine Run, the 76th did in fact come under some sporadic infantry and heavy artillery fire. For new recruits, this may have been the first serious danger they experienced. Of these recruits, one veteran noted, "As they hugged the ground, and listened to the whizzing of bullets and screeching of shells, the roar of artillery, and the quick crack of the sharpshooters' rifles, they believed that Mine Run was the decisive battle of the war."[6] The veterans teased their inexperienced comrades, while also perhaps remembering *their* first time under fire. As part of the unit guarding the ammunition train at this time, Reeves may not have witnessed any fighting during the Mine Run campaign.

Only nineteen years old, Reeves had been too young to be eligible for the federal draft of 1863. He chose instead to sign up as a substitute, taking the place of Hiram Hezekiah Humphrey, a twenty-nine-year-old, who, like Reeves, lived in the small farm town of Victor in western New York. Surprisingly, 29% of those who served in the army were twenty years old or younger and boys as young as thirteen tried to enlist. William Reeves was not only young but slight, and only 5 feet, 4 inches tall. He had fair skin, brown hair, and green eyes. His mother, Louise Reeves, died when he was twelve years old. His father, Theophilus Reeves, owned a small farm in Victor. William worked as a farm laborer before becoming a soldier. He decided to join the army because he believed in the Union cause, and hoped to earn some money fighting for it.

Hiram Humphrey's family was a prominent one in Victor. Hiram's father, Rufus Humphrey, had served in the army during the War of 1812, and later achieved local notoriety for creating a new type of threshing machine that was widely used in the region.[7] Rufus was also active in antislavery politics. Hiram could easily afford to pay $300—which was roughly the market price for a substitute at that time—to William Reeves, who was then required to serve in the Army of the Potomac for three years or until the war ended. The going rate for a substitute in western New York represented almost a year's wages for a farm laborer like Reeves. He would also receive $13 per month from the federal government, while he remained in the army.

The $300 payment from Humphrey allowed Reeves to begin a new life with his sweetheart, Anna E. Barnett, an eighteen-year-old English immigrant, who also lived in Victor. On August 19, 1863—just six days before Reeves enlisted in the Army—he married Anna at a local Methodist church. Sadly, they spent less than a week together as newlyweds before Reeves was shipped off to Virginia to join Meade's army. Eight months later, as Reeves lay on the sloping lawn of Lacy House near the Wilderness Tavern on the evening of May 4, he thought of how much he missed Anna, whom he hadn't seen since leaving Victor back in August. He wondered if he'd ever see her again. Would they start a family together if he returned home?

In the months before the crossing of the Rapidan River by the Army of the Potomac, it seemed like signing on as a substitute was a good financial decision for Reeves. But now, with a deadly engagement looming—and the boys assured him that the aggressive Bobby Lee would attack them mercilessly in the morning—his calculation didn't seem quite as smart. In the darkness that night, Reeves may have seen, like Henry Fleming at the Battle of Chancellorsville, "visions of a thousand-tongued fear that would babble at his back . . . while others were going coolly about their country's business."[8]

The fear of appearing to be afraid was common among ordinary soldiers. A private in the same brigade as Reeves wrote, "To me, I fight because I am too proud to be called a coward, not that I think my fighting will do any good to the human family."[9] Reeves may have recalled the case of Private Thomas Barton of the 76th, who lost his nerve during the Mine Run Campaign. Barton had his head shaved and a placard with the word COWARD inscribed in large letters and fixed to his back as he was "drummed out of the service of the United States in the presence of his Regiment."[10]

In addition to being afraid, Reeves felt added pressure to honorably perform his duties in the coming fight. Military and political leaders viewed substitutes like Reeves in a negative light, so perhaps he hoped to disabuse them of that prejudice. Colonel Charles Wainwright, also a member of the Fifth Corps, believed most of the substitutes were "simply rascals who never intended to serve, but merely wanted the bounty or purchase money offered." Noting the high rates of desertion among substitutes, Wainwright wrote in his diary, "I do hope they will keep on shooting them just as fast as ever they are caught, for society will be benefited at any rate by so doing."[11] A Provost Marshal, who was responsible for recruiting efforts, said "as a class, the substitutes were either morally or physically unfit for the profession of arms."[12] Among draft administrators, the fear of their unreliability was so high that newly enlisted substitutes were placed under armed guard until ultimately being dropped off at their regiments in Virginia or out West.

One substitute expressed his surprise at this treatment upon being mustered into the service in October 1863. After being given a uniform, he was locked in a room with an armed guard outside, "Before that was done I thought I was a patriot but now I thought I was regarded as a criminal."[13] Private Frank Wilkeson, who ran away from home to enlist in the 11th New York Battery, felt similarly. Before his enlistment, he "imagined that the population of Albany would line the sidewalks to see the defenders of the nation march proudly by, bound for the front, and that we would be cheered, and would unbend sufficiently to accept floral offerings from beautiful maidens." Instead, the crowd didn't cheer and small boys threw mud balls at them. One little fellow yelled to a friend, "Hi, Johnnie, come see de bounty-jumpers!"[14]

Many substitutes—drawn from those men who were ineligible for the draft such as foreign citizens and young men under twenty years-old—did in fact desert after obtaining their money, sadly. High bounty men—volunteers who signed up in return for generous bounties—were also notorious for deserting. Bounty jumping became a huge problem for the Union Army in 1863 and 1864. We also know, however, that Private William Reeves was present for duty during the early morning hours of May 4, 1864. He clearly intended to live up to his contract with Hiram Humphrey.

One unscrupulous draftee, who achieved great fame in subsequent years, most certainly did not live up to *his* end of the bargain with his substitute. The future president, Grover Cleveland, who was twenty-six years old in

June 1863, enlisted a Polish immigrant named George Beniski to serve as his substitute for $300. Cleveland paid him $150 right away with the promise to pay another $150 if Beniski "lived to come back from the war."[15] Like Reeves, Beniski was mustered into the 76th New York in August 1863. Beniski injured himself while doing manual labor early on in his service, and never experienced combat. When he returned home "sick and penniless," Beniski's requests for the remainder of the money were ignored by Cleveland. Years later a columnist wrote, "Such was Grover Cleveland's patriotism during the late unpleasantness."[16]

Cleveland wasn't unique in trying to avoid army service during the latter years of the Civil War. After heavy losses at Antietam and Fredericksburg, the Union Army had a difficult time replenishing its ranks by relying solely on volunteers and statewide recruitment efforts. By early 1863, policymakers decided to introduce a federal draft. On March 3, 1863, President Lincoln signed the Enrollment Act. The legislation required all able-bodied male citizens of the United States—and persons of foreign birth who intended to become citizens—to perform military duties in the service of their country.

Men between the ages of 20 and 45 were the prime target of the draft with married men between the ages of 36 and 46 representing a secondary pool of manpower. There were numerous exemptions, however. Men might claim they were physically or mentally unfit. Or they could hire a substitute—the option chosen by Grover Cleveland, Hiram Humphrey, and many others. Finally, a draftee could pay $300 to the government to avoid service during a particular draft.

"Commutation,"[17] as this latter process was known, was extremely unpopular with men subject to the draft, reinforcing their view of the war as a "rich man's war, but a poor man's fight." Hiring a substitute was a far safer option for the draftee, too, as it protected him from future drafts for three years. Paying the commutation fee wouldn't protect the individual from future drafts. The widespread unpopularity of commutation led to its repeal in 1864. It had only been available option for the first two of the four drafts between 1863 and 1865.

The first federal draft during the summer of 1863 had mixed results. It indirectly promoted volunteering since many local districts tried to meet future quotas by offering generous bounties to volunteers. The arithmetic was somewhat straightforward. The more volunteers a district could entice, the fewer men it would be required to draft. In New York City, the first day of the draft in July 1863 was quickly followed by five days of bloody riots that resulted in 120 deaths. Eventually, Union troops that had fought at Gettysburg were commanded to head north to restore order. Disgusted by the riots, Wainwright wrote, "it was composed entirely of the lowest class of foreigners, not one in ten of whom were subject to the draft."[18] The New York riots angered the ordinary soldiers in the field. According to one observer, veterans "showed an extreme anxiety to be allowed the opportunity of showing the Bowery toughs a little real war from the muzzles of their Springfield rifles."[19]

The July 1863 draft failed to achieve its primary aim in the near term—obtaining enough new recruits for the Union Army. Across the North, 39,415 of the draftees never even acknowledged their draft notice, which was 14% of the total. Of the 252,566 who were examined, an incredible 164,395 (65%) were exempted for a wide variety of maladies.[20] Older Americans wondered what had happened to the fitness of the younger generation. All told, the July draft of 1863 yielded just 9,881 draftees and 26,002 substitutes. There were also 52,288 men who paid the $300 commutation fee, generating over $15,000,000 for the government, which put those funds toward procuring substitutes later in the year. In New York, the largest state in the Union, the draft resulted in 2,300 draftees and 6,998 substitutes.[21]

There seemed to be a variety of options for avoiding the draft. In addition to paying the government $300 or hiring a substitute, one could skedaddle to Canada. The most prospective soldiers, however, tried to get exemptions for mental or physical disabilities. A potential recruit might be disqualified if he could somehow prove he was suffering from "Manifest mental imbecility" or "Insanity" or "Epilepsy." Some draftees deliberately knocked out their own teeth, since Civil War infantrymen needed to be able to bite off the tip of the paper cartridges then in use for a muzzle-loading weapon.

The draft regulations listed fifty-one different categories of disabilities that would exempt a citizen from serving. And the surgeons associated with the Enrollment Boards had a very difficult time distinguishing the genuinely disabled from the shirkers. Colonel James Barnet Fry, Provost Marshal General for overseeing the entire federal draft, believed "the large number of exemptions defeated . . . the object of the law."[22] By the summer of 1863, most American men viewed serving in the Union Army as something to be avoided, if at all possible. Those who did answer the call to arms were an increasingly small tribe.

Private Reeves was one of the relatively few who answered the call though it's true he received a considerable amount of money to do so. Enrollments of eligible men in his Upstate New York district—the 25th representing Yates, Livingston, and Ontario Counties—had been compiled during June and July 1863. The draft for Reeves and Humphrey's town of Victor was held in Canandaigua, New York, on Wednesday, July 29, 1863. A huge crowd of citizens gathered around the courthouse to witness the drawing of names. A blind man, who was also blindfolded in order "to render assurance doubly sure," selected the names from a mechanical wheel. At this time, Hiram Hezekiah Humphrey's name was drawn. Once the draft was complete, those new conscripts in attendance lined up in procession and paraded throughout the streets. Afterwards, the conscripts assembled in a local park to hear speeches from local dignitaries.[23]

Humphrey received his official draft notification sometime during the first week of August. Since Humphrey and Reeves both lived in the same small town, it's rather likely they already knew each other and were easily able to agree to a substitute contract by August 15 or so. Reeves then got married to Anna before reporting for his examination on August 25. As a substitute, he was placed under guard after having been mustered into the service that day. Reeves was transported to Rikers Island in New York City and then taken to Alexandria, Virginia, before joining the 76th New York on September 6, 1864, in the field between the Rappahannock and Rapidan

Rivers. It's doubtful he received a warm welcome from the veterans, who treated substitutes with scorn.

Union Army officers began cracking down on bounty jumpers just as Reeves began his military service. This wasn't coincidental. With the influx of new recruits—conscripts, substitutes, and high-bounty men—during the late summer and autumn of 1863, General Meade believed the safety of the army and the most vital interests of the country required the prompt execution of deserters that would "deter others from imitating their bad conduct." According to Meade's records, the Army of the Potomac found 402 soldiers guilty of desertion from July 1, 1863 to December 31, 1863. Of those, 94 were sentenced to be shot, though only 25 were executed.[24]

The military sketch artist Alfred Waud declared desertion to be "the greatest crime of the soldier, and no punishment too severe for the offense."[25] Private Wilkeson, who witnessed five new recruits being instantly killed by guards as they jumped out of their train on the way to the front, agreed that the new soldiers—many of whom were bounty jumpers—"had to be severely disciplined, and that entailed punishment."[26] After the execution of one deserter, a newspaper editor wrote, "I hope this fearful lesson will be a warning to those misguided men who think they can shrink from the duty they owe their country by the base act of desertion."[27] One grizzled sergeant noted in 1863, "The monotony of camp life is to be broken by the shooting of a deserter . . . Military discipline must have its course."[28]

General Meade ordered the execution of five "substitute-deserters"—as the press called them—just four days after Reeves joined the army. Hoping for mercy, these unfortunate deserters appealed to the kindly President Lincoln, who remained unbending in this instance, telling Meade "please let them know at once that their appeal is denied."[29] All five men were immigrants who allegedly deserted on numerous previous occasions to pocket the bounty money. The execution seemed uniquely American as the deserters were of different religions, standing "side by side, each uttering prayers for their souls."[30]

Table 2.1 The Five Executed "Substitute-Deserters"–August 29, 1863

Name	Age	Country of Origin	Family status
George Kuhna	22	Germany	Unmarried
John Felane	26	Italy	Wife and family
Charles Walter	28	Germany	Wife and child
George Keinese	24	Italy	Wife and child
Emil Lai	30	Germany	Wife

According to Waud, the five men "all suffered terribly mentally, and as they marched to their own funeral they staggered with mortal agony like a drunken man." The doomed souls marched behind their coffins until they reached their designated open graves. The men then sat on their coffins as they were blindfolded. They died instantly after their executioners fired a volley. Waud believed there was "no doubt that their death [had] a very salutary influence on discipline."[31] Regarding the execution of another deserter, a veteran wrote, "The day of execution has come. The bugle sounds the call to fall in, and the whole division forms . . . Oh, what must be the poor culprit's thoughts when he hears that call, for it is the signal for him that his last hour on this earth has come."[32]

Private Reeves witnessed the tragic execution of a deserter from his own regiment in December 1863. Private Winslow N. Allen joined the 76th at approximately the same time as Reeves. Upon joining the regiment in September 1863, the officers of his company discovered Allen had deserted the very same unit in the spring of 1862. This unlucky coincidence eventually led to Private Allen being tried, convicted, and sentenced to death by a military court. The execution took place in the field on December 18, 1863 with the entire regiment in attendance.

On that sad day, Allen appeared calm and even ate a hearty dinner just one hour before his execution. As he headed to the execution site, Allen told the officer that accompanied him, "Captain, you have been kind to me, which I can only return by my prayers for your welfare."[33] They then marched in procession to the location where Allen's fellow soldiers gathered around a freshly dug grave that had an open coffin in front of it. Allen was placed at the foot of the coffin with his eyes blindfolded and his hands pinioned. Once the charges had been read aloud, the Captain told Allen, "Winslow, I can go no further with you; the rest of your dark journey is alone. Have you any last word for your wife and child?" Allen replied, "No, only tell them that I love them all!"[34] These were his last words. Shortly after he uttered them, a single shot rang out and Private Winslow N. Allen lay dead upon his coffin. The new recruits, no doubt, were deeply moved by this grim spectacle.

The United States government required a great deal of its ordinary soldiers, who often found it difficult to cope under the tremendous strain. Those who successfully deserted lived out their days with feelings of shame in addition to the lasting condemnation of their fellow citizens. Those deserters who were caught suffered humiliating deaths in front of their friends and colleagues. The loyal soldiers, who remained with their units, contended with the tedium of camp life, which was occasionally interrupted by the terror of skirmishes or massive battles. Some of them attempted to leave the service by faking illness or injury. "Look for me home in the course of six or eight days," a private from Reeves's brigade wrote to his wife, "for to the hospital I mean to go and from there to Washington and from there home . . . I am as patriotic as any man, but I do object to fooling away time here when this war could be ended in a month just as well as not."[35]

For the officers and men on the front lines, the odds of surviving a big engagement were fearful. "This business of getting killed is a mere question of time," an aide to General Warren observed, "it will happen to us all sooner or later if the war keeps on."[36] At Gettysburg, the 76th lost 32 dead soldiers and another 16 who died of wounds. The regiment also had 116 wounded and 70 missing, for an overall casualty rate of 64%. It could always be worse, however. The 24th Michigan at Gettysburg suffered a casualty rate of 73%. Many of the wounded lost limbs or were seriously maimed—the pain experienced by the severely wounded in a Civil War battle, where surgery was often performed in understaffed field hospitals—is incomprehensible. Some of the soldiers listed as "missing" had been captured and would end up in gruesome prison camps where the mortality rate was roughly 17%.

On the eve of the Battle of the Wilderness, Reeves at least felt some confidence in the officers directing the movements of the 76th New York. General Warren, who commanded the Fifth Corps, was seen by Grant as a possible successor to General Meade as commander of the Army of the Potomac. Grant believed Warren to be "a gallant and able man" who was "thoroughly imbued with the solemnity and importance of the duty he had to perform."[37]

Reeves's division commander, Brigadier General James Wadsworth, was brave and beloved by his men. In 1862, the antislavery Wadsworth ran for governor of New York as a Republican, but lost. While not trained as a professional soldier, his sense of duty and moral courage inspired the rank and file. One member of the 76th explained why the men were happy Wadsworth led their division, "His disinterested patriotism in leaving his large and lucrative business to fight for principle without pay; his gallant conduct in crossing the river at Fredericksburg, in the face of the enemy; his kind care of the troops, all tended to give him a firm lodgment in the heart of each man of his command."[38] Upon arriving in the Wilderness, another member of Reeves's regiment reported, "General Wadsworth has been riding among the troops of his division and passing a word with us. The old gentleman is as good natured as ever. He wears the regulation cap, rides a light gray horse, his gray hair cut short and side whiskers closely trimmed. The boys all like the old 'Abolish.'"[39]

The 76th formed part of the brigade of Brigadier General James Rice, a teacher prior to the war, who then rose through the ranks to become a general. A graduate of Yale University with the highest honors, Rice formerly taught school in Natchez, Mississippi, where he became a staunch abolitionist. One soldier, who served under Rice, said the men referred to him as "Old Crazy" because he got too excited in the heat of battle. His bravery in the face of some of the fiercest fighting of the war won the admiration of his peers. It was Colonel Rice's brigade—he took over command after Colonel Strong Vincent had been shot—that held the extreme left of the line on the second day at Gettysburg, thereby playing a central role in the Union victory. Rice won his promotion to brigadier general for his valor on that crucial day. [40]

Finally, the regimental commander of the 76th, Lieutenant-Colonel John Cook, also demonstrated fortitude in the early battles of the war, assuming the command of the 76th at Gettysburg, where he was slightly wounded, but remained in the field. Cook's bravery at Gettysburg—just like that of Warren, Wadsworth, and Rice—was recognized by the soldiers of the Army of the Potomac. If courage alone could lead the Union to victory in the Wilderness, then Reeves could feel optimistic as he eventually fell off to sleep that night. All these men would be severely tested in the morning.

THREE

Confederates on the Turnpike

P rivate William Reeves and the boys of the 76th New York rose before
4:00 A.M. on the morning of May 5. As they enjoyed a quick breakfast of fried pork, hardtack, and coffee, they didn't know that Confederate
General Richard Ewell's infantry was moving east down the Orange Turnpike to within two miles of their camp. The Union cavalry inexplicably
had failed to maintain a patrol farther down the Turnpike that could've
alerted the Fifth Corps to the proximity of the enemy. General Warren
remained unaware that his troops were in grave danger that morning.

Shortly after 5:30 A.M., Warren "mounted his big, logy dapplegray
wearing his yellow sash of a major-general,"[1] and began following two of
his divisions down Parker's Store Road—a narrow, winding, wooded road
that traveled southwesterly from Lacy House on the Orange Turnpike to
Parker's Store on the Orange Plank Road. Warren's engineers had been
working urgently to widen the road so that 24,000 men of the Fifth Corps,
along with their guns and wagons, could all fit during the journey. As
Warren and his party rode along the Turnpike before entering Parker's
Store Road, a staff officer approached and informed the general that Rebel

infantry had been spotted on the Turnpike and were forming a line of battle, roughly three quarters of a mile from Union Brigadier General Charles Griffin's First Division. A large cloud of dust had been seen in the distance to the west of Griffin's position.[2]

The news surprised Warren, though "his thin, solemn, darkly sallow face was nowhere lightened by even a transitory flare," according to an aide, who witnessed the scene.[3] The youthful corps commander immediately ordered one of his staff officers to "tell Griffin to get ready to attack at once."[4] Warren then wrote General Meade informing him that Griffin would hold the Turnpike until additional troops could come up in support. Warren had no idea of the size of the force confronting him, and didn't know if he should continue with the planned march for the day.[5] The prospect of getting attacked on his right flank, while marching through the Wilderness via Parker's Store Road, had been a concern of Warren's even before he heard about the sighting of Ewell's troops.[6]

Lieutenant General Richard Ewell—fondly known as "Old Bald Head" by his men—also made an early start on the pike that morning. "The general was usually very thin and pale, unusually so that morning," a Confederate officer wrote, "but bright-eyed and alert. He was accustomed to ride a flea-bitten gray named Rifle, who was singularly like him, if a horse can be like a man."[7] By 6:00 A.M., Ewell situated one of his divisions in the woods along the Turnpike just two miles from Wilderness Tavern, where most of Warren's Fifth Corps bivouacked during the night of May 4. Ewell's men were in good spirits, even though they had only eaten a few crackers and a bit of meat on the previous day. Initially, Lee ordered Ewell to strike the enemy wherever he could find him. On the morning of May 5, however, Lee changed his mind. Instead, he told Ewell to avoid bringing on a general engagement until General Longstreet's First Corps came up. After having made his presence known to the Union Army, Ewell began building up his defensive line in the woods on both sides of the Turnpike.[8]

Warren faced a dilemma upon hearing the news of Confederates advancing on his flank. It might possibly be a small demonstration by Lee to delay the movement of the Union Army through the Wilderness. Yet, if it was a larger force, Warren would have to realign his divisions so they faced the enemy. Also, gaps between divisions would need to be closed up. This latter maneuver would require time. The density of the forest made it very difficult to make a snap assessment during the early morning hours and any fighting in those woods would be like a "scientific bushwhack," as one staff officer described it.[9] A mistake might be career-ending (or worse) for the thirty-four-year-old general.

At 7:15 A.M., General Meade arrived at Warren's headquarters at Lacy House. He had received Warren's message and ordered him to suspend his march along Parker's Store Road and instead prepare to "attack the enemy with his whole force." Meade, who likely believed most of Lee's army was located farther away at the Mine Run works, told Warren, "if there is to be any fighting this side of Mine Run, let us do it right off."[10] Meade then sent a message to General Grant, who remained behind at the farmhouse near Germanna Ford, telling him that Warren had been directed to attack the Confederate force. Grant replied, "If any opportunity presents itself for pitching into a part of Lee's army, do so without giving time for disposition."[11]

Right after sending this order, Grant headed south on the Germanna Plank Road to be closer to the action. An officer who saw Grant riding by noted, "He was on a fine, though small, black horse, which he set well, was plainly dressed, looked the picture of health, and bore no evidence of anxiety about him. His plain hat and clothes were in marked contrast with a somewhat gaily dressed and equipped staff."[12] The Lieutenant General eventually arrived at Lacy House where he set up a joint command post with General Meade on a nearby knoll. The pugnacious Grant wanted to ensure that the defensive-minded Meade and Warren attacked the enemy as soon as possible.

Before Warren's orders had been suspended, he intended to move his troops in conjunction with a general deployment of the Army of the Potomac over an uneven line roughly seven miles long from Wilderness Tavern to Shady Grove Church. The Second Corps, commanded by General Hancock, was to move to Shady Grove Church and then extend its right to Warren's Fifth Corps, which would be located at Parker's Store, an abandoned country store. The Sixth Corps, led by General Sedgwick, would move to Wilderness Tavern and would extend its left to Warren. Once the line was in place, the army then was to be "held ready to move forward."[13] Now ordered instead to attack right away, Warren had considerable work to do. At 7:50 A.M., Warren rode off to talk with General Wadsworth, commander of his Fourth Division, who had already traveled a mile down Parker's Store Road. Wadsworth's lead brigade was the Second, led by General Rice—this was the brigade that Reeves's 76th New York belonged to.

The pressure made Warren irritable. When one of his staff members suggested a good location for the placement of a battery, Warren said sharply that when he wished to have suggestions from an aide, he'd ask for them. Wadsworth was forming his battle line to the right of Parker's Store Road, when Warren reached him. Looking west into the woods, Warren said to Wadsworth, "Find out what's in there."[14]

At the opening of the Virginia Campaign of 1864, Major General Gouverneur Kemble Warren seemed destined for greatness. Named for Gouverneur Kemble—a former Congressman and friend of his father—Warren graduated second out of forty-four in his class at West Point. In just two years from 1861 to 1863, he rose from lieutenant to corps commander in the Army of the Potomac. One of his fellow officers described him as having "a little of the look of an Indian, and evidently is of a nervous temperament."[15] He also had an odd sense of humor and could often be overheard "laughing and laughing again while alone in his tent over a small volume of limericks."[16] A contemporary journalist characterized Warren as "a man of maps and surveys when other officers rest, but horse and sword 'when blows the blast of war.'" The writer added that Warren was a soldier "whose first glance at the pivotal time and place on the battle-field is worth ten thousand men to the general commanding, to whom after a gallop like tempest, he shall give his opinion of the situation and suggest the movement that snatches victory from the jaws of disaster."[17]

A mathematics professor at West Point before the war, Warren was appointed Lieutenant-Colonel of the Fifth New York Volunteers—a well-known Zouave unit—in May 1861. Civil War Zouave regiments, with their colorful uniforms, were modeled on French Army units that originated in North Africa in the early 19th century. Warren later wrote that he entered the war to defend his country and do his duty. He immediately exhibited bravery and talent. Promotions followed in rapid succession. Sadly, he became discouraged after the Army of the Potomac experienced several early setbacks. After the disastrous Battle of Fredericksburg in December 1862, Warren wrote, "What have we done as a nation to suffer as we do? There must be a just God. Why does he permit these things? Is he the jealous God to us now that visits the sins of the fathers upon the children?" He then declared, "I know that all would go right if we had ability and unity in our counsels and perhaps we may yet have them both."[18]

Warren voted for Abraham Lincoln in 1860, and was opposed to slavery. Yet, he also made it clear in a letter to his brother that he fought for the Union and not the abolition of slavery. Writing in July 1862, a particularly dark time for the Union, Warren said Lincoln should "discard the New England and Greeley abolitionists entirely." He believed the Army "suffered enough now in hardships and perils to no longer act out any abolition program. It is fighting for the Union which is unattainable without allowing the Southern people their constitutional rights, for it is otherwise degrading them."[19] Despite his politics, Warren remained critical of slavery and even chastised Robert E. Lee on the eve of the Battle of Gettysburg for "carrying colored people into slavery like any King of Dahomey."[20]

Warren became Chief Engineer of the Army of the Potomac on June 8, 1863, less than a month before Gettysburg. He later befriended the new commander, General George Gordon Meade, who took over on June 28, 1863. On the second day of the Battle of Gettysburg, Meade said to his chief engineer, "Warren! I hear a little peppering going on in the direction of that little hill off yonder. I wish you would ride over and if anything serious is going on, attend to it."[21] Warren rushed to Little Round Top and noticed immediately the position required troops to defend it. He helped bring forces to secure Little Round Top, thereby saving it in the nick of time and protecting the Union left flank for the remainder of the battle. Warren's efforts were an essential contribution to the Union victory. Today, there is a majestic statue honoring Warren on Little Round Top. A prominent civil engineer at the time said, "but for Warren's military coup d'oeil and prompt acceptance of responsibility, Gettysburg might have been known as the grave of the Union."[22]

Shortly after his triumph, Warren took over as temporary commander of the Second Corps, while General Hancock recovered from a nasty wound he received during Pickett's Charge on the third day at Gettysburg. Upon receiving the promotion, Warren told his wife, "I feel as if while before I but climbed, now I have wings. Patriotism and honor shall be my impulses, and justice my rule and guide of action as far as a mortal like myself can be ruled by it."[23]

One general serving under Warren wrote in his diary at the time, "We have the bullyest little general in the army and his name is Warren. I venture a prophecy on him—that he will in time command us all, although he is my junior by ten years."[24] Further down the ladder, a private in Warren's corps described him as "ever present, cool, calculating, heroic, and determined."[25] When General Meade reorganized the Army of the Potomac in March 1864, Warren became the permanent commander of the Fifth Corps and Hancock returned to head up the Second Corps.

During the Mine Run campaign in late 1863, Warren made a controversial battlefield decision. On November 30, he had been prepared to attack Lee's works shortly after dawn. At the last moment, after a careful examination of the enemy's position, Warren determined an assault would be hopeless and called off the attack. When Meade heard the news, he remarked, "My God. General Warren has half my army at his disposition."[26] Meade later *seemed* to support Warren's decision, telling his wife, "I would rather be ignominiously dismissed and suffer anything, than knowingly and willfully have thousands of brave men slaughtered for nothing."[27] Nevertheless, in a letter to Grant's chief of staff in June 1864, Meade criticized Warren's actions at Mine Run. Regardless of Meade's mixed feelings, the ordinary soldiers respected Warren for his tough call. In this instance, it actually took considerable courage *not* to fight. "The slaughter would have been great and we feel thankful to have been spared," a grateful colonel said of the decision. An officer from a Pennsylvania regiment wrote, "Had the two armies fought at Mine Run the result would have been the greatest slaughter in the history of the United States."[28]

Shortly after the campaign, Warren shared his thinking with his wife, Emily, "We cannot carry all the breastworks the rebels can build by assault, and military science seems to be ignored in our plans. We throw away skill and rush in like savages . . . There seems to be an infatuation, a destiny, that rushes our men at a breastwork as a moth does at a candle."[29] At West Point, Warren studied under Dennis Hart Mahan, a professor of military engineering, who "rebelled against the callous disregard for life that he saw to be implicit in the use of the massed frontal assault."[30]

The aborted Mine Run attack may have been on the minds of Warren, Meade, and Grant on the morning of May 5 in the Wilderness, though for different reasons. Warren believed it was foolish to "throw away skill and rush in like savages."[31] Meade, unfortunately, was now expected to show more aggression under the watchful eyes of Ulysses S. Grant, who made his reputation out West by determined fighting at Shiloh, Vicksburg, and Chattanooga. In a message to Grant at 9:00 A.M., Meade assured his boss there would be no hesitation, "I think, still, Lee is making a demonstration to gain time. I shall, if such is the case, punish him, if he is disposed to fight this side of Mine Run at once, he shall be accommodated."[32]

There would be hesitation, however. After the suspension of the day's march, Warren's division commanders were slow to link up and form a line of battle in the impenetrable woods surrounding the Orange Turnpike and Parker's Store Road. Once Grant was established at his new headquarters—where he sat on a log, smoking cigars and whittling—he exerted his authority on the impending battle. Grant refused to shrink from a fight with Lee in the woods.[33]

At 10:30 A.M., Warren wrote his division commanders, "Push forward a heavy line of skirmishers followed by your line of battle, and attack the enemy at once and push him." Delay would no longer be tolerated by the Union high command. In his 10:30 A.M. directive to Wadsworth, Warren advised that "General Griffin will also attack. Do not wait for him, but look out for your left flank."[34] This was clearly Grant's thinking. Griffin and Wadsworth believed it would be madness to move forward in those woods with their flanks unprotected. Despite his recent order, Warren agreed with his division commanders. Grant felt otherwise.

While Warren, under pressure from Grant, urged his generals to attack, the surgeons of the Fifth Corps set up their field hospitals and prepared for an influx of wounded. Meanwhile, the troops lay in the woods waiting for the battle to begin. "We passed the time lying about in small groups, talking and loafing in the shade of the trees," one soldier said, "Jokes and stories were exchanged, but some spoke seriously with one another, committing some keepsake to a comrade's care." Ominously for Warren's men, the opposing lines were so close that at some points "the noise of felling trees for building breastworks was plainly audible."[35] Officers of the Fifth Corps began sending messages to Warren about the arrival of increasing numbers of Confederates, who were manning their works. By 11:00 A.M., Wadsworth's skirmishers began exchanging gunfire with Rebels in the woods. Wadsworth, by this point, arrayed his main body of soldiers in two lines of battle with the men lying down among the thickets. One soldier heard some officers under an oak tree, "chattering and chaffering in the highest spirits."[36] The 76th New York was positioned at Higgerson's Field on the extreme left of Wadsworth's line of battle.

Warren sympathized with his division commanders who insisted on making connections on their left and right before attacking the enemy. Unlike Grant and Meade, Warren knew the ground and appreciated the difficulty of moving large numbers of men over the narrow roads and uneven terrain of the Wilderness. In addition, Grant and Meade had no idea about the size of the force that was in front of them. As the morning progressed, Warren learned the force was probably a considerable one. He later wrote that Meade and Grant "thought it only an observing brigade of the enemy opposed to me that we might scoop and that by taking time they would get away." Disagreeing, Warren believed, "we had no certain means of knowing" the size of the Rebel force, and "It would do well to move only with matters well in hand, as the repulse of my force would make a bad beginning."[37] At the very least, Warren intended to wait for Brigadier General Horatio Wright's division from the Sixth Corps to help secure Griffin's right flank on the Turnpike before giving Griffin the final order to advance. By midday, neither Griffin nor Wadsworth had attacked the enemy. Grant and Meade lost their patience.

Grant's desire to hit Lee right way in the Wilderness made sense, too, however, despite the reluctance of his generals. With each passing hour, Ewell improved his defenses, while bringing up more men. And all the while, Lieutenant General A. P. Hill's Third Corps was streaming down the Orange Plank Road, around Warren's left. As one military strategist observed, "The Union generals had too often delayed their attacks for everybody to come into line. The chance of inflicting damaging blows before the enemy had concentrated and prepared for the attack had too often been thrown away in this manner, and this was not the time to repeat these tactics."[38] A conversation between Meade and Grant on the eve of the campaign illustrated the latter's approach. According to a leading journalist, General Meade told Grant "that he proposed to maneuver thus and so; whereupon General Grant stopped him at the word 'maneuver,' and said, 'Oh, *I never maneuver.*'"[39]

Around noontime, Meade and Grant made it clear to Warren they expected their orders to be implemented immediately. The conversation grew heated, though we don't know exactly what was said. Most of the important orders from Meade and Grant to Warren that day were verbal. Warren promptly ordered his division and brigade commanders to attack all across the line. Lieutenant Colonel William Swan soon found himself in the midst of a roiling controversy, after bringing the attack order to General Griffin's First Brigade commander, Brigadier General Romeyn Ayres, who faced Ewell's men just north of the Orange Turnpike.

Ayres, an experienced and highly regarded veteran who served in the Mexican War, believed it was unwise to attack at that precise moment.

With General Wright's division still not in place to protect his right flank, Ayres knew it would be disastrous to move forward. Instead, Ayres preferred to remain on the defensive rather than attack under such unfavorable circumstances.

Griffin visited the front and agreed with his brigade commander. Swan then relayed that message back to Warren, who still insisted that Griffin and Ayres go forward as ordered. Swan later wrote of his exchange with Warren, "I remember that he answered me as if fear was at the bottom of my errand." According to Swan, "Warren had just had unpleasant things said to him by General Meade," who "had just heard the bravery of his army questioned" by General Grant.[40] Warren admitted Meade had snapped at him, "We are waiting for you." One of Warren's aides, Major Washington Roebling, would later report that Grant threatened to cashier Warren on the spot, if he wouldn't give the final order straight away.[41] The leaders of the Army of the Potomac were losing their cool as they blindly attempted to confront two of Lee's army corps in the Wilderness. So far, Lee appeared to be winning the psychological battle.

Shortly before 1:00 P.M., Generals Griffin and Wadsworth finally began moving their divisions forward to confront Ewell's troops. General Rice's Second Brigade was at the far left of Wadsworth's line and the 76th New York made up the left of Rice's line of battle. Because Grant decided to attack without protecting Rice's left flank, the 76th was "in the air"—a military term meaning unprotected and susceptible to being encircled. The 76th might also be subjected to enfilade fire into its flanks as it moved toward the enemy. Rice wisely threw out three companies of the 76th—B, F, and K—as skirmishers to cover the left of the line as best he could. Private Reeves belonged to Company C, which was directed to move west with the remainder of the regiment.

Captain Charles Watkins, who served with distinction at Gettysburg, commanded Company C of the 76th New York Infantry. Before his troops headed into the woods, Watkins told them to fire deliberately and fire low. He also encouraged them to take careful aim. This was especially difficult in the Wilderness, however, where the enemy remained unseen.

After giving the order "forward, march," Watkins urged his men to close any gaps.

Overall Union forces confronting Ewell consisted of six brigades— roughly 12,000 men—covering slightly under a mile and a half from right to left. The line stretched from Ayres's brigade, situated north of the Turnpike, to Rice's brigade, located on the perimeter of Higgerson's Field, facing northwest. Upon receiving the attack order, Rice's men picked themselves up off the ground and pushed off from Higgerson's Field into the dense woods. As they advanced, a wild turkey "broke from a thicket ahead of them," startling some of the men. They were anxious—a soldier reported, "One who has never been through it cannot realize the tensity of that hour in the Wilderness: we knew it was the beginning of the end, victory for us at last or victory for them."[42]

The soldiers experienced formidable difficulties moving through the thick underbrush—almost immediately, some of the men got lost or separated from their line. One staff officer remembered, "The density of the woods prevented orders from being given by brigades. The staff officers had difficulty in carrying the orders to regimental commanders."[43] Throughout their march of almost a mile, Rice's soldiers could not even see any Rebels, though they knew they were there. One veteran suspected this would be "a weird, uncanny contest—a battle of invisibles with invisibles."[44]

The Confederates in those woods, lying in wait for the 76th New York, were Brigadier General Junius Daniel's North Carolinians. Daniel's brigade formed part of Major General Rodes's division in Ewell's Second Army Corps. He attended West Point, and trained his men extremely well. "Daniel's Brigade" was highly regarded in the Army of Northern Virginia. Rice's men now faced an unseen, but disciplined force in those tangled thickets.

As Private William Reeves headed deeper into the woods, he wore a cap, a faded blue jacket, and trousers. He carried a British-made Enfield rifle musket; on his belt, he had a bayonet, a cartridge box, and a cap box. His Enfield rifle was considered a good weapon with a reported range of 900 yards. Unfortunately, bullets fired from the rifle traveled in a somewhat curved trajectory, which made it difficult for the average soldier to manage. Under Civil War battlefield conditions, the soldiers needed to be much closer to the enemy to hit their targets. In the confined spaces of the Wilderness, the opposing sides were likely to be within at least fifty yards of each other before firing. [45] Reeves hadn't practiced much with his Enfield, so the risk of him shooting over the heads of the enemy was high. One soldier recalled that instead of target practice, the troops, while in camp prior to the spring offensive, "were marched to and fro and made to perform displayful evolutions." [46] Both the Yankees and the Rebels used rifle muskets that fired minié balls, which created nasty wounds. Experienced Civil War veterans could load and fire four rounds per minute and those minié balls would obliterate an advancing line. Any soldier who got hit directly in the head or the chest by a minié ball would almost certainly die.

Private Reeves didn't know what lay ahead in those woods as he bush-whacked through the Wilderness shortly before 1:00 P.M. on May 5, 1864. He heard the felling of trees by the Confederates who had been bolstering their breastworks for hours. And he knew that Union skirmishers had already exchanged fire with Confederate troops. It was clear to everyone in Company C that a large Confederate force was up ahead. Reeves's breathing got heavier as he advanced and his hands were shaky, which wouldn't help his aim, if called upon to fire his weapon, in the difficult conditions of the forest. If he hoped to finally see the "elephant" [47]—as many green troops did during the Civil War—he now knew he would get his chance.

It was a crystal clear day, though warmer than Reeves was accustomed to. And the light green leaves and birdsong, usually such pleasurable features of a perfect spring day in Virginia, seemed surreal with a terrible battle now looming. So, the fight to save the Union was finally about to commence. Had Reeves given some keepsakes to any of his comrades, in case he was killed? Did he pray before leaving Higgerson's Field and heading into the woods? Was he afraid as he descended ever farther into the Wilderness?

FOUR

The Elephant Appears

T he minié ball tore through Private Reeves's left cheek and exited his right cheek.[1]

He didn't feel pain at first, just an odd tingling sensation and numbness. It was the dollops of dark red blood dripping all over his faded blue uniform that told him he had been shot. He instinctively touched his left cheek, and felt the warm, open wound. A quick jolt of adrenaline surged through his body when he realized the severity of the injury. While the orifice of entry was small, the exit hole was about three inches in diameter. The hollow, cone-shaped minié ball flattened upon impact, leaving large exit wounds.

His pale face was smeared with sweat, blood, and gunpowder. The weather was extremely hot for early May. Though desperately thirsty, taking a sip of water from his canteen would be difficult. Blood, with its unpleasant metallic taste, was now pooling in his mouth.

In addition to shredding tissue, the minié ball had shattered the bones of both his cheek and jaw. In technical terms, Reeves had received "a compound comminuted fracture of the inferior maxilla by a conoidal ball, which entered the left cheek half an inch anterior to the angle of the jaw, and emerged at a point nearly opposite."[2] Bone fragments filled both his mouth and the exit wound.

The right side of Reeves's face looked horrific, but it appeared far worse than it was. The ball exited his face, and didn't appear to have hit an artery. Talking was difficult due to the trauma to his jaw, but if Reeves could be safely transported to a secure hospital, he had a reasonable chance of surviving his injury.[3]

Not too far from where Reeves was hit, Private Frank Wilkeson witnessed another young soldier who received a similar wound. "His head jerked, he staggered, then fell, then regained his feet. A tiny fountain of blood and teeth and bone and bits of tongue burst out of his mouth. He had been shot through the jaws; the lower one was broken and hung down. I looked directly into his open mouth, which was ragged and bloody and tongueless."[4] Given the even greater extent of this injury, it's unlikely the unfortunate soldier survived. An inch or two could be the difference between survival and death.

The soldiers of Company C hadn't seen the enemy until it was too late. Trudging through the woods, they came to within twenty-five yards or so of the Rebels before getting a fleeting glimpse of them. Many of the Northerners shot too high—Reeves never even had a chance to fire his Enfield musket—before the 53rd North Carolina Infantry Regiment hit them with a well-timed and accurate volley. According to the official report for the brigade, "The underbrush was very dense, and the men found difficulty in making their way through it; the enemy, still unseen, poured in a very destructive fire."[5] Some men of the 76th were killed instantly. Those who could run did so, fleeing over uneven terrain toward Parker's Store Road. Union guards posted along the way prevented the demoralized troops from leaving the battlefield, allowing only the wounded to pass.[6]

Quite a few of the men were captured by the Rebels. Given the seriousness of Reeves's injury, that would have been a death sentence. As a prisoner, he wouldn't receive the medical care he urgently required. Fortunately for Reeves, he could still walk and run—at least until blood loss weakened him. As Reeves tried to escape his Confederate pursuers, he looked out for his regiment's "primary station," where he'd receive first aid prior to being transported by ambulance to his division hospital, one mile east of Wilderness Tavern on the Orange Turnpike.

Several officers succeeded in rallying 350 soldiers from General Rice's brigade for a second stand a half a mile back, but they were ordered by General Wadsworth to reform even further in the rear. General Warren's aide, Major Washington Roebling, noted that Parker's Store Road at that time was "crowded with stragglers and large crowds of soldiers pouring out of the woods in great confusion and almost panic stricken. Some said they were flanked, others that they had suddenly come upon the rebs lying concealed in two lines of battle in the thick underbrush." Roebling believed the cause of the repulse was "easily accounted for." Rice's men inadvertently ran into Ewell's troops at an angle, which allowed the Confederates to "pour their fire" into Rice's flank. According to Roebling, "the density of the wood made it impossible to repair the line."[7]

With the fighting finally underway, the Wilderness looked like a scene out of Dante's *Inferno*. As the Yankees streamed out of the woods, an artilleryman observed, "The smoke drifted to and fro . . . I saw scores of wounded men . . . The uproar was deafening; the bullets flew through the air thickly." The powder smoke made it difficult for anyone to see more than a few yards ahead. The poor visibility isolated brigades and regiments. And the groans, moans, shrieks, cheers, and Rebel yells that echoed throughout the woods added even greater stress on the troops, who were desperately fighting for survival.[8]

The sights and sounds of the moment overwhelmed Private Reeves's senses. Many of his wounded comrades from Company C were unable to run any farther. They gave up and lay down on the floor of the woods. Reeves knew some of them wouldn't survive the afternoon, but there was nothing he could do to help them. The cracking sound of Rebel musketry remained dangerously close. Reeves kept moving with the mob of men. His sole focus was getting out of those woods alive. One soldier remarked that "the Battle of the Wilderness more closely resembled a riot than a battle."[9]

It really *was* a different sort of battle. "Your typical 'great white plain,' with long lines advancing and maneuvering, led on by generals in cocked hats and by bands of music, exist not for us," said General Meade's aide-de-camp, Lieutenant Colonel Theodore Lyman, "Here it is said: 'Left face—prime—forward!' and then *wrang, wr-r-rang*, for three or four hours, or for all day, and the poor bleeding, wounded streaming to the rear. That is the great battle in America."[10] Herman Melville wrote, "Plume and sash are vanities now." For Private Reeves, any thoughts of glory and heroism were distant memories.

After retreating half a mile or so through the thickets, Reeves arrived at the primary station with torn pants and scratched legs. He was thankful the surgeons had chosen a location so close to the front line. He had little strength left and could not have gone much farther. During the last hundred yards or so, he became dizzy and his wound started to throb. The bedlam of the primary station was unlike anything he had seen before. The influx of wounded men was considerably greater than the medical staff had expected. Soldiers in varying levels of distress awaited treatment. Despite the seriousness of his injury, Reeves noticed there were others who were much worse off.

An assistant surgeon, with the help of an orderly, took a closer look at his wounds. The assistant surgeon washed both apertures with a sponge and gave Reeves a dressing made of raw cotton to place on the gaping hole in his right cheek. The patient held the dressing on the wound until he was delivered to the division hospital. Reeves was also given some whiskey—by this point, the pain on the right side of his face was unbearable.

This pit-stop had to be brief with the Confederates in relentless pursuit. The surgeon arranged for Reeves to be taken to the field hospital in a horse-drawn, four-wheeled ambulance. There, he'd receive a more thorough examination of his injury. He'd likely need all the various splinters removed from his mouth and the opening on the right side of his face. The hospitals of the Fifth Corps were extremely busy that day. Between noon and 9:00 P.M., they received, dressed, fed, and sheltered 1,235 men. One division surgeon recalled he remained busy treating the wounded until "long after midnight."[11]

The Union ambulance service and field hospital system improved dramatically over the three years prior to the Wilderness Campaign. At the Second Battle of Bull Run in 1862, there were exceedingly poor systems in place for dealing with the wounded.[12] A witness to the plight of injured soldiers during that battle described it as "the most terrible example in all our history of suffering on the battlefield."[13] Things were so bad that regimental musicians served as nurses and drunken ambulance drivers consumed the whiskey that was intended for the wounded. "The third day after the battle I passed such a night as I had never before experienced in my life," a medical officer wrote, "Long trains of ambulances arrived, carrying wounded from the field of battle back to Washington, and there were but four surgeons to look after them and their many imperious needs. Fifty poor thirsty fellows were crying for water; fifty more were crying with the pain from a jolting ride over nine miles over a corduroy road. Most of them had had nothing to eat for one, two, or three days, save what they had obtained from haversacks of the dead."[14] In aggregate, 3,000 wounded men—unfed and unseen by doctors—remained on the field three days after the battle. Those left behind withstood storms, blistering heat, thirst, and hunger. Their suffering was incomprehensible.

The disaster at Second Bull Run provoked much-needed reforms of the medical services provided to soldiers. Dr. Jonathan Letterman, known as the "Father of Modern Battlefield Medicine," led the way in bringing about improvements. A small, scholarly man, he was the Medical Director of the Army of the Potomac in 1862 and 1863. With the full support of Major General George McClellan, who commanded the Army of the Potomac at the time, Letterman introduced the first Ambulance Corps to the United States Army and also began the system of triage in treating injured Union soldiers. Ambulances would now be attached to specific divisions and their crews would be professionally trained for the first time. His plan also made sure that field hospitals and field dressing stations, run by experienced surgeons, would be set up near the battlefields. The new system allowed ambulance crews to focus on removing the wounded from the field, and enabled surgeons to treat the injured men right way. Finally, Letterman instilled the same esprit de corps among military surgeons and ambulance crews as existed among combat troops. [15]

The Lettermen system worked so well that it became a model for the entire world for more than fifty years after the Civil War. A medical historian wrote, "In the years since Bull Run the Medical Department's field service had evolved from a buzzing confusion to an orderly system. Something approaching a trained Hospital Corps had replaced frightened musicians as stretchermen and callous teamsters as ambulance drivers." [16]

The Union Army that crossed the Rapidan in May 1864 had a field hospital for every division, along with 294 hospital tents for treating the wounded behind the lines. There were also 609 ambulances, 266 wagons, and 3,295 draft animals. At the beginning of the Battle of the Wilderness, an ambulance officer for the Fifth Corps set up his train of ambulances in a central location. He then sent forward several ambulances to each division to ferry the wounded from the battlefield back to the field hospitals. The ambulance crews faced the same risks as combat troops. It was dangerous, underappreciated work.

The field hospitals were organized for each division and were situated next to other divisions from their Army Corps about one and a half miles behind the battle line. A medical officer reported that the hospitals of the Fifth Corps "were located on a slope of open ground by a small creek which crosses the Fredericksburg pike 1 mile east of Old Wilderness Tavern. Water for the hospitals was obtained from excellent springs in the vicinity, tents were pitched, operating tables and kitchens prepared, surgeons and attendants at their posts, and everything in readiness for the reception of wounded an hour before the cases began to arrive." [17] Reeves's division hospital had 25 tents, 36 enlisted men, and at least 3 surgeons, along with several assistant surgeons. On May 5 alone, this division hospital treated 300 wounded soldiers.

An ambulance delivered Reeves to his division field hospital between 1:30 and 2:00 P.M. He was gently removed from the vehicle and placed on the ground, amid a large number of other wounded men, where he waited to be seen by a surgeon. Fortunately for Reeves, he didn't have to wait for too long. Thanks to Letterman, the field hospitals now used a triage system and Reeves's case was seen as somewhat promising. The mortally wounded were quickly identified as hopeless. And the slightly wounded could obviously wait to receive treatment. Reeves had a serious wound that might improve, if given immediate medical attention. Even though his condition looked severe, the ball missed hitting a major artery, and the profuse bleeding from his right cheek would eventually subside. Since there was a very good chance Reeves would survive, he received attention before many of the others.

The sight of severed limbs and sounds of shrieking soldiers terrified Reeves upon arrival at the field hospital. The poet Walt Whitman, who was struck by "the smell of ether, the odor of blood," described a typical scene. "Scores, hundreds of the noblest young men on earth, uncomplaining, lie helpless, mangled, faint, alone."[18] A Union colonel remembered his experience in the Wilderness. "On my arrival at hospital, about 2:00 P.M., I was carried through an entrance to a large tent, on each side of which lay human legs and arms, resembling piles of stove wood, the blood only excepted. All around were dead and wounded men, many of the latter dying. The surgeons, with gleaming, sometimes bloody, knives and instruments, were busy at their work."[19] After his surgery, the colonel recalled, "I was then borne to a pallet on the ground to make room for—'Next.'"[20]

With great tenderness and feeling, Lieutenant Morris Schaff characterized the hospitals of the Fifth Corps during the Battle of the Wilderness, "where the surgeons, with rolled-up sleeves, are at their humane tasks in the operating tents, instruments by them which they handle with skill and mercy, as one after another the mutilated and perforated bodies of the boys who have been willing to risk their lives for the country are brought in and laid on the table before them, their anxious eyes scrutinizing the surgeon's face for a sign of hope as he examines their wounds and feels their fluttering pulses."[21]

Sometime in the late afternoon, Reeves was placed on an operating table—likely an old door or large wooden board. After the surgeon probed the wounds with his fingers, he determined Reeves needed an operation to remove the bone fragments caused by the minié ball. A physician's assistant then administered chloroform for the operation. First, the assistant put a small dose of chloroform on a sponge within a towel folded into the shape of a cone. Next, the cone was held above Reeves's face. It took about five to ten minutes for Reeves to drop off to sleep for the operation. First discovered in 1832, chloroform was widely used during the Civil War. In fact, it was highly unusual for a Union surgeon to operate without using an anesthetic, despite popular myths to the contrary.

Once Reeves had been anesthetized, the surgeon began removing the bone fragments from the wounds with forceps. According to the official report, "a large number of primary fracture splinters" were "extracted through the mouth and the orifice of exit."[22] The biggest challenge for the surgeon was that some of the shards of bone may have been hidden or too small to be seen. Today, an X-ray would identify all the pieces of bone. A Civil War surgeon could only remove what he saw or felt. This surgeon surely did not remove *all* the pieces of bone. Reeves was in grave danger if one of those fragments nicked a nearby artery. Other than that ongoing risk, the operation appeared to be successful.

After the operation, Reeves received a dressing for his wounds. The assistant surgeon affixed a linen or cotton square to the three-inch hole on the right side of his face. The dressings on both apertures were held in place with bandages wrapped under the chin and then over the head. His wound on the right cheek was still bleeding, so Reeves looked very badly injured, even after receiving his medical treatments.

Once his wound was dressed, he was laid on a bed of straw. According to a contemporary medical manual, his care after surgery was "exceedingly simple." The plan for Reeves was "absolute rest, keeping down inflammation by cold fomentations, the relieving of pain by opiates, and the supporting of the system (by liquor and quinine) to enable it to go through the necessary process of suppuration."[23] After his surgery, Reeves swallowed some opium pills, which were widely used for pain. He was also given some beef broth, since his traumatized jaw couldn't handle normal food.

The work of Louis Pasteur and Robert Koch in bacteriology came too late to influence Civil War surgeons. They were also unaware of Joseph Lister's ideas on antisepsis in surgery—the prevention of infection by stopping the spread of germs. Lister didn't publish his breakthrough paper, "The Antiseptic Principle of Surgery," until 1867. The American Civil War was one of the last great conflicts before revolutionary changes in medicine. "We operated in old blood-stained and often pus-stained coats, the veterans of a hundred fights," said a leading surgeon of the time, "We operated with clean hands in the social sense, but they were undisinfected hands . . . We used undisinfected instruments from undisinfected plush-lined cases, and still worse used marine sponges which had been used in prior pus cases and had been only washed in tap water. If a sponge or an instrument fell on the floor it was washed and squeezed in a basin of tap water and used as if it were clean."[24]

When Reeves awoke after the chloroform wore off, he pondered his current situation. It appeared he'd probably survive and would be able to see his wife Anna again. His wound seemed just bad enough to put an end to his fighting days. He might even get to go home, if he was lucky, though he might be assigned to a non-combat role after his recovery. Eventually, he'd return to Victor, New York, and work the farm he'd buy with the money he received for being a substitute. He'd also get to see his father, Theophilus, again. They had become close after his mother died. Perhaps he'd start his own family. He hoped his war wound wouldn't scare the children. Maybe it'd be mostly healed by then.

Private Reeves was proud that he did his duty during his brief skirmish in the woods earlier that afternoon. Even though his mouth was dry and his heart was pounding, he marched straight up to the Confederate line. The description of Henry Fleming's heroism in *Red Badge of Courage* was equally true of Reeves during the attack: "He suddenly lost concern for himself, and forgot to look at a menacing fate. He became not a man but a member. He felt that something of which he was a part—a regiment, an army, a cause, or a country—was in crisis. He was welded into a common personality which was dominated by a single desire. For some moments he could not flee no more than a little finger can commit a revolution from a hand."[25] To march, Morris Schaff later wrote, "on in the face of withering musketry and canister" was a "kind of courage which sets your heart a-beating as your eye follows their fluttering colors."[26]

Sure, he and his comrades retreated after the first deadly Confederate volley. But that was only after it became clear they had been flanked. It was either run or be captured. And getting captured would have resulted in a slow, agonizing death, at some godforsaken prison camp in the Deep South. Anyone would have done what they did.

Reeves worried about the boys from the 76th New York. The volley by the North Carolinians had been absolutely lethal. Those Rebels were good shots. It seemed like half his company had been struck down by gunfire. Many of them surely were killed. Reeves felt guilty for somehow surviving. It had been a terrible, terrible moment in those woods. Reeves would never forget it as long as he lived.

He wondered how the battle was going to turn out. Things had clearly gone very badly for General Wadsworth's division. And Reeves learned things hadn't gone that much better for General Griffin's troops. But he heard with his own ears, by late afternoon, the guns of General Hancock's men on the Orange Plank Road. Maybe they'd have more success. Reeves hated to think of having to evacuate if Grant's army was forced to retreat. The pain in his jaw and cheek was excruciating. Keeping completely still was the only thing that made the pain bearable. He didn't even want to think of being transported to a safer location in a wagon with poor springs over bad roads.

Reeves had every reason to be concerned about the well-being of the men of the 76th New York. The regiment suffered disastrous losses in the woods that afternoon. The regimental commander, Lieutenant Colonel John Cook, received a wound to his right arm and had to give up his command for the remainder of the battle. And Major John Young, who headed up the three companies of the 76th that were thrown out as skirmishers, was wounded and taken prisoner. Almost everyone in those three companies—B, F, and K—was killed or captured. A corporal from Company A named Albert Hilton was killed while carrying the regimental colors. [27] All told, the entire 76th experienced a casualty rate of almost 50% on the afternoon of May 5, 1864. It was roughly the same rate the regiment experienced on the first day of Gettysburg.

The loss of three entire companies—approximately 150 men—was an especially devastating blow to the regiment. Companies B, F, and K had been sent out to protect the left flank of General Rice's brigade as it headed into the woods. When the brigade fell back after getting hit with deadly fire from the North Carolinians, it left the skirmishers unprotected and surrounded by Rebels. One skirmisher observed that "the balls came like rain, but not a rebel could be seen." Private John Northrop of Company F said, "We were perplexed, tired, hungry and hot, besmeared with powder and dust, clothing torn and faces and arms scratched with brush." [28] Major Young did his best to organize pockets of resistance, but the situation was hopeless. Young was eventually approached by a Confederate soldier who said, "Halt! You are my prisoner." When Young kept walking, the Rebel said, "Halt! Or I'll blow your damned brains out." According to the official historian of the 76th, Young finally surrendered, "and paid for his obedience by nearly a year in the prison pens of the South." [29]

Northrop's band of men tried to fight their way out, but they were quickly overwhelmed. Captain Edwin Swan, commander of Company K of the 76th, told his men, "It's no use, better surrender." Northrop recalled that, after laying down his gun, the "Jonnies mixed freely with us to trade canteens, knives, caps, rubber blankets, tobacco boxes, etc." The Union soldiers were then marched approximately two miles behind Confederate lines. Northrop remembered that by the time they got there, "It was very dark, and we were closely guarded and not allowed to speak to the guards." [30] It had been a long afternoon. Many members of the three companies had been killed, but most had been taken prisoner.

The hellish ordeal of the prisoners was only just beginning. As recorded by the 76th regimental roster, at least forty-six of them, who were transported to the notorious Andersonville Prison in Georgia, would die over the next several months. And the death toll was probably much higher than that. Upon arriving at Andersonville sixteen days after being captured in the Wilderness, Private Northrop wrote, "On my right, as we entered, I saw men without a thread of clothing upon their dirty skeletons, some panting under old rags, or blankets raised above them . . . On the left the scene was equally sickening. The ground for several yards from the gate was wet with excrement, diarrhea being the disease wasting the bodies of the men scarce able to move."[31]

According to a Union medical officer's report on Andersonville, the main causes of death at the camp were scurvy and bowel disease. The bowel afflictions—diarrhea and dysentery—were primarily a result of poor nutrition and substandard sanitary conditions. Almost all forty-six prisoners who eventually died at Andersonville had been mustered into the army in the summer of 1863 just like Private Reeves.[32] The regimental historian of the 76th described Andersonville as a "story of cruelties, starvation, vermin, heartless disregard of life, and unparalleled diabolism, which puts to blush every loyal man."[33] Nearly 13,000 Union soldiers would die at Andersonville Prison in 1864 and 1865.

On the afternoon of May 5, the men of the 76th New York learned that one of their most popular officers was killed by the same volley that wounded Reeves. Captain Norman Bartholomew, who bravely led Company E toward the Confederate line, was shot in the arm. The young captain, who hailed from Upstate New York, had married Mary Hontz right before the war. He enlisted in 1861 and earned his captain's bars at Gettysburg for his splendid performance under fire.

Brigade Surgeon G. W. Metcalfe, situated at the same primary station that treated Reeves, heard the commencement of gunfire and soon saw Captain Bartholomew "mounted on the colonel's horse, and supported by a soldier, coming toward me, and bleeding profusely from a wound of the arm near the shoulder joint." Metcalfe recalled he "immediately applied a field tourniquet to his arm, which checked the hemorrhage, administered a stimulant, and placed him in an ambulance in waiting, which conveyed him at once to the division hospital." Metcalfe followed Bartholomew to the hospital to conduct a more thorough examination. There, he discovered "the bone badly fractured, the artery severed, and the nerves contused and torn, but not severed. He was very much prostrated, but not bleeding, the artery being perfectly compressed."[34]

After consulting with some other surgeons, Metcalfe decided to amputate the arm. Unfortunately, Bartholomew continued to get even weaker despite the surgery. He died three hours after losing his arm. In his final moments, he expressed "love for his wife, and satisfaction that he had done his duty." He was buried near the field hospital with "a simple head-board erected with his name, rank, and date of death, inscribed thereon." Metcalfe would later write, "No truer patriot or braver man ever lived than Captain N. G. Bartholomew. He was particularly distinguished, in time of battle, for cool judgment, and, at the proper moment, brilliant, dashing courage."[35]

Reeves was especially disheartened about the fate of his comrades in Company C. Privates Mortimer Richey, Horace Smith, and William Towers, who all mustered in around the same time as Reeves, were among the many men who had been shot in the woods. Private Peter Wagner, who enlisted at Canandaigua, New York, and was mustered in on August 25, 1863—the exact same place and date as Reeves—was shot, too. Privates Newton Baldwin, Mathew Devine, and the company musician, Chauncey Barnes, were among the unlucky soldiers of Company C who were captured. Devine would die of disease at Andersonville Prison on September 8, 1864. Baldwin somehow managed to survive the horrors of the prison, and would return to military service in early 1865.

For many of the men of Company C, the fighting ended within minutes after it started. For the rest of the Army of the Potomac, the Battle of the Wilderness was only just beginning. What may have looked like a catastrophe to Private William Reeves was merely an opening gambit by Lieutenant General Ulysses S. Grant.

FIVE

Raging Fire at Saunders Field

General Warren's regrettable assault on Ewell's line lasted from 12:50 P.M. until approximately 2:15 P.M. Three brigades of General Wadsworth's division and two brigades of General Griffin's division suffered heavy losses and were driven back to where they started earlier that morning. The Union men found it more difficult coping with the trying conditions of the forest than the Rebels. Shortly after the fighting subsided, a Union officer "found the pike blocked with ambulances and with wounded on foot, who continually enquired 'How far to the 5th Corps Hospital?'"[1]

Like Rice's brigade, Colonel Roy Stone's Bucktails—a brigade of five Pennsylvania regiments forming part of Wadsworth's division—fled after being surprised by a murderous volley in the woods. Stone's men, situated to the right of Rice and the left of Brigadier General Lysander Cutler's Iron Brigade, began the attack by trudging through a small valley, using axes to cut through impenetrable thickets and vines. Soon, Stone's brigade lost touch with both Rice and Cutler, while becoming bogged down on marshy ground. A veteran remembered his regiment "had not progressed far through the swamp when, without seeing a single foe, a sheet of fire opened on the line—if line it could be called." The engagement didn't last long, roughly twenty minutes or so. Stone's troops couldn't effectively respond to the gunfire of the invisible enemy. A call for retreat resulted in chaos as the Pennsylvanians tried to extricate themselves from "that champion mud hole of mud holes."[2] The stampede turned into a rout with the soldiers not knowing which way to run.

Just twenty-seven years old, the bearded Colonel Stone worked as a director of lumbering operations at a firm in northern Pennsylvania before the war. At Gettysburg, the young brigade commander was shot in the hip and arm during the hard fighting of the first day. His unit fought gallantly, losing 850 of its 1,250 soldiers. Stone wrote of his men at Gettysburg, "They fought as if each man felt that upon his own arm hung the fate of the day and the nation."[3] A superior praised the Bucktails and Stone, "They repulsed the repeated attacks of vastly superior numbers at close quarters, and maintained their position until the final retreat of the whole line. Stone himself was shot down, battling to the last." When Stone returned to his men in March 1864, a soldier wrote, "The boys gave him three hearty cheers and throwed their hats in the air . . . We fairly worship him."[4]

The stellar performance of Stone's Bucktails at Gettysburg made it difficult to comprehend their disorderly flight from Ewell's troops in the woods south of the Turnpike. One soldier provided a pathetic account of a brief exchange of gunfire, "About this time a shot was fired down on our right. Our new men fire into these woods and then away they ran to the rear pell mell like a flock of scared sheep."[5] Some of the veterans blamed the rout on Stone and several of his officers for being drunk. "Tell to the world if you can," a Bucktail later wrote, "why then two fighting brigades were thus advanced to this position in this hell hole, without connection on either flank, and officers drunk."[6] The retreat of the Pennsylvanians had dire consequences for the Iron Brigade that was on their right. And Stone's drunkenness would have grave implications later in the afternoon.

The Iron Brigade, which consisted of mostly western regiments commanded by the fifty-seven-year-old Cutler, experienced some success during the initial moments of the assault by the Fifth Corps. According to Cutler's official report, he "continued to drive the enemy until it was ascertained that the troops on both flanks had left and that the enemy was closing in his rear, when he was obliged to fight his way back losing very heavily in killed and wounded."[7] Cutler's men, at first, "pushed forward with cheers, and the force opposed to them gave way."[8] In the Wilderness, unfortunately, success could instantly become a disaster, as the Confederates poured through the gaps between Union brigades. "Stone's brigade gave way soon after meeting the enemy," Cutler wrote, "thus letting the enemy through our line."[9] The westerners were forced back, though they redeemed themselves somewhat by seizing three flags and 289 prisoners.

The setback for the Iron Brigade was demoralizing, despite Cutler's explanation. Originally known as the "Black Hats" for their distinctive headgear, they later earned the name "Iron Brigade" after Major General George McClellan had declared they "stood like iron" in September 1862. The first day of Gettysburg may have been the brigade's finest hour. After the bloody opening to the battle, only 671 out of the brigade's 1,883 troops were still available for service. Right before the shooting of the heroic Major General John Reynolds at Gettysburg, he shouted to his beloved Iron Brigade, "Forward Men! Forward for God's sake, and drive those fellows out of the woods!"

Cutler, described as a "slim, tall, erect thoroughly soldier figure," was somehow able to organize an orderly retreat under impossible circumstances.[10] It was still a shock, however, to see one of the finest brigades in the Union Army humbled in such a short time. Amid the carnage in the forest "were scores of tall black hats scattered among the bodies which lay in the smoldering grass."[11] The Bucktails, the Iron Brigade, and the 76th New York, which had all won so much glory on the first day at Gettysburg, retreated speedily after coming under fire during the opening moments of the Battle of the Wilderness. It was an inauspicious beginning to Ulysses S. Grant's Overland campaign.

As General Wadsworth's three brigades streamed out of the woods, they regrouped on the sloping lawns surrounding Lacy House. Schaff, who was present among the stunned men, reported that Wadsworth brought them into order, "and it only took a moment, for once out of the woods and where they could see their colors, all rallied save now and then a man whose heart was not made for war." Wadsworth, Schaff remembered, "was deeply mortified and in high temper" as he reorganized his men. The old commander, who led many of these troops during the first day at Gettysburg, couldn't comprehend why they ran after coming under fire for such a relatively short amount of time. [12]

Fighting in the Wilderness caused even the most hardened veterans to become fearful. One soldier noted "there had been wood-fights before, but none in which the contestants were so completely concealed as in this." An officer sadly recalled losing a quarter of his men without ever having seen the enemy. In addition to the deafening sounds and lack of visibility, the troops were extremely anxious about being surrounded. [13]

A staff officer for Brigadier General Romeyn Ayres wrote, "in all this wood fighting our troops seem to have been greatly alarmed whenever the noise of a contest to the right or the left told them that there was fighting in the rear of a prolongation of their own line. Such noises seem to have caused more disturbance than a foe directly in front." This fear of being surrounded by an unseen enemy was compounded by the fact that retreating was difficult over the rough terrain of the woods. Ayres's staff officer recalled that one brigade's confusion soon spread the calamity to adjacent troops, though he dryly added, "every soldier, however, seemed to know the way to the Lacy house." [14]

There was one other obvious reason why these brigades that had won everlasting fame at Gettysburg didn't perform as well in the Wilderness. They weren't really the *same* fighting units. All three of the brigades serving under Rice, Stone, and Cutler, had been wrecked during the Battle of Gettysburg. Throughout late 1863 and early 1864, they were gradually restored to fighting strength. At the opening of the Overland Campaign in May 1864, green troops constituted a large proportion of the fighting strength of these brigades.

One representative regiment of the division as a whole consisted of 343 new men and 323 veterans on the eve of the Overland Campaign.[15] Private William Reeves, who joined up in August 1863, was typical of the new men. An officer on Warren's staff told Schaff of one such recruit after the failed assault, "I can almost see the boy's face yet. The shattered division was just moving back to the line when I noticed the youngster in his place going to what may have been his death, with pallid face and trembling lips, yet with his head erect and eyes to the front, going to meet Fate like a gentleman and soldier."[16]

General Charles Griffin's division had an equally disastrous time of it straddling the Turnpike, during the initial attack. The ill-tempered Griffin, who Colonel Wainwright described as an "inveterate hater," had been reluctant to engage with the Rebels until General Horatio Wright's division from the Sixth Corps could arrive to protect his right flank. Wright became entangled in the woods north of the Turnpike, and didn't arrive until 3:00 P.M. It was too late.

Like many of the top commanders on both sides, Griffin attended West Point, and served in the Mexican War. Despite his bad temper and salty vocabulary, his troops respected him as a brave and honest leader. For the early afternoon assault on Ewell, Griffin positioned a brigade led by Brigadier General Joseph Bartlett just south of the turnpike with another led by Ayres north of the pike. A third brigade, commanded by Colonel Jacob Sweitzer, would provide support.

Just like Cutler's men on their left, Bartlett's troops experienced encouraging success at first, driving the Rebels through the woods. A Union officer wrote, "On we went, o'er briar, o'er brake, o'er logs, and o'er bogs, through underbrush and overhanging limbs, for about three-quarters of a mile, yelling like so many demons."[17] But then, once again similar to Cutler's experience, gaps appeared on Bartlett's flanks and the Rebels capitalized on the opportunity. With both flanks of Bartlett's brigade coming under enemy gunfire, it was compelled to fall back. The retreat was orderly at first, but it rapidly gave way to chaos.

An officer remembered, "the impression soon gained ground that we were hopelessly flanked and liable to be surrounded and captured, and then the line broke up into little knots which falling back some distance, would turn and face the enemy, and then again fall back."[18] One of the reasons why Bartlett was outflanked was that General Ayres's brigade was unable to keep pace with it. Ayres's men, who attacked north of the Turnpike, were easily encircled by the Confederates due to the absence of Wright. One needn't be Carl von Clausewitz to see the dire consequences of Grant's order to Warren to go forward with the attack, without waiting for Wright. During the engagement south of the pike, Bartlett's "horse was killed, part of his clothing was shot away, but he fortunately escaped with a few bruises," according to one of his soldiers.[19]

Ayres's first line consisted of the 140th New York Infantry on the left with several regiments of U.S. Regulars on the right. His second line on the left included the 146th New York Infantry, a Zouave unit like the 140th that wore distinctive red and blue uniforms. The 146th was commanded by Colonel David T. Jenkins, who had led Griffin's pickets at dawn that morning. Jenkins was the first officer to tell Warren that Ewell's troops were on the Turnpike. Before the attack, Ayres told Colonel Jenkins he could remain with the pickets as they moved to the rear. But Jenkins insisted on leading his regiment in the coming fight.[20]

Right before 1:00 P.M., the 140th New York marched across Saunders Field under deadly fire from Brigadier General George Steuart's Virginians and North Carolinians. The Regulars on the right couldn't maintain their line with the New Yorkers. Undaunted, the men of the 140th continued their march under a deluge of lead. Soon, they engaged in violent hand-to-hand combat with the Rebels in the woods just west of the field. Young men from Upstate New York, who only months earlier may have been working as clerks or day laborers, were now using their weapons to club or bayonet their enemies. With terror in their eyes and faces blackened by gunpowder, they'd have been unrecognizable to their friends and family back home. They were now state-sanctioned killers.

As the 140th faced near-certain destruction, Colonel Jenkins led the 146th forward to assist them, yelling "Attention! Take arms! Fix bayonets! Forward march!"[21] Among the attackers was a young lieutenant, Robert

Warren—the youngest brother of Gouverneur Warren. Jenkins's men withstood a merciless volley of minié balls as they crossed Saunders Field. "Many threw their arms wildly into the air as they fell backward, the death-rattle in their throats," one of the soldiers remembered, "Others, wounded more or less severely, reeled in their tracks and collapsed upon the field or staggered to the rear in search of aid." In no time at all, the survivors were grappling with the Rebels, "men ran to and fro, firing, shouting, stabbing with their bayonets, beating each other with the butts of their guns. Each man fought on his own resources, grimly and desperately."[22]

Suddenly, an overwhelming Confederate force, announced with piercing Rebel yells, appeared in the gap to the right of the two New York regiments. A soldier from the 146th wrote, "The result was a complete rout, and escape to the rear became the only alternative to being killed or captured. So dense was the smoke and so confusing the noise and excitement of the battle that men lost their heads completely, rushing directly into the enemy's fire in the belief they were going to the rear."[23]

Captain W.H.S. Sweet diagnosed the problem several years later, "I knew of the danger of being flanked, as by charging over the open field we broke the continuity of our general line of battle and the rebels were adepts in finding gaps. Twenty paces to the rear, enabled me to look over the open field we had just crossed. We were not only flanked, but doubly flanked. Rebel troops covered the open field. We were in the bag and the string was tied."[24] Miraculously, some of the men were able to escape the encirclement. Nevertheless, the Wilderness appeared to be an inhospitable environment for launching offensive operations.

Veterans of the attack never forgot the horror of Saunders Field. One recalled, "the wounded limped painfully along or crawled over the ground on hands and knees. Many fell an easy prey to the Virginians and North Carolinians, whose appearance in such overwhelming numbers had wrought havoc with our regiment."[25] Many of the men died on the field and others ended up in southern prisons, where they eventually succumbed after much suffering. The next time the roll was called for the 146th New York, only

254 enlisted men out of 556 responded to their names. Only ten commissioned officers out of twenty-four remained in the field.

The last time the soldiers of the 146th saw their regimental commander, Colonel Jenkins, he was leaning on his sword wiping sweat and blood from his face with a handkerchief. He'd been in the midst of the heaviest fighting and advanced to within a few feet of the enemy's breastworks. He then seemed to disappear without a trace.

Captain James Jenkins—the brother of the missing Colonel—wrote to a cousin about the matter just two days afterward,

> I write to you that you may break the sad news that I have to write as gently as possible to mother. My dear, brave brother David is wounded and in the hands of the enemy. I have made every exertion to learn the extent of his injuries, but can learn nothing. I have every reason to think, however, that it was nothing further than a wound in the lower part of the leg, but which prevented him from getting off the field . . . General Griffin assures me that David cannot be worse than a prisoner wounded and no doubt he will be paroled soon. I am nearly crazy with excitement and want of rest . . . For God's sake be careful how you break the news to mother. Give her every hope for the best.[26]

A week later, James sent his mother a hopeful message, "I have some cheering news to give from David. A prisoner who has just been taken saw him a few days ago, and says he has only one slight wound in the head and that he was walking around. He described David perfectly, saying that he wore a red cap trimmed with gold lace, the only one of the kind in the army except our brigade. And there was no other field officer taken from this brigade . . . It has cheered me up wonderfully . . . No doubt there will be an exchange soon." Over a month after this note, James informed his mother, "I do not think that David is among the officers exposed to our fire at Charleston. A list of their names was published and David's did not appear among them, though I almost wish it might have in order to relieve our anxiety. I cannot but think the Colonel mentioned at passing through Lynchburg referred to him, but cannot account for our not hearing from him before this in some way or another."

The waiting to hear definitive news was agonizing. In July, a Union prisoner named Griffith Williams reported that he had seen Colonel Jenkins shot and killed in an attempted escape from a Confederate prison. Soon after, that report was contradicted by a letter from Sergeant George Williams, who said he heard some Rebels had discovered the body of Colonel Jenkins in the woods and eventually buried it there. Sadly, an article in the *Utica Morning Herald* confirmed that grim account, "Colonel Jenkins was shot on the battlefield of the Wilderness and died there during the battle." According to the report, a Rebel soldier attempted to assist Jenkins, but it was no use. The same soldier witnessed the burial of the Union officer. At long last, the Jenkins family knew the fate of David, the brave, young colonel of the 146th New York.[27] Many families experienced similar pain and anxiety as they awaited news about their loved ones, who went missing after combat in the Wilderness.

A staff officer for General Warren candidly described the debacle on the Turnpike, "Griffin's Div. made a splendid attack, losing most of his regulars, gaining a few hundred feet of worthless ground & inflicting small loss on the enemy."[28] A captain from the 140th New York stated, "The battle that had opened under such favorable auspices for it had accomplished no real good, while it cost the sacrifice of more than half of that gallant body of men—the result of the failure of the troops on our right to come up to our support."[29] The 140th lost 265 out of 529 men during the brief engagement that afternoon.

General Griffin knew all along the assault would end in disaster, if Wright wasn't in position to protect his right flank. Overcome with rage, the division commander mounted his horse, and headed down the Turnpike to discuss the matter with Grant and Meade. Arriving at headquarters at 2:45 P.M., Griffin was stern and angry. In a diary kept at the time, Meade's aide-de-camp, Lieutenant Colonel Theodore Lyman, described Griffin's outburst, "Says in a loud voice that he drove back the enemy, Ewell, ¾ of a mile, but got no support on the flanks, and had to retreat—the regulars much cut up. Implies censure on Wright and apparently also on his corps commander, Warren. Wadsworth also driven back."[30]

Brigadier General John Rawlins, Grant's chief of staff and confidant, "got very angry, considered the language mutinous and wished him put in arrest," according to Lyman. Grant shared Rawlins's view, asking Meade, "who is this Gen. *Gregg*? You ought to arrest him." Meade, notorious for his own violent temper, very calmly replied, "It's Griffin, not Gregg; and it's only his way of talking." Rawlins, who had only recently joined the Army of the Potomac after having served out West with Grant, later asked Lyman about Griffin. Lyman informed him that "his reputation as an officer was good."[31] After his tantrum, Griffin returned to his men to organize their defenses.

General Warren was also frustrated by the failed assault. In his official report, he wrote that his corps attacked Ewell "impetuously" and that "the attack failed because Wright's division, of the Sixth Corps, was unable on account of the woods to get up on our right flank and meet the division (Johnson's) that flanked us."[32] Warren blamed Grant and Meade for being too impatient, and later said, "If General Grant would only have accepted my suggestion to let me deploy my whole corps, and wait until Sedgwick with one division [Wright's division] could reach and assault the enemy's left flank, towards which I knew he was moving, then my advance would certainly, I think, have been a great success, and Ewell's corps alone and unsupported must have been driven from the field."

Warren was surprised that a fine tactician like Lee exposed one of his own corps in this way. After defeating Ewell, Warren believed "Hill's corps could then have been beaten in its isolated position." With Longstreet not yet on the field, "if General Lee had made any attempt to hold on in the Wilderness we should have finished him there."[33] Alas, none of that came to pass. In despair, Warren admitted, "all of my suggestions were received with contumely and scorn that was positively insulting."[34]

Writing many years later, Grant inexplicably declared that Warren had "attacked with favorable though not decisive results."[35] This statement is obviously untrue, though it does illustrate how easy it was to forget what happened under the confusing conditions of the Wilderness. Lieutenant Colonel William Swan, a staff officer for General Ayres, noted that most of the official reports weren't produced until several months after the battle. Such reports, Swan argued, offered "a confused tale about confusion." Regardless, Swan believed victory had been within the Union's grasp, "but the exposed flank was fatal to success."[36] Speaking of the assault in general, Swan added, "I myself feel that it was the beginning of a reckless (brutal it used to be muttered in those days) way of fighting battles by hurrying into action one division, one brigade, or even a single regiment at a time, which characterized every contest from the crossing of the Rapidan to the battle at Cold Harbor."[37]

Surprisingly, historians have tended to be far more forgiving of Grant than Warren on this particular tactical disagreement. Warren, an engineer by training who was familiar with the ground and had a better sense of the size of the opposing force, merely wanted more time to deploy his entire corps alongside an extra division on his right. Properly executed, Warren may have overwhelmed Ewell. Grant, on the other hand, who was unfamiliar with the terrain and the deployment of enemy forces, insisted on pushing into the woods without worrying about being outflanked. Many writers simply characterize this as Grant's western-style aggressiveness, and imply that Warren's fastidious preparations were characteristic of the Army of the Potomac's dysfunctional culture. It's difficult, however, to not view the order to attack—which resulted in over 3,000 casualties—as impulsive and irresponsible.

At approximately 2:30 P.M. at Saunders Field, as the wounded were being carted away, "a new horror was added to the awful holocaust."[38] It was especially hot that afternoon—almost 90 degrees according to local weather stations—and the constant volleys for over ninety minutes eventually ignited the underbrush on the forest floor resulting in brush fires that spread to the grass of Saunders Field. The wadding from the paper cartridges came out of the guns hot and landed on dry leaves, thereby sparking the ground fires. "As the fire advanced it ignited the powder in the cartridge-boxes of the men and blew great holes in their sides," a soldier from the 146th New York wrote, "The almost cheerful sounding 'Pop! Pop!' of the cartridges gave no hint of the dreadful horror their noise bespoke."[39]

On the eve of the Wilderness campaign, Union soldiers spoke of their fear of being wounded in the midst of a forest fire. Now, their fears became a reality. "The wounded tried desperately to crawl to the road or the bare gully," a New Yorker remembered, "but many were overtaken by the flames and perished miserably, some when safety seemed almost within their reach."[40] As the flames kept spreading, the soldier painfully recalled that the clearing had become "a raging inferno, in which many of the wounded perished and the bodies of the dead were blackened and burned beyond all possibility of recognition, a tragic conclusion to this day of horror."[41] Another wounded soldier, who luckily survived, reported, "The ground, which had been strewn with dead and wounded, was in a few hours blackened, with no distinguishable figure upon it."[42] A North Carolinian wrote of the fires, "I have neaver Saw Such a Site in no Battle as I have in this I have Saw lots of Dead bodes Burnt into a crips . . . I Saw one man that was burnt that had the picture I suppose of his little Daughter in his pocket . . . I neaver Saw enny thing that made me feel more Sorrow."[43]

For the soldiers of both armies—most of whom were extremely religious—the presence of fire on such an already gruesome battlefield made them feel as if they were in the midst of hell on earth. The more literate of the soldiers likened the Wilderness to Dante's *Inferno*. Horace Porter, one of Grant's aides, memorably described the scene, "Forest fires raged; ammunition trains exploded; the dead were roasted in the conflagration; the wounded roused by its hot breath, dragged themselves along, with their torn and mangled limbs, in the mad energy of despair, to escape the ravages of the flames . . . It was as though Christian men had turned to fiends, and hell itself had usurped the place of earth."[44]

Less than twenty-four hours earlier, before the fighting even started, a Union veteran presciently told his comrades around a campfire, "I am willing to take my chances of getting killed, but I dread to have a leg broken and then to be burned slowly; and these woods will surely be burned if we fight here."[45] The daring sketch artist with the Army of the Potomac, Alfred Waud—a good friend of Gouverneur Warren—wrote of "some poor fellows, whose wounds had disabled them, who perished in that dreadful flame. Some were carried off by the ambulance corps, others in blankets suspended to four muskets, and more by the aid of sticks, muskets, or even by crawling."[46] Carrying his sketch pad and pencil while frequently under fire, Waud produced several noteworthy drawings of the Battle of the Wilderness, including some showing the wounded being rescued from the flames. One of the sketches appeared in the June 4, 1864, issue of *Harper's Weekly*.

The Wilderness was a particularly high-risk environment for forest fires. The floor of the woods had an abundance of leaves, twigs, vines, and small shrubs. And the grasses on Saunders Field added even more fuel to the conflagration. Scientists who study forest fires say that a "classic fire triangle consists of fuel, oxygen, and heat."[47] With temperatures unseasonably warm for Virginia in early May, all three conditions were present. It's also not surprising the fires broke out in the afternoon after the underbrush had been heated by the sun for several hours. Contemporaries blamed the extensive timber consumption of local iron furnaces and gold mines for the susceptibility of the Wilderness to fire. That was certainly part of it, but the region's unique environment dated back to the intensive tobacco farming of the 18th century, which exhausted its soil and produced a landscape of stunted trees and tangled underbrush.

Union soldiers feared fire above all other horrors on the battlefield. Private Frank Wilkeson, who claimed he witnessed much of the fighting near the Turnpike, remembered that "the wounded were haunted with the dread of fire. They conjured the scenes of the previous year, when some wounded men were burned to death, and their hearts well-nigh ceased to beat when they detected the smell of burning wood in the air. The bare prospect of fire running through the woods where they lay helpless, unnerved the most courageous of men, and made them call aloud for help."[48] Chillingly,

Wilkeson added, "I saw many wounded soldiers in the Wilderness who hung on to their rifles, and whose intention was clearly stamped on their pallid faces. I saw one man, both of whose legs were broken, lying on the ground with his cocked rifle by his side and his ramrod in his hand, and eyes set to the front. I knew he meant to kill himself in case of fire—knew it as surely as though I could read his thoughts."[49] Union veterans, who fought at the Wilderness, always remembered the fires that raged there. Of all the many dangers they faced, fire was the most terrifying and indelible. And fires would break out again on May 6 and May 7, increasing the anxiety of the soldiers, while also disrupting the course of operations.

After Griffin left headquarters in a rage, Grant decided to accompany Warren to the front, to get a better sense of the conditions. The wounded lay on both sides of the Turnpike and smoke lingered over the tops of trees. Gunfire could still be heard to the west. After the brief visit to the front lines, Grant had then "learned from personal inspection the exact character of the locality in which the battle was to be fought," according to Porter.[50] It's worth noting that *before* he knew the character of the locality, he ordered Warren forward against the professional judgment of Griffin, Ayres, Wadsworth, and Warren himself—all of whom were familiar with the situation.

Grant returned to headquarters, where he resumed his cigar smoking and whittling. He'd soon be preoccupied with the Brock Road/Orange Plank Road intersection, about three miles due south. There were urgent decisions to be made as Brigadier General George Getty, with only three brigades of his division, held on at the intersection until Hancock's troops came fully into line. If Confederate General A. P. Hill seized the crossroads before Hancock's Second Corps arrived, then he'd be able to split Grant's army in two. Schaff wrote, regarding the imminent clash, "I believe that no crossing of country roads on this continent ever heard, or perhaps ever will hear, such volleys."[51]

SIX

Confederates on the Orange Plank Road

"There are but one or two square miles which lay in front of the Brock Road and had the Orange Plank Road as a central avenue, in the two days of the battle of the Wilderness . . . Nearly every square yard had its fill of blood, and on nearly every square yard was Northern and Southern blood intermingled."
—Lieutenant Colonel William Swan

Robert E. Lee arose before dawn on May 5. At breakfast, according to an officer, the general "displayed the cheerfulness which he usually exhibited at meals, and indulged in a few pleasant jests at the expense of his staff officers as was his custom on such occasions." Lee seemed surprised "that his new adversary had placed himself in the same predicament as 'Fighting Joe' had done the previous spring. He hoped the result would be even more disastrous to Grant than that which Hooker had experienced."[1]

Lee intended to pin down Grant's army in the impenetrable woods with two of his corps—the Second Corps led by Ewell and the Third Corps commanded by Hill. Once Longstreet's First Corps finally arrived the next day on the morning of May 6, Lee believed he'd be able to outflank Grant's left and drive him back across the Rapidan. Just as Stonewall Jackson's flanking maneuver helped defeat Hooker at Chancellorsville, Longstreet might be able to rout the Army of the Potomac exactly one year later. Lee was highly confident on the morning of May 5. One observer felt it was "a confidence which was well founded, for there was much reason to believe that his antagonist would be at his mercy while entangled in these pathless and entangled thickets, in whose intricacies disparity of numbers lost much of its importance."[2]

Major General Henry Heth, who commanded a division in Hill's corps, believed Lee had no intention of retreating to Richmond and trying to withstand a siege. Lee's reasoning appeared to be, Heth imagined, "What will I gain by retreating? I cannot expect any material gain in strength. This is as good a time and as good a place to settle this issue as I can expect to find." General Lee, Heth added, "was the most belligerent man in his army."[3]

It was a risky strategy, which explains why Lee had preferred that both Ewell and Hill avoid bringing on a general engagement on May 5. Without Longstreet, Lee's army would be dangerously outnumbered. And the Orange Turnpike and the Orange Plank Road were separated by almost three miles, which would make it almost impossible for Ewell and Hill to assist one another if either one was in serious danger. If Grant managed to overwhelm one of Lee's two corps on May 5, then it might be an irreparable disaster for the Army of Northern Virginia. Indeed, Lee's decision to advance on Grant's army that morning was so audacious that it caught both Meade and Grant by surprise. They had assumed, quite reasonably, that Lee wouldn't advance beyond his works at Mine Run.

Lee continued riding with A. P. Hill, who advanced down the Plank Road that morning with Heth's and Major General Cadmus Wilcox's divisions of his corps. Hill's other division, commanded by Brigadier General Richard Anderson, remained in the rear and wouldn't advance to the Wilderness until the following day. Hill's men appeared to be in good spirits—laughing, joking, "and with not the least idea in the world of anything else but victory."[4] Heth's division led the column and soon his skirmishers ran into troopers from a New York cavalry regiment commanded by Lieutenant Colonel John Hammond. The Rebels pushed the

New Yorkers back past Parker's Store at around 8:00 A.M. While Meade was trying to deal with the gathering threat on the Turnpike, he now faced another emergency on the Plank Road.

Ambrose Powell Hill, affectionately known as "Little Powell," was one of the most fascinating commanders in the Confederate Army. A Virginian who grew up in nearby Culpeper, Hill had been an indispensable division commander under Stonewall Jackson. After Jackson's death, he was promoted to commander of the newly created Third Corps. Just thirty-eight years old at the Wilderness, Little Powell was short and slight and wore his hair long. He liked to don a red shirt during battle and was loved by his men.[5] Hill's troops were always very well-trained and disciplined.

Critics believed Hill performed better as a division commander than as leader of a corps. His aggressiveness and impulsiveness often resulted in tremendous success when leading a smaller unit as he demonstrated at Antietam. As a corps commander, Hill had underperformed at Gettysburg and Bristoe Station. The added responsibility of coordinating multiple divisions had been difficult for him to master thus far. "The great responsibilities of the lieutenant generalcy seemed to have told upon his naturally buoyant spirits," a non-commissioned officer observed, "and there was ever a gravity about him that he maintained until the day of his death."[6]

Hill struggled with a serious health issue that affected his performance at Gettysburg. While on break from West Point in 1844, he contracted gonorrhea, which later resulted in prostatitis—a painful condition that involves the inflammation of the prostate. The symptoms could be quite incapacitating. Urination was difficult and could make it impossible for him to get a full night's sleep. It also made him susceptible to infections, which led to fevers and chills.[7] Of Lee's two corps commanders in the Wilderness on May 5, Ewell had only one leg and Hill had a chronic and increasingly debilitating illness. Lee hoped both could overcome their ailments and be at their best that day. By riding with Hill, Lee would be able to offer timely guidance to his most junior corps commander.

The fighting between Hill's skirmishers and Hammond's troopers foreshadowed what lay ahead later that afternoon. As the Confederates arrived at Parker's Store on the Plank Road—about three miles from the Brock Road intersection—they observed the carnage from the recent delaying action conducted by the New Yorkers at 8:00 A.M.[8] One scene revealed a Union soldier, who had been shot in the head with his dead horse lying on top of him. A Rebel veteran observed that another trooper "had a sword thrust through his body, and two others, in their terribly gashed heads, gave evidence that they had gone down under the saber. The rest of them, and all three of our men, had been killed by balls. Not a living thing was seen about the place."[9] Hammond's troopers had dismounted to fight Hill's skirmishers, but were eventually overwhelmed. One of Hill's men wrote, "The enemy's officers behaved with the greatest gallantry, on horseback encouraging the men, and exposing themselves to hold their line; finally they gave way."

With the Union cavalry unit cleared from its path, Hill's divisions continued their march down the Plank Road to Widow Tapp Farm, about a mile from Brock Road. Lee and Hill set up their headquarters at this location around midday—just before Warren attacked Ewell at the Turnpike. Lee reminded Hill at this time to avoid a general engagement, if at all possible. The small property, where Lee and Hill would be situated for the next two days, was rented from the Lacy family by Catherine Elizabeth Tapp. After the death of her husband, Vincent Tapp, in 1857, Catherine lived there with her two daughters and a granddaughter, while her sons served in the Confederate Army.[10]

Lee was unsure of the strength of the enemy defending the crossroads, and didn't know that, near midday, it was being held by only three brigades from General George Getty's division. Getty, like many of the senior officers on both sides, attended West Point and served in the Mexican War. A formidable opponent, he once said, "I always obey an order. If I was ordered to march my division across the Atlantic Ocean, I'd do it. At least, I would march them up to their necks in the sea, and then withdraw and report that it was impractical to carry out the order."[11]

Getty's chief of staff described his nature as "thoroughly loyal, loyal to his country, to his superiors, to his companions in arms, to any and all who had claims upon him."[12] Nevertheless, Lee might have seized the strategic location if he decided to act more boldly. Uncharacteristically, Lee hesitated. In the early afternoon, Hill had two divisions consisting of between 12,000 and 14,000 men facing Getty's understrength division of about 6,000 soldiers. Hancock's Second Corps, still several miles away, would not arrive until later.

As it turned out, Getty made it to the crossroads just in the nick of time. Rebel skirmishers advanced toward Brock Road minutes after Getty's men ran into place. "Soon a few gray forms were discerned far up the narrow Plank Road moving cautiously forward," a Union staff officer wrote, "then a bullet went whistling overhead, and another and another, and then the leaden hail came faster and faster over and about the little group until its destruction seemed imminent and inevitable."[13] Getty steadied the first unit, until more of his men came into line and started firing toward the woods. "Dead and wounded rebel skirmishers were found within thirty yards of the crossroads, so nearly had gained it," the staff officer added, "and from these wounded prisoners it was learned that Hill's corps, Heth's Division in advance, supported by Wilcox's Division, was the opposing force." Getty decided to wait for Hancock's troops before attacking and commanded his men to entrench in the meantime. He told them, "We must hold this point at any risk. Our men will be up soon."[14]

Around 2:00 P.M., the Confederate States of America luckily avoided a catastrophe. Generals Lee, Hill, and Jeb Stuart, along with their staffs, were plotting strategy under a shady tree at Widow Tapp Farm. A small group of Union men emerged from the adjacent woods and saw the generals sitting nearby. Lee jumped up immediately and then Stuart got up, "looking danger straight in the face." Hill remained seated the whole time. Startled and perhaps unaware of the identity of the Confederate leaders, the Union men turned back and disappeared into the woods again. The Northern men missed a unique opportunity to deal the Confederacy a fatal blow.[15]

Heth's entire division kept advancing toward Brock Road and continued its skirmishing with Getty's troops. Lee presumed Grant and Meade wouldn't have failed to protect such an important crossroads with a powerful force. Eventually, Lee sent a staff officer to Heth, who said, "The General is desirous that you occupy the Brock Road if you could do so without bringing on a general engagement." Heth responded, "Say to the General that the enemy are holding the Brock Road with a strong force; whether I can drive them from the Brock Road or not can only be determined by my attacking with my entire division, but I cannot tell if my attack will bring on a general engagement or not. I am ready to try if he says attack."[16] According to Heth, this exchange was between three and four o'clock in the afternoon. By that time, one of Hancock's divisions had arrived to support Getty. And more were on the way. By delaying, Lee now faced a much larger force at the intersection of Brock and the Plank Road.

❖

Hill's march down the Orange Plank Road on the morning of May 5 caught Grant and Meade unawares. With Hill now threatening his left and Ewell endangering his right, Grant decided to take control of his army around 10:00 A.M. At their new headquarters, near an old building that had been erected for crushing gold, Grant and Meade assessed the recent intelligence from the field.[17] According to Porter, "as soon as General Grant learned the situation, he followed his habitual custom in warfare, and, instead of waiting to be attacked, took the initiative and pushed out against the enemy."[18]

Meade then issued a flurry of directives. As we saw earlier, Warren was ordered to attack without delay on the Turnpike. And that's the moment when Getty headed to the crossroads with three of his brigades, arriving with only minutes to spare. Meade also ordered Hancock to "move up the Brock Road to the Orange Court Plank . . . and be prepared to move out the Plank Road toward Parker's Store."[19] This order didn't reach Hancock until 11:40 A.M. The delay in communications between Hancock and Meade caused problems throughout that first day in the Wilderness. After the discovery of Ewell's troops on the Turnpike earlier in the morning, Meade had sent orders to Hancock to halt at Todd's Tavern. Unfortunately,

Hancock didn't receive *that* order until 9:00 A.M. By that point, some of his troops had already marched past Todd's Tavern. Redirecting those troops up Brock Road would take precious time.[20]

Critics wondered why Hancock's Second Corps, an elite unit consisting of 28,000 soldiers, was so far away from the rest of the army in the first place. Years later, Roebling believed Grant sent "Hancock on a wild goose chase to head off Lee's retreat, saying that Lee would be afraid to attack him and his big army."[21] Grant and Meade's decision to revise their original plan put immense pressure on Hancock. He needed to countermarch back to Todd's Tavern and then move an entire corps up an extremely narrow country road. Inexplicably, Meade seems to have misunderstood how far away Hancock was from the Brock Road/Plank Road junction throughout the morning and early afternoon. When Hancock personally arrived at the crossroads at 1:30 P.M. to discuss the developing situation with Getty, Meade wrongly believed he had the entire Second Corps with him. This was just one of several misunderstandings at headquarters that day.[22]

Major General Winfield Scott Hancock may have been the finest soldier in the Army of the Potomac. Tall, handsome, and majestic on the battlefield, Hancock received the nickname "superb" from General McClellan after an engagement earlier in the war. Upon being promoted to corps commander for his outstanding service at Antietam and Chancellorsville, Hancock fought splendidly and heroically at Gettysburg. Over the course of those three bloody days, Hancock was everywhere, brilliantly leading the Union men to a hard-fought victory.

Hancock's bravery in the face of enemy fire was legendary. Before Pickett's Charge, a soldier remembered, "As soon as the cannonade opened, Hancock mounted his horse, and with his staff behind him and his corps flag flying, rode slowly along the front of his line that every man might see that his general was with him in the storm." The soldiers stayed close to the ground to avoid "the bitter hail," but could look up "at that calm, stately form, that handsome, proud face, that pennon bearing the well-known trefoil; and found courage longer to endure the pelting of the pitiless gale."[23]

When a junior officer told him to get down, Hancock replied, "There are times when a corps commander's life does not count."[24] In a poem about Hancock titled "On the Photograph of a Corps Commander," Herman Melville wrote,

> Nothing can lift the heart of man
> Like manhood in a fellow-man.
> The thought of heaven's great King afar
> But humbles us—too weak to scan;
> But manly greatness men can span,
> And feel the bonds that draw.

A minié ball eventually struck Hancock in the groin during Pickett's Charge. This excruciatingly painful injury put him out of action for several months and would make it difficult for him to ride a horse. Before the Virginia Campaign of 1864, he asked his superiors if he could ride in a spring wagon on occasion until his wound was fully healed. He experienced severe pain in the Wilderness, and insisted on riding his horse during the battle. He wrote, "I suffer agony on these occasions, but must go into action on horseback or ask to be relieved."[25]

With General Warren engaged on the Turnpike, Meade sent yet another order to Hancock at 1:30 P.M., "Attack them; Getty will aid you. Push out on the plank road and connect with Warren."[26] The communications breakdown between them continued, regrettably, with Hancock not receiving that directive until 2:40 P.M. Getting frustrated, Meade sent his aide, Lieutenant Colonel Theodore Lyman, to personally deliver an order to Hancock that read, "The commanding general directs that Getty attack at once and that you support him with your whole corps, one division on his right and one division on his left, the others in reserve; or such dispositions as you think proper, but the attack up the plank road must be made at once."[27] Lyman left at 3:15 and delivered it at 3:25 P.M. Getty believed it was unwise to attack until Hancock was fully up, but also felt he must obey the order. This was somewhat similar to Warren's dilemma earlier that day along the Turnpike. At 4:15 P.M. Getty threw his three brigades forward against Hill's men.

Fortunately, several regiments from Hancock's corps soon joined the assault. Immediately prior to the attack, the troops from the Second Corps had been preparing breastworks as they arrived at the junction. Forming an infantry line on the narrow Brock Road, which was heavily wooded on both sides, was extremely difficult. Between 4:00 and 5:00 P.M., Hancock methodically began sending his troops into the developing conflagration.[28]

The crossroads at that hour instantly became the epicenter of merciless fighting. Eight brigades of Rebel troops—four from North Carolina, one each from South Carolina, Georgia, and Mississippi, and one made up of Virginia and Tennessee troops—performed remarkably well against great odds. Schaff described the scene from the Union perspective, "Soon crash after crash is heard, cheers, volleys, and more wild cheers, and in a little while gray smoke begins to sift up through the tree-tops; and in a little while, too, pale, bleeding fellows, limping or holding a shattered arm, some supported by comrades, others borne on litters, begin to stream out of the woods."[29] An officer from a Pennsylvania regiment wrote of his men as they advanced, "Ah, what young, bright, childish faces, full of sweetness, smiles, enthusiasm and hope. Not a cheek blanched, not a coward in all the noble band. Six hundred boys with less than two months of drill and discipline, in their first battle, yet as steady, confident and reliable as the oldest veterans."[30] As the combat intensified, his men "fell on every side, but still the Regiment passed steadily on. One by one the boys fell—some to rise no more, others badly wounded."[31]

Hancock sat on his horse directing the troops amid the smoke and deafening noise. Regarding the battlefield conditions, Hancock said, "No movements of the enemy could be observed until the lines were almost in collision; only the roar of the musketry disclosed the position of the combatants to those who were at any distance, and my knowledge of what was transpiring on the field, except in my immediate presence, was limited, and was necessarily derived from reports of subordinate commanders."[32]

Initially, Getty's men sustained shockingly high casualties as they blindly advanced toward Heth's troops. The Vermont brigade, led by Brigadier General Lewis Grant, was decimated by the first volleys, and "lost many valuable lives."[33] Over one thousand courageous men from the Vermont brigade would fall defending the crossroads that afternoon. It's impossible to provide an accurate narration of the chaos that prevailed at the intersection between 4:15 and 8:00 P.M. One Vermonter remembered, "There was nothing of brilliancy or maneuver in it. The contending forces could not see each other until within a few paces."[34] The historian of a North Carolina regiment recalled that at one point, "the brigade lay down behind a line of dead Federals so thick as to form partial breastworks, showing how stubbornly they had fought and how severely they had suffered."[35]

With two of Getty's brigades struggling north of the Plank Road, Hancock sent in the brigade of Brigadier General Alexander Hays to assist them. Hays and Hancock had been in the same class together at West Point. Lyman described Hays as "a strong-built, rough sort of man, with red hair, and a tawny, full beard: a braver man never went into action."[36] Immediately facing deadly resistance from Heth's troops, Hays asked for reinforcements. Hancock told a staff officer, "I will send him a brigade in twenty minutes. Tell him to hold his ground. He can do it; I know him to be a powerful man."[37] While encouraging his men to hold on, Hays was shot in the brain.

Ulysses S. Grant, who had been a year ahead of Hays at West Point, became distraught upon hearing the news. While whittling pine sticks back at headquarters, Grant told his officers in a low voice, "Hays and I were cadets together for three years. We served for a time in the same regiment in the Mexican war. He was a noble man and a gallant officer. I am not surprised that he met his death at the head of his troops; it was just like him. He was a man who would never follow, but would always lead in battle."[38] The fight between Hill and Hancock would continue to rage for hours. The slaughter on both sides was frightening. "Of those that survived," one soldier wrote, "many had not beheld the enemy; yet the tangled forest had been alive with flying missiles; the whistling of the bullets through the air had been incessant; the very trees seemed peopled by spirits that shrieked and groaned through those hours of mortal combat."[39]

When the fighting began on the Plank Road, Grant decided to send an additional force from the Fifth Corps to assist Hancock and Getty. Wadsworth, hoping for redemption after the poor showing of his division earlier that afternoon, pleaded with Grant to allow him to take his men through the dense woods, so they could "fall upon the flank and rear of Hill."[40] Shortly after four o'clock, Grant gave the order sending Wadsworth to the Plank Road. Brigadier General Henry Baxter's brigade from the Fifth Corps' Second Division would accompany Wadsworth. They were expected to depart at 5:00 P.M., but didn't leave until 6:00 P.M. That lost hour would prove to be significant.[41]

The fifty-six-year-old James Samuel Wadsworth from Geneseo, New York, took a highly unusual path to becoming a division commander in the Army of the Potomac. Before the war, he ran a land business consisting of 70,000 acres, while also overseeing a large personal estate. After Fort Sumter, Wadsworth eagerly volunteered as an unpaid aide-de-camp to help save the Union and abolish slavery. President Abraham Lincoln averred no man had "given himself up to the war with such self-sacrificing patriotism as Gen. Wadsworth."[42]

Wadsworth, described by a colleague as "rather tall, an eminently handsome man of commanding presence, but showing gentle breeding," was educated at Harvard, where he was a classmate with Senator Charles Sumner, and later attended Yale Law School.[43] He wasn't much of a scholar, however, and never practiced law. Always a man of action, he inherited his estate and land business, and frenetically managed his commercial interests for most of his career. A friend described him in 1838 as "a fellow of a great deal of character & ability, and one of those restless spirits who cannot live without excitement. He is always flying from one end of the country to the other, speculating in land, shooting & pursuing all sorts of adventures which life in the backwoods affords."[44]

His substantial wealth eventually made him a power broker in New York politics. In the 1850s, he became a committed opponent of the extension of slavery. Eventually joining the Republican Party, he campaigned on Lincoln's behalf during the election of 1860. Wadsworth later wrote, "At the outbreak of this rebellion I was barely a Republican, that is, only opposed to the extension of slavery. I have slowly come to the conclusion that the time has arrived to strike it down forever. This is the rebellion of an aristocracy, base, selfish & degraded, but still distinctly formed aristocracy. We cannot put down the rebellion & save the aristocracy & we ought not do, if we could."[45] Wadsworth strongly believed the "rebellion can only and ought only to end in the total overthrow of slavery."[46]

The New York aristocrat contributed to the war effort in a variety of different capacities. Upon the outbreak of hostilities, the Governor of New York appointed Wadsworth as a Major General of Volunteers, a rank he wasn't qualified for. Even Wadsworth admitted, "As against a graduate of West Point or an officer of the regular army of fair reputation . . . I can on no account allow my name to be presented as a candidate."[47] He soon sent a letter of resignation and instead joined the staff of Brigadier General Irvin McDowell, who was based at Robert E. Lee's former Arlington estate. After a commendable performance at the Battle of Bull Run, Wadsworth was promoted to brigadier general and was given a brigade to command. In 1862, President Lincoln appointed Wadsworth as military governor of Washington, D.C., where he shored up the capital's defenses and sought solutions for dealing with an influx of runaway slaves. On one occasion in this role, Wadsworth released an accused spy named Patrick McCracken, who had been captured by the Union Army near the Wilderness of Spotsylvania, in return for a promise not to aid the enemy. McCracken would be true to his word and would eventually repay Wadsworth for that merciful deed.

By 1863, after a failed campaign to become governor of New York, Wadsworth was back in the field, commanding a division at the Battles of Chancellorsville and Gettysburg. Not everyone believed Wadsworth deserved a field command. Colonel Charles Wainwright, who served with Wadsworth under General Warren in the Wilderness, thought

Wadsworth was woefully deficient in military matters. In 1863, Wainwright wrote in his diary, "Wadsworth having been defeated in his efforts to be governor of New York gets the First Division as a balm." Wainwright then snidely added, "I know nothing of his natural ability, but it ought to be very great, as he knew nothing of military matters before the war, is not a young man, and has had no experience in battle to entitle him to so high a position."[48]

Wainwright may have been rivalrous, but his concerns were legitimate. Wadsworth did lack experience as a field commander. It's true his bravery was unquestioned, and his leadership skills were highly regarded. Yet, his courage could seem like recklessness at times. During the Battle of Chancellorsville, a soldier predicted, "he'll be killed before [the war] closes," after Wadsworth stood up in a boat, while being fired upon by the enemy.[49] Successfully commanding a division on a Civil War battlefield required much more than courage alone.

Compared with West Point trained officers, Wadsworth was relatively unskilled at handling large bodies of men under combat conditions. Was this a factor in the subpar performance of his division south of the Turnpike on the afternoon of May 5? In fairness to Wadsworth, managing troops in those woods was almost impossible, even for experienced commanders. The fighting in the Wilderness was done by companies and regiments rather than by brigades and divisions. Wadsworth's brigade commanders—Rice, Stone, and Cutler—hadn't been trained at West Point either. It's not entirely clear whether or not this was a liability during the initial engagement. In the case of General Rice, when he had been promoted to lieutenant colonel earlier in the war, several officers signed a petition protesting his inexperience.[50]

At Gettysburg, Wadsworth led the First Division of General Reynolds's First Corps. The fighting during the opening hours of that battle was arguably the deadliest of the entire war and Wadsworth played a conspicuous role on the first day—he even took over command of the First Corps temporarily after Reynolds was shot. His division, which included the Iron Brigade and the 76th New York, lost over half of its men—2,209 out of

3,504 engaged—during the battle. Like Gouverneur Warren, Wadsworth was later honored with a monument at Gettysburg.

After Gettysburg, Wadsworth was critical of General Meade's decision to not aggressively pursue Lee's army. He told the Committee on the Conduct of the War that "General Meade did not, perhaps, appreciate fully the completeness of his victory. The terrible slaughter of our men produced, of course, a great impression upon the officers of our army."[51] At a Council of War on July 12, just over a week after Lee's defeat, Wadsworth voted in favor of a renewed attack on the Army of Northern Virginia. Gouverneur Warren, the army's chief engineer who also voted in favor, made an especially compelling argument for a new assault. Meade's corps commanders voted against such an attack, however, and Lee eventually escaped to Virginia.

Wainwright reported that Wadsworth openly expressed his frustration about the decision. Later, Lincoln's secretary, John Hay, also noted Wadsworth's anger over letting Lee escape.[52] In his diary, Wainwright wrote of Wadsworth, "There is something to be admired in the old man's earnestness, and did it concern no life but his own, it would be grand. His only idea seems to be that war means fight. Yonder are the enemy; pitch in. I know nothing about the left of our line, but Lee's position in front of us is very strong . . . My opinion is most decided that we could not carry it."[53] Wadsworth might have been brave and aggressive, but he wasn't perceived as being prudent, in this instance.

What motivated Wadsworth, a man of enormous wealth and responsibilities, to risk his life on behalf of his country? Unlike Robert E. Lee, who was almost the exact same age, Wadsworth wasn't a professional soldier. No one would have thought twice about it, if he volunteered in a civilian capacity to assist the war effort, while still managing his business in New York. Early in the war, Wadsworth explained his motivations, "my obligations to my country and to posterity are manifest as the sun at noonday. I cannot avoid them and continue to respect myself even—nor shall I try to do so. Duty is with me—results with God."[54] This sense of duty is evident in a letter he wrote to his wife just hours before crossing the Rapidan River into the Wilderness:

May 3rd, 9 P.M.

My Dear Wife:

I have just received your most kind letter of April 30th (Saturday). We have just received marching orders to move at 12 tonight and all is bustle and confusion. Still I withdraw my mind from the scene and duties of the hour a few moments, my dear wife, to tell you that we are all well (Tick [his son, Craig] is with me) and in the best spirits. We feel sure of a victory. I wish I could tell you how much I love you and our dear children, how anxious I am that all should go well with you, that you will all live in affection and kindness, and that none of our dear children will ever do anything to tarnish the good name which we who are here hope to maintain on the battlefield. Write a kind letter to dear Jimmie if he is not with you, with all the love and affection I can express. Kiss Nancy and Lizzie and believe me, my dear wife, fondly and truly yours,

Jas. S. Wadsworth[55]

Roughly forty-two hours after having written that letter, an exhausted Wadsworth had been beaten badly in the woods. The dismayed squire of Geneseo now hoped for a second chance against the Rebels. His considerable force when combined with Hancock and Getty's troops might be enough to overwhelm Lee's right flank. Much would depend on whether or not Wadsworth's men could bushwhack their way through the woods before darkness.

Regarding Wadsworth's departure for the Plank Road, Schaff wrote years later, "There is no occurrence of the day that I remember with more distinctness than the setting off of Wadsworth's command that afternoon. I can see the men now moving down the field in column to the road, and then following it up the run for a piece toward Parker's store."[56] The soldiers marched quietly, having been ordered to do so by Wadsworth, and could hear the incessant gunfire at the crossroads almost three miles away. The troops were arrayed in three lines. Baxter's brigade led the way with

Stone's men to his left. The second line consisted of Cutler's Iron Brigade, with Rice's men in reserve. Roebling, from Warren's staff, directed them in finding their way to the Plank Road. Their progress, in the impenetrable woods, was snail-like.

Wadsworth, who believed the earlier rout in the woods was merely a case of bad luck, may have been personally eager to rejoin the fight, but his soldiers were wary. They had been stunned and then severely roughed up by the Rebels only several hours ago. Many of the regiments were at half-strength. And not all of the missing men were casualties. A large percentage of Wadsworth's men remained in hiding behind the lines, resistant to joining another engagement so soon after the debacle of the early afternoon. Stone's Bucktails seemed to be in particularly bad shape. The men appeared to distrust their officers, who in turn blamed the troops for their earlier poor performance. Many of the Pennsylvanian officers smelled of cheap whiskey and appeared to be drunk.[57]

Wadsworth's men had been marching for only fifteen minutes before they were fired upon by Wilcox's soldiers of Hill's corps. The Rebels yelled as they discharged their volley. Baxter's men immediately responded to the skirmishers with a volley of their own. And then chaos broke loose in the Wilderness. Stone's men, still traumatized by the events of the early afternoon, began firing wildly at the unseen enemy. All of a sudden, "the whole Wilderness roared like a fire in a canebrake," reported one regimental historian.[58] The front lines suffered considerable losses.

After discharging their weapons, Stone's Bucktails turned and ran. A staff officer for Wadsworth later admitted, "[Stone's] brigade broke in a disgraceful manner on seeing the fire of Baxter's skirmishers in front of them. They were stopped, however, by the exertions of their own officers, and Cutler's bayonets behind them."[59] Stone, who had been drinking commissary whiskey all afternoon, made matters considerably worse by behaving erratically. "As soon as the rebels fired upon us," a Bucktail remembered, "one would have thought old Stone had gone crazy. Hat off, and his coat thrown back on his shoulders, he rode down behind his line of 'tails,' which a line of western troops had stopped. Cursing and swinging his sword he drove them back to our line again."[60] The Pennsylvania commander was mortified his men had run two times in one day. A soldier later explained that the troops fought badly due to "a lack of confidence in their leaders for they knew a drunken leader was worse than none."[61]

In the twilight of the woods, it didn't take much to create panic in the Union ranks. Wadsworth and his staff did their best to restore order. Yet, Stone defied Wadsworth's command to cease firing and be quiet. Instead, he urged his troops to cheer for Pennsylvania. Shortly after, Stone fell off his horse, breaking a pelvic bone that had been injured at Gettysburg. Stone was removed from the field, and his Bucktails would now be without a commander. Precious moments were lost before Wadsworth's men could resume their march to the Plank Road with Stone's demoralized men now placed in reserve.

The Rebels became alarmed when Wadsworth's division finally approached the Plank Road around nightfall. Having sent in all of their reserves, Hill's officers worried they couldn't hold on much longer against superior numbers. A Rebel colonel pleaded, "If night would only come."[62]

All that was available to throw against Wadsworth's troops was a tiny force of 125 men from the Fifth Alabama Battalion. One southern writer remembered, "They went in with a cheer, and whatever was before them was driven back, and night settled down on the dreadful field—our lines all held."[63] Regarding the fighting at the crossroads, Major General Humphreys wrote, "darkness and the dense forest put an end to it, fortunately for Hill, whose troops were shattered and his lines disjointed; an hour more of daylight, and he would have been driven from the field, for Longstreet and Anderson were many miles distant."[64]

Roebling recalled that "the resistance of the enemy had not been severe." Sadly, he added, "It had been hoped that we would form connection with the 2nd Corps that evening, but darkness came on too soon."[65] The division stopped for the night about a half-mile from the Plank Road. The right of the line, which included Reeves's 76th New York Infantry regiment, was quite close to Widow Tapp Farm, where Lee and Hill oversaw the battle. The left was about a half mile from Brock Road. Only half the soldiers of Stone's brigade were still present after the day of fighting. With the Rebels nearby, Wadsworth's men would be required to "sleep on their arms" that night.

Schaff described the scene north of the Plank Road at dusk, "their position had been reached practically in the dark and they were so close to the enemy that both spoke in whispers, and all realized the inevitable renewal of the struggle in the morning."[66] According to Humphreys, the enemy lines were so close that "many men from both armies, in looking for water during the night, found themselves within opposing lines, and were made prisoners." Indeed, one observer said that, "the combatants drew water from the same brook."[67]

The senior officers at Grant's headquarters inexplicably believed Wadsworth had succeeded in his mission to the Plank Road. Congressman Elihu Washburne, a friend of Grant's who witnessed the battle, wrote in his diary, "Just as night fell Wadsworth's division fell on Wilcox's division Hill's Corps and drove them a mile. That was a grand movement and it was directed by General Grant. Wadsworth was celebrated nobly today."[68] Around the fire that night, Grant and his officers "were full of rejoicing at Wadsworth's success and left unsaid no word of praise for his promptness, courage, and patriotism."[69]

The truth was much different. Wadsworth's troops, still shaken from the disaster earlier in the day, had been stymied by the dense woods and Rebel skirmishers, who instilled fear in the Union ranks. General Wilcox of Hill's Corps believed Wadsworth should have been successful, if the movement had been "directed with ordinary skill and courage."[70] Had Wadsworth arrived at the Plank Road an hour earlier, he may have helped Hancock and Getty drive Hill from the field. Instead, the Northern generals would have to wait until morning. With Longstreet likely up by then, the Union advantage would disappear. The Army of the Potomac missed a tremendous opportunity to destroy an entire corps of Lee's army on May 5. Looking back on the day, an exhausted Wadsworth must have been disappointed in his performance and that of his men.

As the firing died down around the crossroads after 8:00 P.M., a soldier from the Iron Brigade remembered lying down "surrounded by dead and dying rebel soldiers." The wounded suffered terribly and "their moans and cries were harrowing." The Union men gave their wounded enemies water, but were haunted by one dying Rebel who kept crying, "My God, why has thou forsaken me!"[71]

SEVEN

Nighttime in the Wilderness

T he survivors from both sides never forgot the horrifying night spent in the Wilderness after the first day of battle. "Night put an end to the bloody strife, & drew a sable curtain over the dead, the mangled, & the dying," said a North Carolina officer, who captured the sights and sounds of the evening, "Ambulances & litters brought the wounded to the rear, & the surgeons were soon busy cutting out balls, amputating limbs, & dressing ghastly wounds. The cries of the sufferers, the rumbling of wagons & artillery & ambulances, the hurrying to & fro of men & animals, the neighing of horses and mules, the glare of the ruddy campfires, all made a scene difficult to describe, but never to be forgotten."[1]

There was no moon that night. The woods became even darker with each passing hour. Ambulances were on the move and the scent of burnt leaves and shrubs filled the air. Along the Turnpike, both sides were dug in—within a pistol shot of one another—lying behind their recently constructed breastworks. Behind General Ewell's lines, 1,200 Union prisoners began their trek to Orange Court House, Virginia, which was twenty miles to the west. Roughly 150 of those captives came from the 76th New

York Infantry. "Had I been one of the unfortunate prisoners," remembered Morris Schaff, "I know that I should have wished over and over again, as I trudged along that night, that I was lying dead back on the field with my fellows, rather than about to face a long term in Confederate prisons, so greatly did I dread them after seeing the wrecks that came down the James from Richmond when I first went to Fort Monroe."[2]

Forest fires remained a danger. "Throughout the night," a Pennsylvanian wrote, "as the fires, which had blazed since the early afternoon, drew nearer and nearer to the groans of the poor unfortunates who lay between the lines, their shrieks, cries, and groans, loud, piercing, penetrating, rent the air, until death relieved the sufferer."[3] Death and suffering were everywhere. Making matters worse, the soldiers knew the slaughter would begin again at dawn. The historian of the Vermont brigade—the unit with the highest casualties on May 5—reported, "the burial parties and stretcher-bearers sought through the thickets for the killed and wounded, at risk of their own lives, for the enemy's pickets fired at every light or sound. In the debatable ground between them lay hundreds of dead and dying, whom neither army could remove. The men in the lines of battle lay on their arms behind their low breastworks, and got but brief and fitful rest."[4] The Vermonters eventually succeeded in retrieving the body of Colonel Newton Stone at around 11:00 P.M. and burying him at midnight.

Sometime after 10:00 P.M., Lieutenant Schaff headed over to Lacy House—where Robert E. Lee's father "Light Horse Harry" Lee wrote his Revolutionary War memoirs in 1809—for a meeting with General Warren, Lieutenant Colonel Frederick Locke, and John Milau. Schaff described Locke, who served as Warren's adjutant general, as "unpretentious, much reflecting, and taciturn." Milau, the chief surgeon for the Fifth Corps, had a joyful personality and was a dear friend of George McClellan. The four men began writing up a report on the losses for the day, in a large, high-ceilinged room with tallow candles burning on the table. Schaff was well-acquainted with Warren, who had been his mathematics instructor at West Point. Describing his commander that evening, Schaff wrote, "Warren was still wearing his yellow sash, his hat rested on the table, and his long, coal-black hair was streaming away from his finely expressive forehead, the only feature rising unclouded above his habitual gloom of his duskily sallow face."[5]

At one point during their work, Milau reported a figure from data he had just compiled from the various field hospitals nearby. Looking at his adjutant, Warren immediately responded, "It will never do, Locke, to make a showing of such heavy losses." Shocked at this attempt to underreport casualty figures, Schaff later wrote, "in my unsophisticated state of West Point truthfulness it drew my eyes to Warren's face with wonder, and I can see its earnest, mournfully solemn lines yet. It is needless to say that after that I always doubted reports of casualties until officially certified."[6]

It had been a trying day for Warren. He lost the confidence of both Grant and Meade earlier in the afternoon at the Turnpike. And then he resisted orders a second time. When Meade tried to coordinate another assault at 6:00 P.M. with Sedgwick and Warren advancing in unison against Ewell, Warren chose not to attack the fortified positions of the enemy. Warren was in close contact with Grant and Meade at the time, so presumably they accepted his decision. [7]

Nonetheless, the weight of command was negatively affecting him in the dimly lit room at Lacy House. No doubt, to his staff, it appeared self-interested and unethical to report misleading casualty figures. But Schaff's account also shows Warren was still shaken by the heavy losses earlier in the day. Theodore Lyman later described Warren as "certainly the most tender-hearted of our commanders. Almost all officers grow soon callous in the service; not unfeeling, only accustomed, and unaffected by the suffering they see. But Warren feels it a great deal."[8]

The casualties during the first day of fighting were indeed truly frightening—ranking May 5 at the Wilderness with Antietam and the second day of Gettysburg as among the costliest single days of combat during the war up to that point. A Confederate soldier wrote of "many who groaned in agony or met terrible death all alone in the dense woods" or groups of men who charged "only to be slaughtered in heaps."[9] Throughout the evening, the dead remained scattered throughout the woods. It was too dangerous to remove them, while the armies still confronted one another. Private Wilkeson recalled "the dead men lay where they fell. Their haversacks and cartridges had been taken from their bodies. The battlefield ghouls had rifled through their pockets. I saw no dead man that night whose pockets had not been turned inside out."[10] Walt Whitman wrote of "the bloody promenade of the Wilderness" where the dead lay "strewing the fields and woods." He famously added, "the dead, the dead, the dead—our dead . . . Somewhere they crawl'd to die, alone, in bushes, low gulleys, or on the sides of hills."[11]

"Somewhere they crawl'd to die, alone." Whitman described a typical unnamed dead solider, who crawled "aside to some bush-clump, or ferny tuft, on receiving his death shot—there sheltering a little while, soaking roots, grass and soil, with red blood—the battle advances, retreats, flits from the scene, sweeps by—and there, haply with pain and suffering (yet less, far less, than is supposed) the last lethargy winds like a serpent round him—the eyes glaze in death—none recks—perhaps the burial-squads, in truce, a week afterwards, search not the secluded spot—and there, at last, the Bravest Soldier crumbles in mother earth, unburied and unknown."[12]

Of the war in general, Whitman predicted, "Future years will never know the seething hell and the black infernal background of the countless minor scenes and interiors, (not the official surface-courteousness of the Generals, not the few great battles) of the Secession war; and it is best they should not—the real war will never get in the books . . . It was not a quadrille in a ball room."[13] In his poem "The Armies of the Wilderness," Melville wrote,

> None can narrate that strife in the pines,
> A seal is on it—Sabean lore!
> Obscure as the wood, the entangled rhyme
> But hints at the maze of war—
> Vivid glimpses or livid through peopled gloom,
> And fires which creep and char—
> A riddle of death, of which the slain
> Sole solvers are.

We will perhaps never be able to comprehend the fear and suffering and *courage* in those haunted woods that night. Yet, it is an essential part of the Wilderness story. It's hard to imagine the trauma of that suffering—on both sides—isn't still with us today in some way or another.

For the survivors of the first day of slaughter, their emotions must have been overwhelming. Many of their comrades had just been killed or maimed or taken prisoner. Corpses lay nearby, while ambulance crews did their best to find and carry off the badly wounded. The men were hungry and thirsty. And they were *tired*, yet knew they faced more murderous fighting in the morning. In the darkness of the woods, it was impossible to know where the enemy might be at sunrise. There'd be very little sleeping that evening. The nervous strain of the men must have been near the breaking point.

Getty's troops suffered the most on May 5. Among the Vermonters "the carnage was fearful." The Vermont brigade, consisting of five Vermont regiments commanded by Colonel Lewis Grant, had crossed the Rapidan River on May 4 with 2,800 men. On the afternoon of May 5, a thousand Vermont soldiers fell and fifty of the brigade's finest line officers were killed or wounded. In one Vermont regiment, a colonel, who was shot in the head, was replaced by a lieutenant, who was soon shot as well. Wadsworth's division had also suffered extremely high casualties with the 76th New York experiencing similar losses to the Vermont regiments. Overall, Warren's Fifth Corps, Sedgwick's Sixth Corps, and Hancock's Second Corps had all endured inordinately high casualties. Only Burnside's Ninth Corps, consisting of four divisions of predominantly green troops, escaped relatively unscathed. The luck of Burnside's men would change. The pugnacious Ulysses S. Grant intended to deploy them in the gap between the Turnpike and the Plank Road on May 6. [14]

While the fighting subsided with darkness, the frenetic activity at the field hospitals continued throughout the night. At the hospitals of the Fifth Corps, where Private William Reeves tried to rest, surgeons and medical assistants worked tirelessly to treat a much larger number of wounded than had been expected. The hospitals of the Fifth Corps attended to over

1,200 wounded soldiers between noon and 9:00 P.M. on May 5 and performed over 700 surgical procedures. According to an official report, each wounded man had about eight minutes on the operating table. Many of the wounded went unrecorded, of course. Some dutiful soldiers preferred to remain in the line, despite having been injured. Regarding mortality rates, a surgeon observed that "the relative proportion of killed was also large being nearly 1 to every 5 wounded."[15] All of the soldiers dreaded being killed and then abandoned on the field—"dying a lonely battlefield death, buried by strangers in graves far from home."[16]

Such was the fate of Corporal Albert Hilton, who was the color bearer for the 76th New York at the time of his death. Hilton mustered in as a private in 1861, and was later wounded and captured during the first day of Gettysburg. Hilton escaped and was promoted to corporal on the eve of the Wilderness Campaign.

Corporal Hilton marched into the woods, along with Private Reeves, during the early afternoon of May 5. After two color bearers of the 76th were seriously wounded, Hilton seized the colors, but was then immediately shot dead. Several weeks later, Hilton's father sent a letter to the authorities inquiring about his son, who hadn't been heard from since crossing the Rapidan. In early June 1864, Lieutenant Herschel Pierce from the 76th replied to Hilton's father,

> I am in receipt of your letter of May 22, 1864 asking information in relation to your Son Albert. He was killed in the Battle of the Wilderness May 5th, 1864. There is no doubt about it.
>
> He was Color Corporal and was shot through the Body and fell forwards on his face on the Colors of the Regiment. I did not See him after he fell, except for a few minutes. We were fighting all along the line for Several Days in Succession. He was buried in the Wilderness by the Ninth Corps as they afterwards occupied the same grounds fought over by the fifth Corps, by a change of corps in the prosecution of the Battle.

Many years later, a comrade of Hilton's remembered that he "Saw him when he was Shot I was very near him and Saw him double over and fall he was carrying the colors at the time. I could not get to him as the enemy was a little too much for us just then."[17]

It had been a tragic day for Private William Reeves, who spent an uncomfortable night at the field hospital, a mile or so behind the lines. He'd been shot within minutes of the opening of the campaign. And many of his comrades had been killed, wounded, or taken prisoner. In some ways, Reeves had been lucky. He didn't crawl to his death all alone, never to be discovered by his family. He hadn't been taken prisoner like so many of the unfortunate men of the 76th that day. And he wasn't left maimed on the field, worrying if he'd be burned alive by creeping forest fires. Remarkably, being confined to a field hospital wasn't the worst possible outcome for a soldier in the Army of the Potomac at the opening of the Overland Campaign. And though his wound was painful, it didn't seem anywhere near as serious as those suffered by many of the others in the hospital.

Yet, residing in a Civil War field hospital was a pretty traumatic and gruesome experience, nevertheless. "A single night spent under such conditions was a torment," one soldier recalled, "The pleadings for water of fever-parched invalids, the moans of those racked with pain, the mutterings and sometimes violent outcries of the delirious, the not uncommon noisy, gurgling respiration of those in the clutch of death, the curses and anathemas of worn-out, helpless ones who could get no rest in the midst of such a horrid Babel, linger in the memory as though an uncanny vision." The former patient added, "it demands the stoutest heart in the soundest body to be brought face to face with all the unspeakable things pertaining to the living and the dead that may be encountered in a temporary army hospital."[18]

Reeves would have to make the best of it, however. He knew the battle would continue in the morning. A lull in the fighting would be required before the wounded could be transported to more secure hospitals in northern cities for advanced treatment. Reeves learned that the outcome of the battle on the following day might depend on the 76th New York and the rest of Wadsworth's men, who were poised to attack General Hill's flank at sunrise. If he were honest, he'd have to admit that he didn't like their chances. The conditions in those woods seemed to favor the more experienced Rebels. He'd seen it clearly himself. Reeves wondered why the Union officers had failed to learn from the debacle earlier that afternoon near the Turnpike.

It had been a discouraging day for Ulysses S. Grant. Undaunted, the Union general-in-chief remained remarkably calm, despite the poor results of his first encounter with Robert E. Lee. Schaff, who witnessed Grant at the close of the fighting on day one, remarked that he "was not troubled, and he issued orders with the same even, softly warm voice, to attack Lee impetuously early the next morning all along his line." The young staff officer wondered, however, if Grant had been disappointed to discover "the Army of the Potomac's one weakness, the lack of springy formation, and audacious, self-reliant initiative." [19]

During the afternoon of May 5, Lyman described Grant as "looking sleepy and stern and indifferent," yet added, "That he believes in his star and takes a bright view of things is evident." [20] Around the campfire at head-quarters that evening, with his staff officers and General Meade, Grant was surprisingly sanguine about the outcome of the first day and looked forward to continuing the fight. He told his men that the engagement on May 5 had not been a true "test of strength" and that Lee had failed in trying to hit the Union Army in the flank. Grant may not have been aware of the true extent of his casualties at the time. They were considerable and far greater than those suffered by Lee. And the arrival of both Burnside and Longstreet would have the net result of making Lee relatively stronger on day two. Two thirds of Burnside's corps consisted of raw recruits, while Longstreet's men were among the best fighters in either army.

So far, Grant had failed to coordinate his assaults on both the Turnpike and the Plank Road. Forcing Warren to attack without Wright protecting his right flank resulted in a missed chance to drive Ewell back. Later in the afternoon, Meade's order for Getty to attack Hill without waiting for support from Hancock also led to atrocious losses. Meade's desire to prove his aggressiveness to Grant illustrated the weakness of having the commander of the Army of the Potomac report directly to the general-in-chief of the Union armies in the field. The friction between Grant and Meade led to Union troops being deployed piecemeal throughout the day. This undermined the primary Union advantage—its superior numbers. For Grant to be successful, he would need to try something different on the following day.

All things considered, the Confederates fought more effectively in the woods than the Federals. The Rebels fired their guns more accurately and were better able to cope with the difficult terrain. Traditionally elite northern units, like the Iron Brigade and Ayres's Regulars, struggled in the thickets and swamps of the Wilderness. And yet, despite Confederate advantages and Union mishaps, Hancock came tantalizingly close to overwhelming Hill's men on the Plank Road right before dark. If Hancock arrived at the crossroads an hour or two earlier, he may have succeeded in destroying Lee's right. With nightfall, Union forces were well-positioned for success at sunrise. Everything would depend on whether General Longstreet's First Corps would be up in time to relieve Hill's men. An English historian summarized the first day of the Battle of the Wilderness by writing, "The 5th, then, must be adjudged a day of lost opportunities, lost chiefly by the impatience of the Union commander. But this first day of battle had certainly impressed every officer and man in the army with the fact that the command was in strong hands. There was something remorseless even in Grant's mistakes."[21]

Robert E. Lee had surprised Grant, and inflicted considerable damage on the Army of the Potomac. He took incredibly bold risks to do so. Isolated on the Turnpike, Ewell was fortunate that Warren and Wright hadn't been allowed to go forward together. And Hill was substantially outnumbered on the Plank Road, which prevented Lee from closing the gap in his center. Initially, Lee sent Wilcox to connect with Ewell, but had to recall him to reinforce Heth. After the bloodbath at the crossroads, Hill's men were huddled together in disarray.

Hill's soldiers would be vulnerable to another attack by Hancock at sunrise, if they weren't replaced in the line by Longstreet's men by then.

Lee seemed confident his "Old War Horse" would arrive in time to attack Grant's left at first light. Lee, like Grant, fancied his prospects for day two of the contest. Confederate Brigadier General Edward Porter Alexander summarized the situation perfectly, "May 5th was Grant's day. Every hour of daylight was to him a golden opportunity to crush an inferior enemy which had rashly ventured within reach. May 6 was going to be anybody's day, after Longstreet arrived."[22] Unlike Grant, Lee had almost no margin for error.

In Grant's conversations with Meade and his staff around the fire that evening, he expressed anxiety about providing relief to the wounded, and urged his medical officers to do everything in their power to care for those who were suffering. Years later, Grant professed horror at witnessing the suffering of maimed soldiers under his command. After the first day of the Battle of Shiloh, in April 1862, Grant found shelter at a log house that had been converted to a field hospital. In his memoirs, Grant wrote, "all night wounded men were being brought in, their wounds dressed, a leg or an arm amputated as the case might require, and everything being done to save life or alleviate suffering." The general found the agony of his men "more unendurable than encountering the enemy's fire," so he left the hospital, and settled under a tree, in the driving rain, for the remainder of the evening.[23]

The plan for the following morning that Grant and his officers devised that night in the Wilderness was remarkably straightforward. The entire army would attack all across the line at 4:30 A.M. sharp. Grant hoped to maintain the initiative and perhaps destroy Lee's right flank before Longstreet could arrive. Intelligence from Rebel prisoners had revealed that Longstreet was expected at some point on the morning of May 6. With this in mind, Hancock and Wadsworth would attack Hill at 4:30 A.M. With any luck, they'd overwhelm the Rebels with superior numbers. General Burnside's Ninth Corps would appear on the field early to plug the gap between Warren and Hancock. And Warren and Sedgwick would assault Ewell at the Turnpike at 4:30 A.M. to prevent him from sending reinforcements to Hill and possibly Longstreet, if he was up by then. Finally, Burnside's Fourth Division of African American troops would guard the wagon trains in the rear.[24] After laying out the plan, Grant retired to his tent for an early bedtime. According to Porter, headquarters was eerily still after "the shock and din of battle which had just ceased, and which was so soon to be renewed."[25]

Meade left Grant to meet with his corps commanders at 10:00 P.M. His tent was only two hundred yards away. This meeting lasted about thirty minutes, and consisted of Meade laying out the plan he had recently discussed with Grant. Warren, Sedgwick, Hancock, Burnside, and various staff officers were all in attendance.

As the meeting broke up, Burnside, who was expected to have three of his divisions in motion by 2:00 A.M. said, "Well, then, my troops shall break camp by half-past two!" He then calmly left, disappearing into the thickets. When he was gone, Major James Duane, Meade's chief of engineers, told the remaining men, "He won't be up—I know him well!" Everyone seemed to agree. Lyman believed Burnside "had a genius for slowness."[26] Complicating matters further, Burnside technically outranked Meade and therefore reported directly to Grant. This represented yet another clumsy command deficiency in Grant's army.

Recognizing that Burnside's slowness might jeopardize the synchronization of the assault, Meade sent Grant a note at 10:30 P.M. requesting that the attack be postponed to 6:00 A.M. instead of 4:30. He also noted that "It appears to be the general opinion among prisoners that Longstreet was not in the action today, though expected, and that his position was to be on their right or our left." Meade added, "I have notified Hancock to look out for his left."[27] Grant's secretary sent a reply to Meade before 11:30 P.M. stating the attack could be postponed until 5:00 A.M., but no later. Grant did not want the enemy to gain the initiative.

One of the biggest challenges for Grant was deciding how best to deploy Burnside's Ninth Corps, which consisted of about 22,000 troops—only 6,000 of whom had "any seasoning as soldiers," according to Humphreys.[28] Major Roebling, described by Lyman as one who "goes poking about in the most dangerous places, looking for the position of the enemy, and always with an air of indifference," reported that he went to Grant's headquarters at 11:30 P.M. to discuss Burnside's orders with one of Grant's staff officers.[29] They eventually decided that Burnside would try to seize the heights at Chewning Farm, which was located between Hancock's right and Warren's left. Roebling was ordered to lead two of Burnside's divisions through the thickets to Chewning Farm at 4:00 A.M.[30]

Major General Ambrose Burnside didn't have the best reputation among the senior officers of the Army of the Potomac, to say the least. He attended West Point and rose rapidly through the ranks early in the war. Despite Burnside's mixed performance at Antietam in September 1862, Lincoln appointed him commander of the Army of the Potomac, after McClellan was dismissed in November 1862. Several weeks later, Burnside led the army to a humiliating and disastrous defeat at Fredericksburg. The Union lost 13,000 men compared with only 5,000 for Lee's army. After learning about the catastrophe, Lincoln famously said, "if there is a worse place than hell, I am in it."

Burnside failed as a leader of an entire army, and was relieved of his command in January 1863. He later was assigned to the Department of the Ohio, and had some success out west. After campaigning in Tennessee, under Grant, in late 1863, he returned east on the eve of the Overland Campaign, to once again command the Ninth Corps.

Morris Schaff, a usually congenial observer of men and events, was quite critical of Burnside, writing that he "represented a well-recognized type in all armies, the California-peach class of men, handsome, ingratiating manners, and noted for a soldierly bearing." Such appearances were deceiving, according to Schaff, who added that these men "in times of peace, not only in our country but everywhere, invariably land in high places, and who almost as invariably make utter failures when they are given commands on the breaking out of war."[31]

The public expressed high hopes for Burnside and his Ninth Corps prior to the Wilderness Campaign. On April 25, 1864, Burnside's men were enthusiastically cheered as they marched through Washington, D.C., on their way to join the rest of the army. Lincoln watched the spectacle from the balcony of the Willard Hotel. As Burnside's African American troops marched in front of Lincoln, they yelled, "Three cheers for the President!" This marked the first review of black troops by Lincoln. "These colored troops were greeted with cheers and applause," wrote a prominent D.C. journalist, "as they passed the central crowd along Fourteenth street, and such shouts as 'Remember Fort Pillow!' were flung out to them as they marched by. All of the troops cheered lustily the President and Burnside as they caught sight of them, and Uncle Abraham smiled benevolently down upon them."[32]

Walt Whitman, who was there, wrote "the 9th Corps made a very fine show indeed. There were, I should think, five very full regiments of new black troops, under General Ferraro. They looked and marched very well. It looked funny to see the President standing with his hat off to them just the same as the rest as they passed by."[33] The division of roughly 3,000 black troops, many of whom had once been enslaved and had very little combat experience, was led by Brigadier General Edward Ferrero, a former dancing instructor at West Point who later rose to division command during the war.

Ferrero's black troops, having been given the responsibility of protecting the wagon trains at the beginning of the campaign, left Manassas Junction, Virginia, on May 4 to join the rest of the Ninth Corps. By nightfall, Burnside's other three divisions arrived in the Wilderness and settled down near Sedgwick's troops, north of the Turnpike. They had marched forty miles in a day and a half. On May 5 and May 6, Ferrero's men protected the trains and guarded the crossing. Theodore Lyman may have expressed the regrettable views of many senior officers in the Army of the Potomac when he wrote of seeing black troops for the first time, "As I looked at them, my soul was troubled and I would gladly have seen them marched back to Washington. Can we not fight our own battles, without calling on these humble hewers of wood and drawers of water to be bayonetted by the unsparing Southerners?"[34] Lyman also recorded in his diary that the high command didn't trust black soldiers in the line of battle and that's why they were chosen to guard the trains.

On the night of May 5, the African American troops must have been anxious, despite suspecting they might not be heavily engaged in the morning. These men had never experienced battle before. In an emergency, they'd be sorely tested. If Ewell somehow made it around Sedgwick's right, then Ferrero's men would be expected to protect the river crossing. A possible fight with Confederate infantry, who pledged to give "no quarter" to black troops, might be especially murderous.

Just three weeks earlier, Rebel soldiers during the Battle of Fort Pillow yelled, "No Quarter" before massacring almost 200 African American Union soldiers. According to a congressional report, "All around were heard cries of 'no quarter,' 'no quarter,' 'kill the damned . . . ,' 'shoot them down.' All who asked for mercy were answered by the most cruel taunts and sneers."[35] A Union officer wrote, "Many of the colored soldiers, seeing that no quarters were to be given, madly leaped into the river, while the rebels stood on the banks or part way up the bluff, and shot at the heads of their victims."[36] Ferrero's men knew they'd receive savage treatment from Lee's Rebels, if they fought them during the spring campaign. This added stress was exacerbated by a moonless sky over the river's edge after one of the most ferocious days of fighting during the Civil War.

While Ferrero's black troops may have worried about the Confederates outflanking the Union right, General Hancock spent most of his evening planning his 5:00 A.M. assault and meticulously preparing for a possible Rebel attempt to outflank his left. As Meade indicated in his letter to Grant, an examination of Confederate prisoners suggested Longstreet would assault Hancock's left with about 12,000 men.

In order to meet this threat, Hancock appointed the battle-hardened John Gibbon as his left wing commander. Gibbon, who would be responsible for Brigadier General Francis Barlow's division and the corps artillery, positioned Barlow's men defensively on the far left; they would not join Hancock's assault down the Plank Road at dawn. Gibbon spent the entire night protecting against an attack via the Brock Road. By having his men face south, a gap was created between his troops and Hancock's other divisions. Stonewall Jackson's flanking movement had caught the Union by surprise during the Battle of Chancellorsville just one year earlier. Hancock's mission was to prevent history from repeating itself. It's highly doubtful he got any sleep on the night before May 6.

Embarking from Gordonsville, Virginia, Longstreet's two divisions marched twenty-eight miles on May 4 and 5. They reached Richard's Shop, which was another ten miles from Lee's headquarters, at 5:00 P.M. on May 5. Upon arrival, Longstreet received an order from Lee to resume marching at 1:00 A.M. on May 6, so his troops could reinforce Hill's battered men at daybreak. The First Corps originally planned on marching up the Brock Road, but Lee revised his instructions. Longstreet wrote, "The accounts we had of the day's work were favorable to the Confederates; but the change of direction of our march was not reassuring." His weary men took some time to rest and cook supper, after two days of hard marching. When they set off again at 1:00 A.M., darkness and atrocious roads made the night march a difficult one. Despite the trying conditions, a senior officer recorded that Longstreet's soldiers entered the Plank Road at daylight "and filed down towards the field of strife of the afternoon of the 5th."[37] They arrived in the nick of time.

James Longstreet may have been seeking redemption when he arrived at Parker's Store shortly after sunrise. Some of the men from the Army of Northern Virginia blamed Longstreet for their defeat at Gettysburg. They believed he'd been too slow in following Lee's orders on both the second and third days of the battle. Sent out to Tennessee in late 1863 and early 1864, Longstreet was unsuccessful in his efforts to capture Knoxville. After his failure out west, Longstreet hoped to recapture the glory he had achieved at Second Manassas, Antietam, and Fredericksburg, under Lee's command. Despite his recent setbacks, Longstreet remained an outstanding battlefield commander who cared about the safety of his men. Lieutenant General John Bell Hood wrote of him, "Of all the men living, not excepting our incomparable Lee himself, I would rather follow James Longstreet in a forlorn hope or desperate encounter against heavy odds. He was our hardest hitter."[38]

"Old Pete," as Longstreet was nicknamed by West Point cadets, was born in 1821 in South Carolina. He graduated from West Point in 1842—just one year before Ulysses S. Grant, who was a close friend. Longstreet flourished as the leader of the C.S.A.'s First Corps, after Lee took over as commander of the Army of Northern Virginia in 1862. At the Battle of Antietam, Lee remarked, upon seeing Longstreet emerge from the chaos of the battlefield, "Ah! Here is Longstreet; here's my old *war-horse!* Let us hear what he has to say."[39] The nickname, "Old War Horse," stuck and Lee often referred to him by that name. Early in the war, Longstreet's chief of staff described him as "a most striking figure, about forty years of age, a soldier every inch, and very handsome, tall and well proportioned, strong and active, a superb horseman and with an unsurpassed soldierly bearing, his features and expression fairly matched; eyes, glint steel blue, deep and piercing; a full brown beard, head well shaped and poised. The worst feature was the mouth, rather coarse; it was partly hidden, however, by his ample beard."[40] A biographer later wrote, "Longstreet approached war dispassionately. No moral imperatives, no testings of men's characters drove his generalship as they did Jackson's. To Longstreet, victory resulted from preparation—deliberate, thoughtful planning. He believed in the strategic offensive and the tactical defensive. If Jackson was the army's hammer, Longstreet was its anvil."[41]

Sadly, and perhaps unfairly, Longstreet would forever be associated with the Confederate failure at Gettysburg. He believed Lee was wrong to attack heavily defended positions and instead had advised Lee to outflank the Union left. Longstreet was especially critical of the disastrous Pickett's Charge, telling Lee, "General, I have been a soldier all my life. I have been with soldiers engaged in fights by couples, by squads, companies, regiments, divisions, and armies, and should know, as well as anyone, what soldiers can do. It is my opinion that no fifteen thousand men ever arranged for battle can take that position."[42]

Despite Longstreet's excellent professional relationship with Lee, he could be critical of his chief on occasion, describing him as "too pugnacious." At Gettysburg, Longstreet felt "General Lee's pugnacity got the better of his strategy and judgment and came near being fatal to his army and cause."[43] Unfortunately for Longstreet, many Southerners blamed him, but not Lee, for the epic disaster in Pennsylvania in July 1863. Ten months later, the Wilderness represented an excellent opportunity for Longstreet to restore his tarnished reputation.

Robert E. Lee and his senior officers had been preoccupied with the timing of Longstreet's arrival throughout the late evening of May 5 and early morning hours of May 6. Heth's and Wilcox's soldiers decided to rest for the night without making preparations for battle in the morning. They assumed they'd be relieved by Longstreet's men before the Union assault began at dawn. If somehow Hancock attacked *before* Longstreet arrived, then Hill's divisions would be driven and perhaps destroyed. It was extraordinarily risky to leave the lines in such disorder until morning.

Growing more and more concerned about the dangerously broken lines of his men, General Heth went to see A. P. Hill during the evening of May 5. Heth told Hill the troops were terribly mixed up and "the men lay down and were soon asleep." Hill, who appeared to be unwell, replied, "Your division has done splendidly today; its magnificent fighting is the theme of the entire army."

Returning to his initial concern, Heth said, "Yes, the division has done splendid fighting, but we have other matters to attend to just now. Let me take one side of the road and form line of battle, and Wilcox the other side and do the same; we are so mixed, and lying at every conceivable angle, that we cannot fire a shot without firing into each other. A skirmish line could drive both my division and Wilcox's, situated as we are. We shall certainly be attacked early in the morning." Hill responded, "Longstreet will be up in a few hours. He will form your front. I don't propose that your division shall do any fighting tomorrow, the men have been marching and fighting all day and are tired. I do not wish them disturbed."[44]

Hill, who clearly believed Longstreet would arrive *before* dawn, showed great solicitude for the well-being of his exhausted troops. Heth couldn't let it go, however. He raised his concerns with Hill two more times that evening. On the last occasion, Hill said, "Damn it, Heth, I don't want to hear any more about it; the men shall not be disturbed." Heth wanted to raise the matter with General Lee, but couldn't find his tent. On this disagreement,

Heth later wrote, "The only excuse I make for Hill is that he was sick." Hill may have suffered a flare-up of symptoms relating to his inflamed prostate, perhaps brought on by the stress of battle.[45]

Hill had in fact discussed the issue with Lee, who assured him that Longstreet would be up in time. According to Hill's chief of staff, "General Lee's orders were to let the men rest as they were."[46] Lee attempted to speed up the arrival time of Longstreet's lead division, but in the end, he stoically accepted the fact that the First Corps might not be up until shortly after daylight. The Confederate commander went to sleep at midnight with the situation on the Plank Road still highly uncertain. The Army of Northern Virginia had been incredibly lucky throughout the day of May 5. Lee perhaps hoped the good fortune would carry over to the following day. Some observers believed the usually conscientious Lee became more of a risk taker when his "blood was up" from battle.

❖

Only several hundred yards from Lee's headquarters, James Wadsworth spent his night repairing his lines and planning for the morning. Just one year younger than Lee at fifty-six, Wadsworth didn't get a wink of sleep that evening. After an exhausting day of combat, the strain on his nerves was considerable. Unlike Hill, Wadsworth insisted that his officers adjust their lines. After they returned with information on the condition of the troops, Wadsworth remarked "that as our ammunition was pretty well exhausted someone would have to go back to the train for a supply, and also to Gen. Warren for orders." He then turned to his aide, Captain Robert Monteith, and said, "Capt. Monteith, you had better go."[47]

Monteith embarked on a dangerous mission through the pitch-black woods with only the North Star as his guide. Fortunately, he easily found his way to Warren's headquarters to receive his orders. He then headed to the ammunition train where he loaded up ten pack mules with two thousand rounds each. The return journey proved far more perilous, unfortunately.

He was unable to find a guiding star on the trip back to his division. At one point, he saw fires and heard the sound of troops, "Halting my train, I dismounted to reconnoiter, and creeping along the edge of the woods soon discovered that instead of taking the ammunition to our troops I was making straight for the enemy and was then very close to them." Monteith retraced his steps and was eventually able to find his way back to camp, reporting to Wadsworth at 3:00 A.M. He "had barely time to distribute the ammunition when it was the hour to attack," and later wrote that it had been "the most anxious night spent during my service, and the task the most important and difficult to perform."[48]

Warren, who stayed up all night assisting his division commanders with their preparations, told Wadsworth that they'd be advancing at 5:00 A.M. "everywhere on the line." Wadsworth was advised to set his "line of battle on a line northeast and southwest, and march directly southeast on the flank of the enemy in front of General Hancock."[49] Wadsworth's men awoke at first light and only had time for a quick bite to eat. They then waited patiently and silently for the booming signal gun from Hancock's headquarters at the crossroads. Wadsworth's brigades moved out swiftly southward toward the Plank Road—Rice on the right, Baxter in the center, and Cutler on the left. Of the impending battle, a staff officer from the Second Corps told his men, "You are to attack the enemy again this morning. The fate of the best Government in the world may depend upon your efforts."[50]

EIGHT

Lee to the Rear

Robert E. Lee awoke at 4:00 A.M. on May 6. Four hours of sleep would have to be enough for the fifty-seven-year-old. His tent was near the western edge of Widow Tapp Farm, where the artillery pieces of Lieutenant Colonel William Poague were also situated. Surely, General Lee was deeply concerned when he discovered Longstreet hadn't arrived yet. By all accounts, Lee was not an anxious man, though he had a volcanic temper. The whereabouts of Longstreet tested his nerves as he thought about the arduous day ahead. His Army of Northern Virginia was in mortal danger. [1]

The waiting placed an unbearable strain on Hill's officers. Major General Cadmus Wilcox, whose troops had fought so splendidly on May 5, remembered, "twelve, two, three o'clock came, and half past three, and no reinforcements." Finally, Wilcox would wait no longer and wisely sent out an order for some men to go to the front to construct breastworks. But it was too late. The men didn't arrive until daylight and by that time, the enemy was too close for them to do their work unharmed. A Confederate artillerist succinctly described what lay ahead, "We all knew the two divisions would give way if attacked and all knew we would be attacked." [2]

Lee had asked too much of his men thus far in the Wilderness. And he'd have to ask even more of them this morning. His boys would be required to hold on somehow until Longstreet's eventual appearance at an unknown time after Hancock's imminent attack. The Rebel commander, who had once been derisively nicknamed "Granny Lee" for his prudence, had gambled rather recklessly at the opening of the current campaign and was about to pay dearly for it. On this beautiful spring morning in the Virginia woods, Lee faced the possible annihilation of his entire army. Up to this point, he believed Grant had underestimated the fighting ability of the Army of Northern Virginia. Now, Lee wondered if *he* had been the one to underestimate Grant's sheer relentlessness. At daybreak at Widow Tapp Farm, everything seemed to be slipping away.

Hancock's men came charging down the Plank Road, from east to west, just before 5:00 A.M. Wadsworth's troops simultaneously advanced from the north to join them. Very shortly, the "whole front was alive with musketry." Wilcox wrote, "the Confederates were in no condition either to advance or resist an attack. Wilcox, in front, was in an irregular and broken line; Heth's men had slept close in rear, without regard to order." Hill's corps risked being crushed in a vise. Predictably, the Rebel lines soon gave way in "rout and confusion."[3]

Hancock's divisions began driving the Rebels down the Plank Road. Wadsworth's men soon linked up with them there and advanced westward along the road. About thirty minutes after the assault began, Hancock told Lyman, "We are driving them, sir; tell General Meade we are driving them most beautifully. Birney has gone in and he is just cleaning them out be-au-ti-fully!"[4] Later, the commander of the Second Corps estimated he drove the Rebels over a mile and a half. More likely, the Union men drove the enemy about one thousand yards—up to the eastern edge of Widow Tapp Farm. During the first hour of fighting on May 6, the Union plan unfolded perfectly. Ulysses S. Grant was on the verge of accomplishing something earlier Union commanders had failed to do: defeat Robert E. Lee on Virginia soil.

"There is no glitter or parade about him," said an
observer of Ulysses S. Grant in 1864.

ABOVE: The hero of Little Round Top,
Gouverneur Kemble Warren.
RIGHT: A sketch of a gunshot to the jaw.

Alfred Waud's "Wounded escaping from the
burning woods of the Wilderness."

A. P. Hill liked to don a red shirt in battle and was loved by his men.

ABOVE: Winfield Scott Hancock may have been the finest soldier in the Union Army. LEFT: Lincoln said that "no man has given himself up to the war with such self-sacrificing patriotism as Genl. Wadsworth."

In the Wilderness, James Longstreet hoped to make
amends for recent defeats in Tennessee.

ABOVE: Grant told General Meade, "Lee's army will be your objective point. Wherever Lee goes, there you will go also."
BELOW: Grant's Night March.

Wounded soldiers from the Wilderness Campaign.

A general hospital in Washington, D.C.

Walt Whitman wrote, "I sit by the restless all
the dark night, some are so young . . ."

The grave of Private William Reeves. *Photo by the author.*

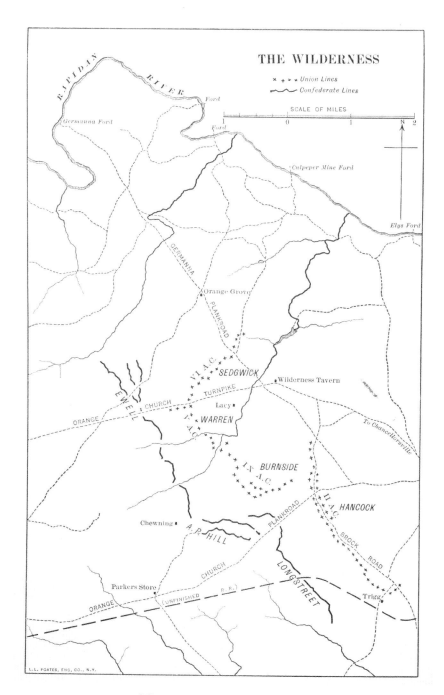

The Wilderness battlefields.

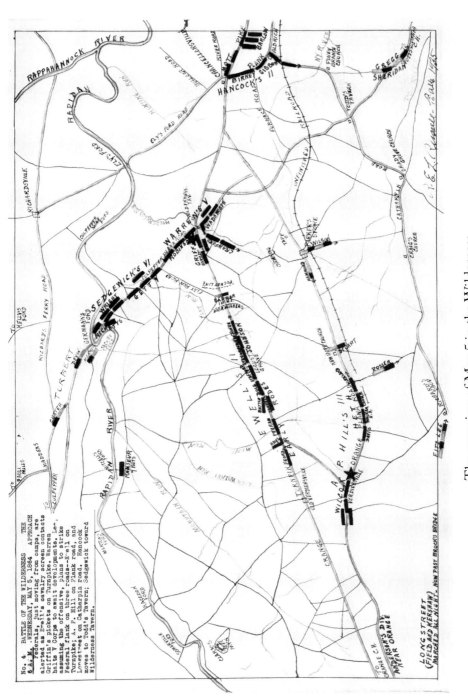

The morning of May 5 in the Wilderness.

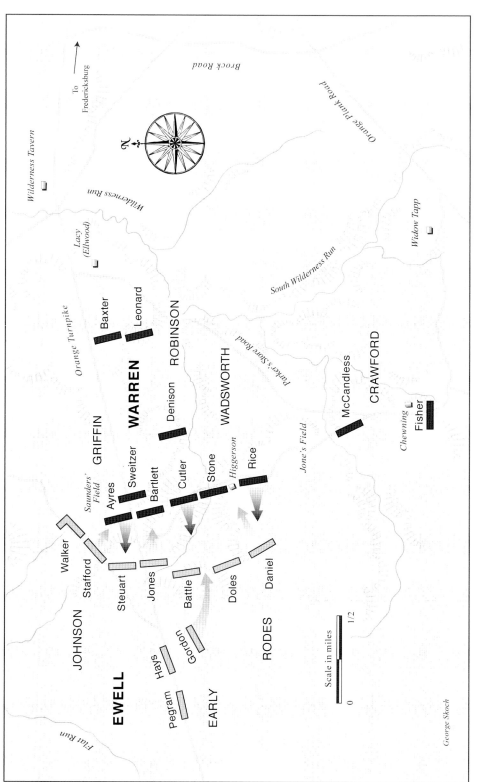

The Battle of the Wilderness begins. *Map by George Skoch.*

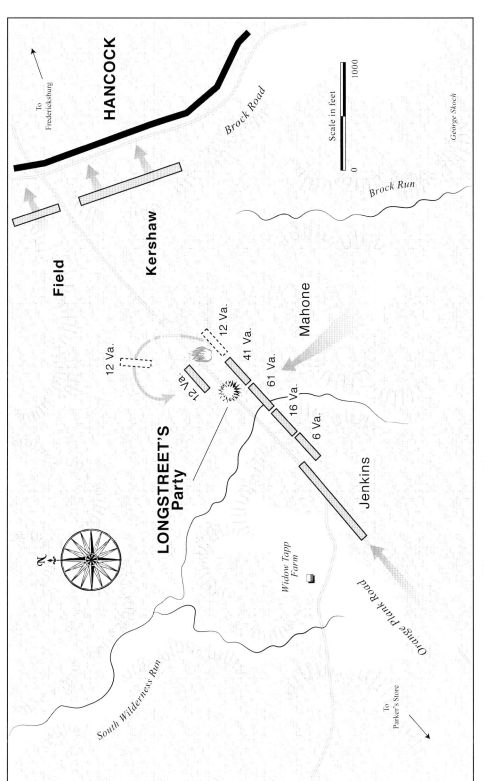

The wounding of James Longstreet. *Map by George Skoch.*

Whitman said, "The journey from the field till they get aboard the boats at Belle Plain is horrible."

The Rebels fought tenaciously before giving way. On both sides of the Plank Road, Confederate troops began falling back—slowly at first and then more rapidly. "We were forced back in disorder," said Brigadier General James Lane. "Brave men are sometimes forced to turn their back to the foe."[5] Brigadier General Samuel McGowan's South Carolinians, who had fought so bravely on May 5, were pushed back toward Widow Tapp Farm. It was impossible for them to defend their position.

Colonel John Stone's Mississippi brigade found a way to stand firm against the wave of bluecoats, in the woods north of the road. At first, Stone's men broke just like the others, but the gritty colonel stopped them and shouted, "Steady, men! Steady! Form on your colors."[6] As things got increasingly desperate, the Mississippians placed slightly wounded Union men in front of nearby trees with the hope that Union sharpshooters would stop their fire. That morally questionable tactic appeared to work.

Other than a few pockets of resistance, Heth's and Wilcox's men ultimately collapsed before the Union onslaught. Heth told his brigade commanders to take their men to the rear to regroup. One artillerist observed, "the men were ordered to run, and the signs are they obeyed, with all the means which God and nature had put into their feet."[7] McGowan's South Carolinians soon came retreating in disorder across Tapp's field right in front of the disapproving gaze of Robert E. Lee, who was on horseback near Poague's guns.

"My God!" Lee said, "Gen. McGowan is this splendid brigade of yours running like a flock of wild geese?" McGowan defensively replied, "They just want a place to form and they are ready to fight as well as ever."[8] A young private, who witnessed the exchange, remembered Lee "expressed himself rather roughly to us, especially to us unfortunate file-closers; but I am not sure but his anger implied a sort of compliment to our past performances."[9] Lee urged Hill's retreating troops to rally, "Go back men, you can beat those people."[10] Morris Schaff described Lee at that precise moment, "By all accounts, Lee's face was a sky of storm and anxiety, and well it might be, for Catastrophe was knocking at the door."[11]

Given the crisis, Lee's ill humor made perfect sense. With the Yankees quickly approaching his position, Lee asked his officers, "Why does Longstreet not come?" The Rebel commander then ordered his adjutant, Colonel Walter Taylor, to prepare for the immediate withdrawal of the wagon trains at Parker's Store. Brigadier General Porter Alexander thought this "the most critical moment which Gen. Lee's fortunes had yet known."[12] But the day could still be salvaged: an officer brought word from Longstreet that his corps was closing fast.

With Confederate forces in flight and disorder, Colonel William Poague's artillerymen tried to stop the Union advance. Four batteries— 300 men with sixteen guns—made a stand on the western edge of Tapp Farm. Artillery hadn't been used much by either side on the first day, so its deployment here caught the Northerners by surprise. Poague's gunners let loose a storm of over 3,000 solid shot on the unfortunate Yankees, who could no longer advance down the Plank Road. According to a private at the fringe of Tapp Farm, General Hill "rode along the line of these guns, directing them how to fire, which they were compelled to do, while some of our own men were in the path of their projectiles."[13] The guns would keep Union troops at bay momentarily. But Lee and Hill had now run out of options.

Longstreet's troops hurried at a "turkey trot" pace, as they at last reached the Plank Road, where the divisions of Brigadier General Joseph Kershaw and Major General Charles Field deployed side by side—Field on the left and Kershaw on the right. "It was superb," Lee's aide, Colonel Venable, remembered, "and my heart beats quicker to think about it even at this distance of time."[14] Wilcox said, "General Longstreet rode forward with that imperturbable coolness which always characterized him in times of perilous action, and began to put them in position on the right and left of the road."[15] A Confederate private wrote, "Like a fine lady at a party, Longstreet was often late in his arrival at the ball, but he always made a sensation and that of delight, when he *got* in, with the grand old First Corps, sweeping behind him, as his train."[16] Longstreet's men appeared just in time, rejoining their old comrades and their beloved "Old Bob" Lee, after having been apart for eight months. An officer with Hill found it "an inspiring homecoming for the First Corps."[17]

As they got closer to the front, Longstreet's men saw "broken masses of Heth's division, swarming through the woods, heedless of their officers, who were riding in every direction shouting to gain their attention."[18] They had to pass through Hill's field hospitals, where they witnessed "hideous sights, fractured limbs and bloody clothing." Such sights, said one private, "did not add much to our courage."[19] A staff officer for Longstreet, Lieutenant Colonel G. Moxley Sorrel, was shocked by the retreat of Hill's troops and found it appalling. With the men from Hill's corps streaming to the rear, Sorrel felt "it looked as things were past mending."[20]

Once the divisions of Kershaw and Field finally arrived, Longstreet took charge, doing his best to create a new line of battle. In awe of the First Corps' achievement, Sorrel wrote, "I have always thought that in its entire splendid history the simple act of forming line in that dense undergrowth, under heavy fire and with the Third Corps men pushing to the rear through the ranks, was perhaps its greatest performance for steadiness and inflexible courage and discipline."[21] Kershaw's men began to form in the woods south of the Plank Road; Field's soldiers deployed north of the road. Brigadier General John Gregg's Texas brigade, which belonged to Field's division, arrived at Poague's guns at the western edge of Tapp Farm at approximately 6:00 A.M. Sitting atop Traveller, General Lee witnessed their arrival, and told Longstreet, "I never was so glad to see you. Hancock has broken my line."[22] One Texan recalled, "We had to push our way through a dense thicket of underbrush, coming up finally into line of battle on the margin of a small clearing."[23] Another soldier from the brigade remembered "a scene of utter and apparently irremediable confusion, such as we had never witnessed before in Lee's army."[24] Trying to steady his new arrivals, Longstreet yelled above the din, "Keep cool, men, we will straighten this out in a short time—keep cool."[25]

While the Texans rushed past Poague's guns and entered Tapp Farm, Robert E. Lee, with a black cape draped around his shoulders, rode up alongside them. Led by the tough Brigadier General Gregg, severely wounded at Chickamauga seven months earlier, the Texas brigade—three regiments from Texas and one from Arkansas—possessed a stellar reputation for courage under fire. According to Colonel Venable, "the Texans cheered lustily as their line of battle, coming up in splendid style, passed Wilcox's disordered columns, and swept across our artillery pit and its adjacent breastwork."[26]

Deeply moved, an emotional Lee shouted to the men, "Who are you, my boys?" The soldiers replied, "Texas boys." Waving his hat, Lee exclaimed, "Hurrah for Texas! Hurrah for Texas! Texans always move them." A private remembered seeing "the fire of battle in [Lee's] eye, and his form quivered with emotions." A staff officer for the brigade said, "I have often seen Gen. Lee, but never did I see him so excited, so disturbed—never did anxiety of care manifest itself before so plainly upon his countenance. If I mistake not he was almost moved to tears."[27]

The troops began their grim preparations before charging across the field toward the enemy. They expected to be greeted by raging fire from Union musketry. Every last one of the men knew they might be killed or seriously maimed. General Alexander, a particularly reliable observer, wrote of Lee, "the old man, with the light of battle in his eyes . . . rode up behind their line, following them in the charge."[28] General Field recalled, "General Lee . . . seeing, as all did, that the battle was lost to us unless some almost superhuman exertion was made, placed himself at the center of the brigade, saying aloud he would lead them."[29] Many of the men looked on in dismay. "I believe that the one only thing General Lee ever did," one private wrote, "that the men in this army thought he *ought not to do*, was going under fire."[30] Longstreet believed that Lee, by this point, was "off his balance."[31]

As Lee went forward, the Texans became increasingly alarmed. Many of them shouted across the line, "Go back, General Lee, go back! Lee to the rear." Some of the men added, "We won't go on unless you go back." A sergeant then grabbed the reins of Traveller and pulled Lee back toward Poague's guns. Lee appeared to come to his senses, "I'll go, my men, if you will drive back those people."[32] Venable escorted Lee behind the lines. Lee then consulted with Longstreet, who urged him to go even farther back. Lee replied, "Can't I too, die for my country?"[33] Years later, one of Lee's sons recalled a conversation in which the commander of the Army of Northern Virginia admitted that, "it brought tears to his eyes when he saw men willing to face death if he would go to a place of safety."[34]

Fortunately for the Confederate States of America, Lee remained safely in the rear as the Texans went forward. According to General Field, the Texas brigade, which consisted of 850 soldiers, was cut down by two thirds in just ten minutes after their charge across Tapp's field. Other, perhaps more reliable accounts, record that the brigade lost half of its men as they cleared the Yankees from the woods past the eastern edge of the clearing. A soldier from the 1st Texas remembered the horror, "Many of our company killed and wounded among whomb my friend Frank Gearing shot in breast, [I] laid him down by a tree and pass on with boys. Had canteen and tin cup perforated by a ball, also one through the breast of coat, and haversack strap cut—struck in face by a piece of tin, off a canister or some arrangement for holding balls by artillerymen . . . Many wounded among whomb was Jno McCarty and myself in right breast glancy shot bled considerably but never left field."[35]

The "Lee to the Rear" episode, as Lee's attempt to lead the Texas brigade is now known, became part of the Lee myth after the Civil War. The Confederate general came to be seen as a holy figure that made heroic sacrifices for the cause of the Confederate States of America. By the late 19th and early 20th centuries, Lee had become even more of a mythical hero than an ordinary man, and the "Lee to the Rear" story appeared to support this larger-than-life image of the general. The Christlike Lee had been eager to sacrifice his life for the Confederacy on the morning of May 6. His loyal followers urged him to "go back." They believed the success of their cause depended on his continued leadership.

The irony is that the "Lee to the Rear" moment during the Battle of the Wilderness shows just how *human* Lee really was. Instead of being cool and unflappable, he was agitated and desperate. He realized he was in danger of losing everything, and he unwisely put himself forward to lead a brigade to stop the Union advance. Longstreet acknowledged his chief was "off his balance." Others reported—and Lee confirmed—that he shed tears during this emotional moment. Lee had been pushed to his breaking point, and he almost did something utterly reckless that probably would have ended in him being shot. The death of the South's finest commander and leader might have been a mortal blow to the Confederacy.

A modern scholar estimates there were 457 casualties for the Texas Brigade that morning out of 850 men present for duty.[36] Given that Lee would have been on horseback—and therefore at greater risk had he led the charge—we can guess that there was considerably more than a 50% chance he would have been killed or wounded if he hadn't gone to the rear. In retrospect, Lee had been extraordinarily lucky he came to his senses in time just as he had been fortunate when nightfall prevented Hancock from overwhelming Hill on the Plank Road a day earlier.

Perhaps a death wish was behind Lee's desire to charge across Tapp's field. His health hadn't been good for over a year. It's probable Lee had a heart attack in March 1863, and he had felt unwell on numerous occasions since then. In a letter to his son Custis, a month before the Battle of the Wilderness, Lee wrote, "I feel a marked change in my strength since my attack last spring at Fredericksburg, and am less competent for my duty than ever." Lee may have also been discouraged by the news that his beloved Arlington estate had been purchased by the United States government for an unpaid tax bill of $92.07 in January 1864. It seemed likely, in May 1864, that his family would never live at Arlington again. The government had already transformed part of his former estate into a "Freedman's Village" for freed slaves from the surrounding area. It is conceivable Lee wanted to bring matters to a conclusion, one way or another, at Tapp Farm shortly after dawn on May 6. Immediately after the war, Lee told a newspaper correspondent, "he would have been pleased had his life been taken in any of the numerous battlefields of which he had fought during this war."[37] That morning in the Wilderness may have been the closest Lee ever came to being killed on the battlefield during the Civil War.

General George Washington also appeared to have a death wish on one occasion during a desperate fight in New York City in 1776. While his demoralized troops were retreating en masse, Washington stood his ground against the impending British assault. One senior officer believed Washington was "so vexed at the infamous conduct of his troops that he sought death rather than life."[38] Fortunately for the future of the United States, his aides grabbed the reins of his horse and removed him from danger.

There had been another instance of a Confederate commanding general attempting to lead troops in the heat of battle, and it too involved Ulysses S. Grant as the opposing commander. Rebel General Albert Sidney Johnston, commander of the Western Department, was shot in the leg while leading a charge during a pivotal moment of the Battle of Shiloh in April 1862. The ball severed an artery and Johnston died on the battlefield. Grant chose not to see Johnston's death as a random and unfortunate accident, however. He believed, instead, that a commander who would put himself at such great risk illustrated the desperation of the Confederates. "Commanding generals are liable to be killed during engagements," Grant wrote, "and the fact that when he was shot Johnston was leading a brigade to induce it to make a charge which had been repeatedly ordered, is evidence that there was neither the universal demoralization on our side nor the unbounded confidence on theirs which has been claimed."[39] Similarly, the "Lee to the Rear" episode wasn't merely one of many "what ifs" during the two days in the Wilderness. Rather, it represented how dire the situation had become for the Confederates shortly after 6:00 A.M. at Widow Tapp Farm.

The Army of Northern Virginia faced an existential crisis at that moment—perhaps its most serious of the war so far. While the heroism of the Texans bought additional time for Lee, Hancock retained the initiative. Longstreet had surely prevented a near-certain defeat for the Rebels. Now, "Old Pete" would try to threaten Grant's left. Despite the disastrous beginning of day two for Lee's army, May 6 still remained anybody's day.

NINE

High Noon on the Orange Plank Road

Even with the timely arrival of Longstreet's men, Winfield Scott Hancock glimpsed a tantalizing opportunity to sweep away Lee's right wing during the early morning hours of May 6. At 6:30 A.M., Hancock expected three of Burnside's divisions would be ready to attack the left of Longstreet's and Hill's forces. He sent a message to Meade at that time requesting Burnside "go in as soon as possible." Unfortunately, "Old Burn"—as he was referred to by the officers of the Army of the Potomac—was nowhere near where he was supposed to be, and wouldn't be ready to attack until later in the *afternoon*, over six hours later. When Hancock learned Burnside wasn't up yet, he responded, "I knew it! Just what I expected! If he could attack now, we could smash A. P. Hill all to pieces!!"[1]

The Union Second Corps general, who now commanded almost half of Grant's army, also intended to send in Barlow's entire division in response to Longstreet's counterattack. In one of the great mysteries of the battle, Gibbon, now commanding Barlow's division and the rest of Hancock's left wing, said he never received the order to advance Barlow's troops. Hancock insisted he did send the order. Both men were highly respected and fundamentally honest, so it was most likely an unfortunate miscommunication.[2]

The consequences were nonetheless regrettable for the Union Army. The inability of Burnside and Barlow to attack Lee at his most vulnerable moment resulted in a missed opportunity. In his memoirs, Ulysses S. Grant wrote, "I believed then, and see no reason to change that opinion now, that if the country had been such that Hancock and his command could have seen the confusion and panic in the lines of the enemy, it would have been taken advantage of so effectually that Lee would not have made another stand outside of his Richmond defenses."[3] Hancock, of course, was well aware of Lee's distress—that's why he was eager for Burnside and Barlow to attack at 7:00 A.M. Grant later stated, "We gained an advantage on the morning of the 6th, which, if it had been followed up, must have proven very decisive."[4] Hancock believed that if Barlow's entire division had attacked as he had ordered, "the result must have been very disastrous to the enemy, in his then shattered condition."[5] He added that he received no assistance from Burnside that morning, despite anticipating such relief shortly after the Union assault at 5:00 A.M.

The story of Burnside's misadventures that morning, as detailed by Morris Schaff, is pretty damning. Washington Roebling had been originally assigned to escort Burnside's men to Chewning Farm, but he was recalled by General Warren. Schaff was instead ordered to lead Burnside's divisions through the woods. The lead division of the Ninth Corps didn't arrive at the agreed meeting place until 5:30 A.M.—an hour and a half later than expected.

To assist with Hancock's attack at 5:00 A.M., it was hoped Burnside's men would head into the woods in the direction of Chewning Farm at 4:00 A.M. Burnside himself didn't arrive at the jumping-off point until 6:00 A.M. Upon Burnside's arrival, Schaff gave him his instructions verbally and remembered, "He was mounted on a bobtailed horse and wore a drooping army hat with a large gold cord around it. Like the Sphinx, he made no reply, halted, and began to look with a most leaden countenance in the direction he was to go."[6]

Both Warren and Meade were upset that Burnside had been delayed. Colonel Wainwright wrote in his diary, "Burnside somehow is never up to the mark when the tug comes."[7] In fairness to Burnside, artillery clogged the roads, which impeded the progress of his soldiers. Meade, who didn't have authority over Burnside, felt unable to intervene to clear the roads. This chain of command anomaly—Burnside reporting to Grant but not Meade—caused just as many problems as Burnside's notorious "slowness."[8]

Just as two of Burnside's divisions finally headed into the woods, the Ninth Corps commander ordered a halt for breakfast. By 9:00 A.M., Burnside had been unable to occupy Chewning Farm and was told instead to go immediately to Hancock's assistance. By midday, Burnside still hadn't attacked the enemy, causing Grant's chief of staff, John Rawlins, to write him tersely, "Hancock has been expecting you for the last three hours, and has been making his attack and dispositions with a view to your assistance."[9] All in all, Burnside had been a colossal disappointment on the morning of May 6.

Perhaps this isn't an entirely judicious assessment of "Old Burn." One of his divisions had been sent to Hancock early in the morning for reserve duty, leaving him with just two for attacking Rebel positions at Chewning Farm. His fourth division, consisting of African American troops, was guarding the wagon trains. And moving through the dense woods between Hancock on the left and Warren on the right was a far more challenging assignment than it seemed. Wadsworth had been similarly bogged down in the exact same forest on the afternoon of May 5. Finally, many of Burnside's men were green. On the eve of battle, one of Burnside's generals wrote, "My regiment is in no condition to take into action, but I must do the best I can. It will be a long and hard fight . . . Give me twenty days and I could make a splendid regiment of this, but man proposes and God disposes."[10] All in all, Longstreet's corps was a significantly more valuable addition to Lee's fighting capability than Burnside's corps was to Grant's.

Not only did Hancock have to worry about Burnside's woes, but he was also preoccupied with his far left flank. Union headquarters had been fearful that Longstreet would march up the Brock Road in Hancock's rear on the morning of May 6. That's why Gibbon was given Barlow's division along with artillery to defend against such an attack. Barlow's men were deployed south of the Brock Road/Plank Road intersection and were facing south. Even after it was clear that Longstreet turned up where Hill had been fighting, there was still a concern that a division under General Pickett might approach up the Brock Road. According to Schaff, "The record seems to show that Meade, Hancock, as well as Gibbon and presumably Humphreys in a measure, all harbored a fear that Longstreet, on the left, would suddenly appear a portentous spectre, forever casting its image on their minds."[11] Specifically, Hancock may have feared the ghost of Stonewall Jackson, who outflanked Hooker's right at the Battle of Chancellorsville resulting in a crushing Union defeat. And yet, at a crucial moment, Hancock decided to overcome his apprehension, ordering Barlow to stop Longstreet's counterattack. But Gibbon, apparently, was determined to stick with the more cautious plan.

Of the miscommunication between Gibbon and Hancock, a historian of the Second Corps wrote, "The history of war abounds in such misunderstandings. No one who knew Gibbon can possibly believe that this accomplished officer conspicuously failed to do anything that was required of him."[12] It may have been an honest error, but it was nevertheless a costly one. Hancock wrote, "it seems that the expected movement of Longstreet on the left flank, on the morning of the 6th, had a very material effect upon the result of the battle . . . This paralyzed a large number of my best troops, who would otherwise have gone into action at a decisive point on the morning of the 6th."[13]

Gibbon's failure to send Barlow forward caused another problem for the overburdened Hancock that morning. With Birney's men having moved west down the Orange Plank Road and Barlow's troops having remained in place south of the crossroads, there was a dangerous gap between the two forces that could possibly be exploited by aggressive and opportunistic commanders like Lee and Longstreet. Those two superior tacticians seldom missed such favorable opportunities for destroying the enemy.

◆

The morning of May 6 began splendidly for James Samuel Wadsworth. His troops swept away the Rebels from the woods north of the Orange Plank Road, and then joined Major General David Birney's men in driving Hill's weary soldiers back down the Plank Road. The 76th New York Infantry, despite suffering devastating losses on the previous day, provided valuable service by attempting to disable a Confederate battery that began firing on the Northerners. Only the belated arrival of Longstreet's First Corps had been able to halt Wadsworth's and Birney's inexorable momentum. By all accounts, Wadsworth was in tremendous form. He rode in front of his men yelling encouraging words like, "Give it to them, Bucktails!" and "Boys, you are driving them; charge!"[14] Throughout the morning, Wadsworth, who had three horses shot out from under him, sat on one of his horses "with hat in hand, bringing it down on the pommel of his saddle with every bound as he rides at the head of the column." He also carried a Revolutionary War saber in his other hand.[15]

After urging Lee to go to the rear, Gregg's Texans came storming across Tapp's field and delivered a savage blow to Wadsworth's troops. According to Schaff, the Texas brigade "dashed at Wadsworth's riddled front, through which the battery had been cutting swaths; and besides that, two 12-pound guns and one 24-pound howitzer had run forward into the Plank Road and were pouring their canister into his huddled and crumbling flanks. Fatigue and want of coherence were breaking down the fighting power of his men, yet they met this shock with great fortitude."[16]

After Gregg's assault, Longstreet's brigades attacked in waves against Wadsworth's forces. The fighting became bloody at close quarters with frequent charges and countercharges.[17] Brigadier General Henry Benning's Georgians "advanced through Gregg's lines, and with yipping cries plunged into the Yankee defenders."[18] Wadsworth's men held their ground at first, but were eventually overwhelmed by Colonel William Perry's Alabama brigade. At 7:40 A.M., an aide-de-camp wrote General Warren, "Wadsworth has been slowly pushed back, but is contesting every inch of ground."[19]

A private remembered, "The Confederate fire resembled the fury of hell in intensity, and was deadly accurate."[20] Another witness said the Union line "began to waver, then break, and finally disrupt in great confusion."[21]

Shortly after 8:00 A.M., Wadsworth's forces came under assault while positioned in four lines adjacent to the Plank Road. The men were densely packed together and stayed low to the ground to avoid Rebel artillery fire. The Iron Brigade, commanded by Brigadier General Lysander Cutler, bore the brunt of an especially vicious Rebel attack. According to Cutler, his men were "badly scattered, a large portion of them taking the route over which they had marched the night before."[22] Over 1,000 soldiers—Cutler's brigade and many Pennsylvanians formerly commanded by Colonel Stone along with numerous stragglers—darted through the woods toward Lacy House. It was an ignominious moment for two brigades that had earned a well-deserved reputation for fearlessness at Gettysburg.

Coincidentally, Schaff, who was on his way to deliver a message to Wadsworth after completing his assignment with the Ninth Corps, ran into Cutler and his men as they were streaming toward Lacy House. Schaff described Cutler as "an oldish, thin, earnest-looking Roundhead sort of man."[23] Cutler had been wounded, and was bleeding on his upper lip. Schaff wrote that he "looked ghastly" and probably felt worse, "for he was a gallant man, and to lead his men back, hearing every little while the volleys of their comrades still facing the enemy, must have been hard."[24] A private, who served under Cutler, offered a different opinion of his commander, "Cutler is an old fool and is never around where there is any danger. He limbers off to the rear as soon as the shells begin to fly."[25]

Cutler did feel awful about the retreat of his soldiers. In a later report to General Warren, he wrote, "When they broke the men started back on the route we went in. I and all my staff commenced rallying them, but were within half a mile of here [Lacy House] before I got anything like order restored . . . I was very much mortified at finding myself separated from the column, and feared that there might be some misapprehension about it."[26] The provost marshal for the Army of the Potomac Marsena Patrick witnessed Cutler and his men returning to Lacy House. He wrote in his diary, "The Old 1'Corps was coming out as I went up, very much broken & Cutler confused."[27]

Shockingly, Cutler told Schaff he believed Wadsworth had been killed in the assault. And a couple officers said, "Yes, we saw him fall." This report at approximately 9:00 A.M. was erroneous, however. Schaff felt they must have seen Wadsworth's horse killed and assumed the general suffered a similar fate.[28]

With the retreat of this motley band of soldiers under Cutler, Wadsworth's force had been cut in two by Longstreet. The first group, consisting of the remnants of Rice's and Baxter's brigades, remained with Wadsworth along the Orange Plank Road just west of the Brock Road intersection. The second group—what remained of Stone's and Cutler's brigades—was now situated on the lawn in front of Lacy House. In just over twenty-four hours, Wadsworth's division that had proudly marched into the Wilderness during the wee hours of May 4 had been wrecked. At the beginning of the campaign, the division's strength had been listed at 8,153. During the early morning of May 6, Meade assumed Wadsworth still had 5,000 men, a number that included Baxter's brigade. After the retreat of Cutler, Lyman believed Wadsworth had just 2,000 soldiers remaining at the Plank Road. Cutler still had another 1,269 demoralized troops at Lacy House.

As an effective fighting force, the 4th Division of the Fifth Corps appeared to be spent. The proud and combative James Wadsworth, who had such high hopes for the campaign, must have felt bitterly disappointed. Headquarters was understandably concerned when they saw Cutler's men streaming out of the woods. Grant's friend, Elihu Washburne, wrote in his diary, "Wadsworth's division seems to have been driven out of the timber into the open field in plain sight. We do not know what it all means. General Grant has gone out in that direction. It is feared it may be serious. Meade has gone there."[29]

Wadsworth eventually steadied his rump fighting force, after the departure of Cutler. Luckily for the survivors of the morning slaughter, a lull in the fighting took place after 9:00 A.M. The time between 8:00 A.M.

until 11:00 A.M. in the woods around the Orange Plank Road was characterized by murderous back-and-forth assaults between the Rebels and the Federals interspersed with occasional lulls. It was impossible for even the participants to remember the details with any certainty. A staff officer said that the official reports of the fighting "make a confused tale, and much of it a confused tale about confusion."[30]

One officer believed the fighting was as severe during that period as at any other time during the day, adding, "Sometimes one party gained a little ground, and then the other."[31] Another infantryman remembered the Wilderness on May 6 as "one seething crackling cauldron of all that a Dante might have conceived of the worst condition of a veritable hell, with nearly two hundred thousand men struggling like infuriated demons."[32] At roughly 9:00 A.M., Hancock ordered Wadsworth to take command of all troops north of the Plank Road, which included regiments from the Second Corps and Ninth Corps in addition to his Fifth Corps men. With a bolstered force, Wadsworth might be able to join with Birney in regaining the initiative.

During the brief respite from fighting, Wadsworth received the unlikeliest of surprises amid all the battlefield chaos and carnage. His son, Captain Craig Wadsworth, nicknamed "Tick," obtained permission from his commanding officer to visit his father in the woods for a couple hours. Craig had apparently heard his father had had two horses shot out from under him already that day, and urged him to be more careful. Schaff described the "high-spirited" James Wadsworth that morning as "more an individual combatant than the cool and trained commander."[33] It's not clear whether Craig had heard false rumors from Cutler and his men that his father had been killed. Wadsworth loved his children, so a visit from Craig ordinarily would have been a pleasant interlude. Surprisingly, the commander soon insisted that his son return to his unit, after Craig pleaded with his father to be less reckless. The younger Wadsworth departed before 11:00 A.M.[34]

Shortly after Craig rode off through the thickets, James Wadsworth had an astonishing discussion with his aide, Captain Robert Monteith. They were talking alone, when Wadsworth told Monteith "he felt completely exhausted and worn out; that he was unfit to command, and felt he ought, in justice to himself and his men, to turn the command of the division over to Gen. Cutler." Wadsworth then asked for a cracker, which Monteith got for him. The squire of Geneseo seemed broken. [35]

It's certainly not surprising Wadsworth was worn out. At fifty-six years old, the relentless stress of leading men in combat for two straight days would have been difficult to bear. He also felt responsible for the tragic losses of so many young men. And we also know he didn't have much sleep over the previous seventy-two hours. Wadsworth realized, perhaps after his adrenaline subsided, he was no longer fit for the immense responsibilities of commanding Hancock's right wing in what was shaping up to be one of the bloodiest and most important battles in American history.

Yet, it was a difficult decision to consider for the brave and dutiful aristocrat, who cared a great deal about his reputation. In a letter to his wife before the campaign, he wrote, "I wish I could tell you how much I love you and our dear children, how anxious I am that all should go well with you, that you will all live in affection and kindness, *and that none of our dear children will ever do anything to tarnish the good name which we who are here hope to maintain on the battlefield.*" [36] [Italics added] Was it merely fatigue or did he fear he was on the verge of suffering a mental breakdown? One wonders if Craig's visit to his father was related to Wadsworth's mental state. Had Craig been alerted by officers close to the division commander that he had been acting erratically in the field? It seems odd that Craig would otherwise have chosen such a crucial moment of the battle to pay a social visit to his dad.

The logistics of turning his command over to Cutler may have ultimately seemed prohibitive to Wadsworth upon further reflection. Cutler was a couple miles away at Lacy House, and would be required to return to the Plank Road to take over Wadsworth's ragtag force consisting of units from the Fifth, Second, and Ninth Corps. A seamless transfer of command might have taken more time than was feasible at that juncture of the battle. The idea must have seemed increasingly impracticable to Wadsworth as he mulled it over. At some point between 11:00 and 11:30 A.M., he heard firing from the left of the road, and returned to the front to prepare his men for another Confederate assault.

As Wadsworth approached the Union front line, he noticed that Birney's men, on his left, were giving way before an unseen enemy force. A Pennsylvania officer believed it was "one of the strangest scenes of army experience. Without any apparent cause that could be seen from the position of the brigade, the troops on our left began to give way, and commenced falling back towards the Brock road."[37] The soldiers didn't appear to be demoralized. Instead, "by far the larger number acted with the utmost deliberation in their movements."[38] Wadsworth responded immediately—some might say impulsively—to the gathering crisis.

First, he ordered a brigade commander to find four additional regiments that would stop the Union men from fleeing to the Brock Road. Then, he rode ahead and discovered the 20th Massachusetts Infantry, which would later be known as the Harvard Regiment, holding a key position in the line. These men were safely dug in behind breastworks. Lieutenant Henry Mali looked on in surprise as General Wadsworth "came galloping up in a very wild and exciting manner." Wadsworth shouted, "What are you doing there, who commands here?" Colonel George Macy stepped forward and answered, "I do, sir, and have been placed here by General Webb with orders to hold this position at any cost." Still agitated, Wadsworth replied, "I command these troops and order you forward." Macy, who wasn't quite sure Wadsworth had the authority to overrule his orders, responded somewhat rebelliously, "Very well, sir, but we are the Second Corps."[39]

This response angered Wadsworth, who began "throwing his arms in the air." After Wadsworth said something indistinguishable, Macy answered, "Very well, sir, we will go." Wadsworth galloped off again to find Rice's men. Colonel Macy then gave orders to his officers, adding "it is certain death. Great God! That man is out of his mind. Gentlemen, you must lead your companies or the men won't go."[40]

The brave Massachusetts men charged straight into a hailstorm of lead from the Rebels. Incredibly, the Union men made it to Confederate lines where "hand to hand fighting ensued, the men using the butts of their muskets." The fighting lasted fifteen minutes before the 20th Massachusetts retreated. Lieutenant Mali recorded that 533 soldiers had gone forward. Only 110 men returned to the Brock Road, when the regiment reformed later that afternoon. Macy was one of the first to be shot. Major Henry Livermore Abbott, who took command after Macy fell, was mortally wounded minutes later. Mali later wrote, perhaps unjustly, "Had Wadsworth left us in our position our line would not have been broken and the result of that day, as far as the second corps was concerned, I believe would have been very different."[41]

Abbott, one of the most respected soldiers in the Army of the Potomac, would be sorely missed by his fellow officers. Lyman saw his friend Abbott right before he died, writing, "Abbott lay on a stretcher, quietly breathing his last—his eyes were fixed and the ashen color of death was on his face. Nearby lay his Colonel, Macy, shot in the foot. I raised Macy and helped him to the side of Abbott, and we stood there until he died." The field hospital was a ghastly site. "Arms & legs lay outside the operating tents," Lyman noted, "and each table had a bleeding man on it, insensible from ether, and with the surgeons at work on him." With Macy in tears, Lyman gathered up Abbott's valuables along with a lock of his hair. He also received a promise that Abbott's body would be returned to Massachusetts.[42]

After leaving the 20th Massachusetts, Wadsworth found the remnants of Rice's brigade. Wadsworth faced a dilemma. Union troops were being attacked from both the front and their left flank south of the Plank Road. Ordinary soldiers instinctively recognized this murderous situation and many of them quite sensibly retreated to the Brock Road fortifications in the rear. Trying to save his force from this desperate predicament, Wadsworth ordered Rice's men to undertake a wheel movement "so as to fire into the enemy on the other side of the road." In the midst of the maneuver, Wadsworth shouted to his aide, Monteith, "I will throw these two regiments on their flank and you hurry forward the 1st Brigade." Waving his Revolutionary War saber high above his head, Wadsworth then encouraged his troops—among them were the 76th New York—"Forward, men! We'll take a thousand prisoners now!"[43]

At that precise moment, Wadsworth lost control of his horse, which ran wildly toward the Confederate line held by an Alabama brigade. A blast may have first killed Wadsworth's horse. As the horse fell, a bullet hit Wadsworth on the top of his head, "his brain spattering the coat of Earl M. Rogers, his aide at his side."[44] When Lieutenant Earl Rogers was later asked by an officer why Wadsworth was allowed to expose himself to such danger, Rogers replied, "My God, Colonel, nobody could stop him."[45]

After the shooting of Wadsworth, his soldiers were driven back to the entrenchments on the Brock Road. The severely wounded Wadsworth remained in the custody of the enemy. It was shortly before noontime. Brigadier General James Samuel Wadsworth had led his men in combat for over thirty hours since the early morning of May 5. His division had been broken to pieces, and he now lay close to death on the Orange Plank Road. Regarding Wadsworth, one officer remembered, "If 'the blood of the martyrs is the seed of the church,' the blood of such men consecrates the corner-stone of our country, and is never shed in vain."[46]

Not too long after Rice's men headed to the rear, a Rebel captain from Georgia "noticed a fine-looking man in the uniform of a general, who was lying on the side of the road in the dust and heat."[47] A surgeon gave the wounded man some water and morphine. They learned their captive was General Wadsworth of New York, who "was said by some of the prisoners who knew him to have been a very brave man."[48] Wadsworth's watch, field glasses, map, and sword were taken from him. One veteran remarked, without exaggeration, that the Union commander may have had "more wealth than the treasury of the Confederate government."[49]

Colonel Charles Marshall, a staff officer for Robert E. Lee, immediately proceeded to the spot where Wadsworth lay. "Supposing that he might wish to send some message to his family," Marshall wrote, "I addressed him and tendered my services. I found, however, that he paid no attention to me, and upon further effort to communicate with him discovered that he was unconscious of what was passing around him. I should not have supposed that such was the case from the expression of his face, which was perfectly calm and natural, the eye indicating consciousness and intelligence."[50] Later in the afternoon, Wadsworth was taken to a Confederate hospital about two miles west on the Orange Plank Road. One wounded prisoner wrote of this hospital, "I cannot conceive of a more dismal place."[51]

After the wounding of Wadsworth, his troops along with Birney's men moved quickly to the rear, so they could protect themselves behind breastworks. Witnessing the retreat, Lyman reported, "the whole line came back, slowly but mixed up—a hopeless sight! American soldiers, in this condition are enough to sink one's heart! They have no craven terror—they have their arms; but, for the moment, they will not fight, nor even rally."[52] Lyman even drew his sword to try to stem the retreat, but it was useless. Marsena Patrick also tried to stop the fleeing men, "I put in my Cavalry & rode down & drove back & sent to Corps multitudes of these fellows, handling them very roughly as an Example—they being in full view of most of the army."[53] After consulting with General Birney, Hancock decided it was best to officially order all of his men on the Plank Road to withdraw behind the breastworks at the Brock Road. This took place shortly after noontime. Hancock's foresight in having the men prepare fortifications on the previous day proved to be a godsend.

It had been a stunning reversal for the Union Army that morning. Hancock came close to victory shortly after 6:00 A.M., and now, six hours later, his force had been routed and was in disarray behind its Brock Road fortifications. The Orange Plank Road at that moment belonged to Robert E. Lee. What Wadsworth didn't know was that the mysterious assault south of the road had come from Longstreet's men, who had surreptitiously outflanked Birney and then rolled up the entire Union line.

The Union Second Corps troops had been surprised and then broke. In his diary, Washburne wrote, "It is true—Hancock driven back and his left turned. It is an awful moment."[54] An awful moment indeed. Demoralized and disorganized, the Federals were in serious danger. Most likely, they would not be able to withstand a timely attack by Longstreet on the Brock Road. Hancock would need at least a couple of hours to reorganize his men. It seemed certain Lee and Longstreet wouldn't allow him any time at all to regroup.

Ulysses S. Grant's spring campaign hung in the balance. Schaff sensed at that moment, "gaunt Slavery, frenzied with delight over her prospective reprieve, snatches a cap from a dead, fair-browed Confederate soldier, and clapping it on her coarse, rusty, gray-streaked mane, begins to dance in hideous glee out on the broom-grass of the Widow Tapp's old field."[55] That determined foe of slavery, James Wadsworth, affectionately known as "Old Waddy" by his men, was now a semiconscious prisoner. It seemed doubtful he'd survive to see his beloved family ever again.

TEN

Robert E. Lee's Enticing Opportunity

With Hancock's troops fleeing to their Brock Road fortifications at midday, James Longstreet intended to capitalize on the enemy's disorganization. He led a column of Rebel soldiers, who were moving easterly along the Orange Plank Road, in pursuit of the retreating Federals. Riding with him were his staff, orderlies, Brigadier General Joseph Kershaw, and Brigadier General Micah Jenkins. Schaff described Jenkins, who commanded a brigade in Longstreet's First Corps, as "a sensitive, enthusiastic South Carolinian" and a "humble Christian."[1]

When Lieutenant Colonel Moxley Sorrel, who had led the flanking movement that rolled up Hancock's men moments earlier, met Longstreet's party on the Plank Road, Jenkins threw his arm around his shoulder, and said, "Sorrel, it was splendid, we shall smash them now."[2] As the officers quickly congratulated themselves on the remarkable success of their attack, Jenkins told Longstreet, "I am happy; I have felt despair of the cause for some months, but am relieved, and feel assured that we will put the enemy back across the Rapidan before night."[3]

As the party continued riding, Longstreet discussed his plan with the officers for following up on their stunning accomplishment. Jenkins's and Kershaw's men would attempt to break Hancock's lines at Brock Road, while another force in the woods would attempt to swing around Hancock's extreme left. "The order to me," Kershaw wrote, "was to break their line and push all to the right of the road toward Fredericksburg. Jenkins's brigade was put in motion by a flank in the plank road, my division in the woods to the right."[4]

The men appeared exuberant and optimistic. They sensed they were about to win a stunning victory. The esteemed biographer of Robert E. Lee, Douglas Southall Freeman, wrote, "Longstreet believed that Grant's army could be hurled back, a broken and confused mass, against the fords of the Rapidan. A triumph, Longstreet thought, akin to that which might have been won the previous year, if Jackson had not fallen, was now awaiting the army. A tragic morning was trending to a glorious noon!"[5] While the officers finalized the plans, Longstreet's aide-de-camp, Lieutenant Andrew Dunn, expressed concern that the First Corps commander was exposing himself to enemy fire. Longstreet replied, "That is our business."[6]

The success of the initial Confederate flank attack, which resulted in the wounding of Wadsworth and the retreat of Hancock's troops, exceeded all expectations. Robert E. Lee had desired an outflanking of Hancock all along, and originally intended to have Longstreet arrive on the morning of May 6 via Brock Road for that purpose. After Hill's corps suffered crippling losses on May 5, however, Lee needed Longstreet to relieve Hill's men via the Orange Plank Road. Once Longstreet prevented disaster at dawn on May 6, Lee could then return to his goal of outflanking Hancock. It's a testament to Lee's aggressiveness that he pivoted so quickly to offensive operations after such a close call at the Widow Tapp Farm during the early morning hours. By all accounts, Lee regained his composure by mid-morning.

Around 9:00 A.M., Lee sent Major General Martin Smith of the engineers to Longstreet to try to find a way around Hancock's left. General Edward Porter Alexander wrote of Smith, "He was a fine tactician, a skillful engineer, and had been noted for gallantry in the defense of Vicksburg, where he had been chief engineer. He was a native of N.Y. and a graduate of West Point of the class of 1838."[7] Smith soon returned to Longstreet around 10:00 A.M. with good news. He had discovered the route of the Fredericksburg and Orange Court House unfinished railroad, which didn't appear on Rebel maps, that ran parallel for a stretch with the Orange Plank Road less than a quarter mile south of it. Confederate troops would be able to move east down the unfinished railroad without being seen by the enemy. And there were natural pathways for heading back up to the Plank Road. It was a promising discovery by Smith.

Longstreet ordered his chief of staff, Moxley Sorrel, to lead four brigades down the unfinished railway, so they could then hit Hancock on his flank. The gallant, twenty-six-year-old Sorrel, described by Schaff as "a tall, trim, graceful young Georgian, with keen dark eyes and engaging face," had never led troops in battle before.[8] Upon giving Sorrel the assignment, Longstreet told him, "Colonel, there is a fine chance of a great attack by our right. If you will quickly get into those woods, some brigades will be found much scattered from the fight. Collect them and take charge. Form a good line and then move, your right pushed forward and turning as much as possible to the left. Hit them hard when you start, but don't start until you have everything ready. I shall be waiting for your gun fire, and be on hand with fresh troops for further advance." Sorrel later wrote, "No greater opportunity could be given to an aspiring young staff officer, and I was quickly at work."[9] He put his force together in an hour. At 11:00 A.M., his men moved down the unfinished railroad for about a half mile and then they set upon Hancock's left. The Rebels, Sorrel wrote, "rolled back line after line." Sorrel rode with Brigadier General William Mahone's Virginians. "Follow me, Virginians! Let me lead you," Sorrel yelled in the heat of the fighting.[10]

The Rebels easily swept away the Federals. "Back pell-mell came the ever swelling crowd of fugitives," one Union soldier remembered, "and the next moment the Sons of Orange were caught up as by a whirlwind, and broken to fragments; and the terrible tempest of disaster swept on down the Union line, beating back brigade after brigade, and tearing to pieces regiment after regiment, until upwards of twenty thousand veterans were fleeing, every man for himself, through the disorganizing and already blood-stained woods, toward the Union rear."[11] Inexplicably, the left wing commander General Gibbon never sent a force down the unfinished railway. The official explanation was that Gibbon was worried about the enemy—possibly Major General George Pickett's division—attacking up the Brock Road. Regardless, the failure to have troops on the unfinished railway was a disastrous mistake. As Gibbon's commander, Hancock also bore some responsibility for this costly error.

❧

About ten minutes past noon, after the rout of Hancock's men, the 12th Virginia Infantry of Mahone's brigade crossed the Orange Plank Road and went about fifty yards into the woods on the north side of the road. This movement was approximately the same time that Moxley Sorrel exited the woods and joined up with Longstreet's party on the Plank Road. Soon, the officers leading the 12th Virginia decided to rejoin their brigade in the woods on the south side of the road. As the 12th Virginia headed back, some Virginians on the other side of the road mistakenly believed they were Union troops and yelled, "Look out, boys, they are coming back! There they come! There they come!" Their brigade commander General Mahone shouted, "Steady men, steady! Get in your places! Get in your places!"[12]

Gunfire erupted but abruptly stopped when the Virginians realized they were shooting at their comrades. Unfortunately, Longstreet's party, which had just entered the woods north of the road about one hundred yards from the Virginians, was caught in the crossfire. A bullet struck Micah Jenkins in the head, knocking him off his horse. Longstreet was then hit, too. "At the moment that Jenkins fell," Longstreet recalled, "I received a severe shock from a minie ball passing through my throat and right shoulder. The blow lifted me from the saddle, and my right arm dropped to my side, but I settled back to my seat, and started to ride on, when in a minute the flow of blood admonished me that my work for the day was done."[13]

The brave Jenkins had been critically wounded and would die two hours later. Right after the shooting, a soldier asked, "Jenkins . . . Mike, do you know me?"[14] Alas, he didn't answer. Years later, Longstreet wrote of Jenkins, "In a moment of highest earthly hope, he was transported to serenest heavenly joy; to that life beyond that knows no bugle call, beat of drum, or clash of steel. May his beautiful spirit, through the mercy of God, rest in peace! Amen!"[15]

Longstreet, who may have been hit by a ball that entered his right shoulder and exited his throat, *appeared* to be fatally wounded as well. Sorrel remembered that Longstreet's staff dismounted the large corps commander—Longstreet stood 6 feet, 2 inches and weighed 220 pounds—and propped him against a tree. Longstreet "almost choked with blood," while he waited for medical assistance.[16]

Longstreet summoned his remaining strength to order Major General Charles Field, a West Point graduate and career officer, to assume command, telling him, "Press them on General Field: press them on, sir!"[17] He also told Moxley Sorrel to go to Lee "and urge him to continue the movement he was engaged on; the troops being all ready, success would surely follow, and Grant, he firmly believed, be driven back across the Rapidan."[18] A British volunteer, Francis Dawson, went immediately to find a doctor. Luckily, he found the First Corps medical director, Dr. John Syng Dorsey Cullen, who rode quickly to the front and was able to stop the bleeding of Longstreet's wound.

As Longstreet was placed in a stretcher and carried to the rear, some nearby soldiers wondered if he was dead. Old Pete raised his hat with his left hand to show them he was still alive. The soldiers cheered wildly for their commander. "The burst of voices and the flying of hats in the air eased my pains somewhat," Longstreet recalled.[19] An officer on the general's staff remembered, "I never on any occasion during the four years of the war saw a group of officers and gentlemen more deeply disturbed. They were literally bowed down with grief. All of them were in tears."[20] Lee, who was riding on the Plank Road, became distraught, when he received the news. "I shall not soon forget the sadness in his face," Dawson said of Lee, "and the almost despairing movement of his hands when he was told that Longstreet had fallen."[21]

Longstreet was transported west along the Plank Road to the Confederate hospital tents at Parker's Store. The semiconscious James Wadsworth, who had been wounded less than thirty minutes earlier at almost the exact same spot, was a fellow patient. While at the hospital, Cullen probed Longstreet's wound and determined it wasn't fatal. Nevertheless, it would be several months before Lee's War Horse could return to his command.

Moxley Sorrel observed that the circumstances surrounding the wounding of James Longstreet were eerily similar to those associated with the shooting of Stonewall Jackson. On May 2, 1863, Lieutenant General Thomas Jackson, one of the finest corps commanders of the Army of Northern Virginia, had been struck by friendly fire while executing a successful flanking movement in the Wilderness during the Battle of Chancellorsville. On May 6, 1864—almost a year to the day later—Lieutenant General James Longstreet, another outstanding corps commander of the Army of Northern Virginia, was also hit by friendly fire during a successful flank attack, less than four miles away from where Stonewall had been hit.[22]

To the 19th-century mind, this couldn't possibly have been a coincidence. One veteran believed the wounding of his chief was a momentous incident, "which must rather be considered one of those mysterious interpositions of the Almighty in the affairs of men deemed necessary to shape for his own purposes the course of human events."[23] If God struck down Jackson and Longstreet at such critical moments, did that mean he did not favor the Confederate cause?

The news of Longstreet's wounding weighed heavily on Robert E. Lee. He didn't know if Old Pete would survive, and felt great sadness for his friend and trusted colleague. He also knew he couldn't afford to lose such a talented commander at that crucial point of the battle. An extremely religious man, Lee wondered if the loss of both Jackson and Longstreet at pivotal moments in the Wilderness was an ominous sign of some kind. Regardless, Lee was determined to carry on the fight. His soldiers needed his trusted leadership now more than ever.

Schaff described the chaos on the Plank Road immediately after the wounding of Longstreet, "Field's and Kershaw's divisions advancing in two or more lines of battle, at right angles to the road, Sorrel's flanking brigades parallel to it, all in more or less disorder, moving by flank to the rear for the time being, preparatory to the execution of Longstreet's order for a second attack on Hancock's left, every step they take bringing them and the advancing organizations nearer utter confusion, and the woods enveloped in heavy, obscuring smoke!"[24] The burden on Lee at that time was considerable. He'd now have to direct the attack on the Plank Road, in addition to serving as the overall commander of the Army of Northern Virginia. For Lee, who had been in the saddle since 4:00 A.M., it had already been a long and exhausting day. And it wasn't even close to being over yet.

Sorrel quickly explained everything that happened thus far to Lee, and added that Longstreet urged Lee to continue the maneuver that was already underway. Lee then asked Sorrel several questions, and praised him for his leadership of the flank attack. Sorrel gathered Lee would delay the attack, writing, "the General was not in sufficient touch with the actual position of the troops to proceed with it as our fallen chief would have been able to do, at least, I received that impression, because activity came to a stop for the moment."[25] Longstreet suspected, "General Lee did not care to handle the troops in broken lines, and ordered formation in a general line for parallel battle." Unfortunately for the Rebels, this would take time and would allow Hancock "time to collect his men into battle order, post his heavy reinforcements, and improve his intrenchments."[26]

General Field believed Grant's army would have been routed if Longstreet hadn't been shot. But once the First Corps commander was knocked out of action, Field agreed with Lee that it was necessary to straighten out the Confederate lines. Some Rebel troops were positioned perpendicular to the Brock Road, while others ran parallel to it. No attack could be made, according to Field, until these troops were realigned.

Wounded and dead from both sides were strewn throughout the no-man's-land between Rebel and Federal forces at the crossroads. Over the previous seven hours, the Army of Northern Virginia and the Army of the Potomac had engaged in some of the bloodiest fighting of the Civil War. Lee shared the view of his officers that one final, concentrated assault might lead to victory. But Lee ultimately decided against an elaborate flanking maneuver this time. Instead, he ordered Field to straighten out the lines, so they could directly attack Hancock's formidable earthworks, which were chest-high. Brute force, instead of maneuver, would now decide the fate of the battle for the Rebels. Ironically, this was a decision that would have greatly appealed to Ulysses S. Grant himself, who was not an advocate of maneuvering, or so he claimed.

While Field went about the painstaking task of straightening Confederate forces on the road and in the woods, Hancock used his reprieve wisely. He ordered his officers to realign their units, resupply the troops with ammunition, and strengthen their already well built breastworks. Unfortunately, much of this effort was complicated by the fact that many of Hancock's field officers had been killed or wounded. Surviving Union troops experienced relief once they made it behind their Brock Road works. The men desperately needed food and rest. Unaware of the wounding of Longstreet, Hancock's men were pleasantly surprised when he didn't follow up on his successful flank attack. During the delay by Lee, Sorrel recalled, "the foe was not idle. He had used the intervening hours in strengthening his position and making really formidable works across the road."[27]

With most of his troops recuperating at Brock Road, Hancock also took advantage of the Confederate delay to attempt to clear the enemy from his immediate front. Colonel Daniel Leasure's brigade from the Ninth Corps, which had been part of Gibbon's force on the far left, was given this dangerous assignment. Hancock ordered Colonel Leasure to sweep across the front of the Union line, while "keeping his right about 100 paces from our breastworks." This bold movement was carried out with "great spirit and success." Leasure's boys confronted a Rebel brigade, but it "fell back in disorder without engaging him."[28] After this successful operation, Hancock could breathe slightly easier.

Shortly after noontime, Lyman rode back to headquarters to report to General Meade on the state of affairs at Brock Road. The news was grim. Lyman noted that Grant, "who was smoking stoically under a pine, expressed himself annoyed and surprised that Burnside did not attack especially as Comstock was with him as an engineer & staff officer, to show him the way."[29] So far, Old Burn failed to have a meaningful impact on the fighting. This allowed Longstreet and Lee to take bigger risks than they might have done had they faced a more substantial threat from Burnside on their flank.

At 1:00 P.M., according to Lyman, the Union wagon trains were ordered back toward Ely's Ford in a precautionary move. At this time, Lyman returned to Hancock, who was resting under some trees. The Second Corps commander, who had been under incredible stress so far that day, admitted he was exhausted. Hancock also told Lyman that his troops "were rallied but very tired and mixed up, and not in a condition to advance."[30]

Meanwhile, Burnside's comedy of errors continued. His men still struggled to find their way through the dense underbrush and swamps. Grant's aide, Horace Porter, caught up with Burnside after midday, and recalled, "A champagne basket filled with lunch had been brought up, and at his invitation I joined him and some of his staff in sampling the attractive contents of the hamper."[31] Burnside was clearly having a more pleasant time than Hancock. Between 1:30 and 2:00 P.M., however, Burnside *finally* made an attack on Lee's left flank in the woods north of the Plank Road. Lyman urged Hancock to attack as well, but the Second Corps commander said "it would be to hazard too much."[32] Hancock, perhaps wisely, sensed he had been lucky to avoid a complete catastrophe at noontime, and still needed precious time for his men to recover their fighting prowess.

Among the soldiers at Brock Road that afternoon were the remnants of James Wadsworth's beleaguered division that had retreated after

Longstreet's flank attack. General Rice ordered Colonel John William Hofmann, who commanded the 56th Pennsylvania Infantry, to reform the division, which now consisted of undermanned regiments from Rice's and Stone's brigades along with just one company from Cutler's brigade. What remained of Private Reeves's 76th New York Infantry was part of this force. Hofmann, a brave soldier who had been a retail clerk before the war, quickly organized the officers and men, placing them in the third line just north of the crossroads. At 4:00 P.M. Hofmann counted 408 men still present for duty. The portion of Wadsworth's division that was still directly engaged with the enemy was now smaller than a regiment.

At 4:15 P.M. Lee's Rebels assaulted Hancock's well-fortified line at Brock Road. A bugler, mounted on Union General Gershom Mott's breastworks, sounded for the recall of skirmishers once he saw the enemy advance. Confederate troops marched up to the edge of the abatis—an elaborate obstacle consisting of rows of trees with pointed tops facing outward—where they halted and began an uninterrupted blast of musketry. Hancock observed that the rifle fire lasted for about thirty minutes. By most accounts, this musketry fire wasn't especially destructive and Hancock was able to effectively deploy artillery, which "delivered a destructive fire as the enemy approached" his line. [33]

Unexpectedly, some of Mott's and Birney's men, positioned just south of the intersection, broke and ran away toward Chancellorsville in disorder. As Hancock recalled, "As soon as the break in our line occurred, the enemy pushed forward and some of them reached the breast-works and planted their flags thereon." [34] It was a dangerous moment for the Federals.

At the same time, some of the breastworks caught fire after dry leaves and twigs were ignited by gunfire. According to some accounts, smaller fires flickered throughout the woods during the early hours of the afternoon. Hancock, who noticed that the woods were burning on his left front at 4:00 P.M., believed these fires spread to his breastworks, which added to the confusion and disorganization among some of Mott's and Birney's soldiers. "The breast-works on this portion of my line were constructed entirely of logs," Hancock reported, "and at the critical moment of the enemy's advance were a mass of flames which it was impossible at that time to subdue, the fire extending for many hundred paces to the right and left. The intense heat and smoke, which was driven by the wind directly into the faces of the men, prevented them on portions of the line from firing over the parapet, and at some points compelled them to abandon the line."[35] Some Union men had their hair "singed, for the smoke and flames were blown directly into their faces." A Rebel soldier remembered the fire "rendered the movements of the troops difficult, while the noise of battle raging in that dense thicket, scarcely drowned the shrieks of the wounded as the spreding fir of the underbrush and leaves caught them. The demon of destruction was in the very air."[36]

Hancock acted quickly to repair the break in his line. He rode through the woods and saw Wadsworth's depleted division now commanded by Hofmann. Hancock yelled, "What troops are those?" After Hofmann told him, Hancock replied, "Just what I want." He then gave Hofmann orders to retake the lost breastworks. "Instantly the lines were formed," one of Hofmann's men wrote, "and, advancing swiftly, rushed upon the intrenchments, which, after a brief but bloody encounter, were freed from the clutch of the enemy, who was pursued far beyond the woods."[37] In his official report, Hofmann wrote, "In the course of ten minutes the enemy was driven from the works and back into the woods from whence he had emerged. Several hundred men now sprang over the works and desired to follow the enemy."[38] Hofmann ordered his men to stop the pursuit, however, a decision that was approved by Hancock.

Repairing the break in the line had been a heroic and unexpected moment for Wadsworth's battered division. They had been involved in most of the fighting in the Wilderness for two straight days and had suffered devastating losses. On several occasions they had been overwhelmed by the enemy. And yet, at one of the most critical moments of the battle, they had been called upon by the "superb" Hancock himself to stop a Rebel breakthrough. James Wadsworth would have been proud of them.

By 5:00 p.m., Humphreys wrote, "the enemy was completely repulsed, and fell back with heavy loss in killed and wounded."[39] Confederate

General Field experienced severe losses and withdrew his forces to the Widow Tapp's field at about the exact same spot where the Texans had charged almost twelve hours earlier that day. Another Rebel commander, General Alexander, noted Lee lacked reinforcements and had to withdraw when faced with Hancock's second line of troops. This was just one of the consequences of Lee having a much smaller force than Grant.

"I have always thought," Morris Schaff later wrote, "that if Grant had been with Hancock at the time of this repulse, he would have ordered an immediate advance. For the Army of the Potomac never had another commander who was so quick as Grant to deliver a counter-blow."[40] Maybe so, though Grant's failure to pursue the retreating Rebels on the second day of the Battle of Shiloh in 1862 seems to contradict this belief. Schaff's comparison of Grant with Hancock mustn't take away from the latter's stellar performance during the two days of intense fighting. Lyman called Hancock and Getty, "the stars of the Wilderness." Describing Hancock's leadership as brilliant, Lyman wrote, "The vigor with which he brought up his men on the 5th through a difficult country, and the skill and rapidity with which he pushed them into action, his punctual and dashing advance on the 6th, and his cheerful courage under reverse, justify the playful praise that General Meade once gave him, 'Bully Hancock is the only one of my corps commanders who will always go right in when I order him.'"[41]

Shortly after Mott's works were briefly seized by the Rebels, Lyman, who was riding to Hancock, was told by an officer that there was no longer communication with the Union left wing. An aide from General Birney rode quickly to headquarters and reported the same news to Meade and Grant. Apparently, Grant and Meade were sitting against a tree when they heard the story. Grant calmly looked up at the aide and said, "I don't believe it." Grant's instinct was correct and the small breach had already been repaired by that time. Nevertheless, Washburne wrote in his diary at 5:25 P.M., "it looks gloomy enough at this time and there are long faces about the H.Q." On a more positive note, Washburne added, "Gen. Meade shows the true patriot and the persistent soldier. He says the hopes of the world rest upon our success and that he will fight so long as there is a man to stand up."[42]

During Lee's attack, Burnside decided to help out of his own accord, which took some pressure off of Hancock's right. After a frustrating morning and early afternoon, Burnside's two divisions finally had some success in driving the Rebels at a critical juncture in the battle. Meade said it was "the best thing old Burn did during the day."[43] Meade hoped Burnside and Hancock might launch a coordinated attack at 6:00 P.M. But after repulsing Lee, Hancock's men were exhausted and almost out of ammunition. Meade's joint attack was canceled. The fighting at the crossroads was over for the day. Lieutenant Colonel William Swan, an aide in the Fifth Corps, would later write, "There are but one or two square miles upon this continent that have been more saturated with blood than was the square mile which lay in front of the Brock Road and had the Orange Plank Road as a central avenue, in the two days of the battle of the Wilderness. Nearly every square yard had its fill of blood, and on nearly every square yard was Northern and Southern blood intermingled."[44]

Robert E. Lee's frontal assault on Hancock's works ended in failure. A tantalizing opportunity for dividing Grant's army was lost. The unfortunate wounding of Longstreet had led to a four-hour delay, which gave the Federals time to prepare. In a memoir published in 1907—thirty-seven years after the death of Robert E. Lee—General Edward Porter Alexander wrote, "the renewal of the attack at the late hour, and without Kershaw's division, was unwise. It was certain to cost many lives, the chances of success were not good, and even had they been, the lateness of the hour would have interfered with gathering the fruit of victory."[45] This was an unusually critical appraisal of Robert E. Lee from one of his loyal commanders.

Privately, Alexander was even more scathing, writing, "This attack ought *never, never* to have been made. It was sending a boy on a man's errand. It was wasting good soldiers whom we could not spare. It was discouraging pluck & spirit by setting it an impossible task."[46] Perhaps similar to Pickett's Charge on the third day of Gettysburg, Lee gambled on a frontal assault of a heavily fortified enemy position. The odds of success seemed low, and the gambit resulted in high casualties that Lee couldn't afford. One Union soldier, writing of the attack, compared Lee with Grant, who was often referred to as a butcher, "But certainly in this instance the epithet butcher, if applied to either, should rest on Lee."[47]

It later became an article of faith among Confederate soldiers that the wounding of James Longstreet upended a potentially devastating blow to Grant's army in the Wilderness. General Field wrote "had our advance not been suspended by this disaster, I have always believed that Grant would have been driven across the Rapidan before night."[48] Longstreet sensed he was on the verge of driving Hancock toward Fredericksburg. Even Edward Porter Alexander, who was one of the few sober-minded Confederate commentators on military affairs, wrote, "From the accounts of those who participated in this attack, experienced soldiers such as Gen. Mahone & others, & from details learned from prisoners, I have always believed that, but for Longstreet's fall, the panic which was fairly under way in Hancock's corps would have been extended & have resulted in Grant's being forced to retreat back across the Rapidan."[49]

The Confederates may have exaggerated their chances of success. Years later, Longstreet wrote to the journalist, William Swinton, "I thought that we had another Bull Run on you, for I had made my dispositions to seize the Brock Road." Swinton replied, "Hancock's left had not advanced, but remained on the original line covering the road." In response, Longstreet "admitted that that altered the complexion of affairs."[50]

There's little doubt Hancock faced severe difficulties after the successful Confederate flank attack. But he still had fresh troops on his left, and they may have been enough to stop another flanking movement by Longstreet's disorganized troops. It's tempting to wonder what might have happened had Longstreet not been shot. Would the possible defeat of Grant's spring campaign have ultimately led to a negotiated peace of some sort?

Perhaps it's more instructive to consider *why* the loss of Longstreet was so costly. Lee commanded an experienced, powerful army, yet he also possessed very little margin for error. Despite its impressive fighting capabilities, the Army of Northern Virginia couldn't overcome the wounding of its best corps commander at midday or the lack of reserves at 5:00 P.M. Poor luck may or may not explain the untimely wounding of both James Longstreet and Thomas Jackson one year earlier. We know for sure, however, that Lee's army was not strong enough in the end to overcome the loss of such valuable commanders. Indeed, Douglas Southall Freeman believed the increasing turnover among Lee's senior officers in general became a glaring liability for him during the Overland Campaign and after.[51]

It had been an exhausting and eventful day for Robert E. Lee. Military historians might say his performance was mixed. He bore some responsibility for the disordered state of Hill's corps prior to the arrival of Longstreet just after dawn. Lee also lost control of himself at Widow Tapp Farm, when it looked like his army might be defeated. He recovered well, however, and initiated the process that ultimately led to Longstreet's successful flank attack. Lee's 4:15 P.M. assault on Hancock's well-fortified lines at the Brock Road seems reckless in retrospect, but he had an unshakable confidence in his men. Many years later, Grant said, "Lee was a good deal of a head-quarters general; a desk general, from what I can hear and from what his officers say."[52] This couldn't have been further from the truth in the Wilderness, where Lee was much closer than Grant to the heaviest fighting. After the battle, Lyman wrote of Lee, "he is a brave and skillful soldier and he will fight while he has a division or a day's rations left."[53]

Lee demonstrated in those woods that he was still willing to attack and take big risks, despite having inferior numbers. Lyman noted that Grant's friend, Congressman Elihu Washburne, who witnessed the Battle of the Wilderness from headquarters, "came down entirely confident that Grant would at once swallow and annihilate Lee; but he wears another face now!"[54] The afternoon had been a very somber time at headquarters for not only Washburne, but Meade and Grant as well. And the battle wasn't over yet, either. Confederate Brigadier General John Gordon discovered Grant's extreme right was unprotected. Around sunset that evening, the Army of the Potomac would face another potentially disastrous crisis.

ELEVEN

Grant's Night March

The second day of combat in the woods was an especially stressful one for Ulysses S. Grant, despite his stoic demeanor that projected tranquility to everyone around him. When Hancock came to headquarters to consult with the commander-in-chief in the early evening, Grant fished through his pockets to find a cigar to give to him. He discovered he had only one remaining. "Deducting the number he had given away from the supply he had started out with in the morning," Horace Porter wrote, "showed that he had smoked that day about twenty, all very strong and of formidable size. But it must be remembered it was a particularly long day. He never afterward equaled that record in the use of tobacco."[1]

Grant experienced anxiety on the inside, but he remained imperturbable on the outside. Porter described another episode at headquarters shortly after General Cutler's men had been driven in around 9:00 A.M. Enemy shells began landing near where Grant was sitting on a log. An officer said, "General, wouldn't it be prudent to move headquarters to the other side of the Germanna road till the result of the present attack is known?" Between puffs of his cigar, Grant replied, "It strikes me it would be better to order up some artillery and defend the present location."[2] The threat was eventually neutralized. Whether that particular anecdote was exaggerated or not, Grant had a reputation for being cool in the most desperate situations on the battlefield.

The lieutenant general's staff reported he remained calm and reserved throughout much of the two days in the woods. Grant told Porter, "The only time I ever feel impatient is when I give an order for an important movement of troops in the presence of the enemy, and am waiting for them to reach their destination. Then the minutes seem like hours."[3] Troop movements, unfortunately, were almost impossible in the woods, as illustrated by both Wadsworth's and Burnside's struggles in the dense thickets between the Turnpike and the Plank Road. In each case, it was many hours before the troops eventually reached their destinations.

Grant spent most of the second day of battle at headquarters near the Turnpike. He believed his communications with his officers would be easier that way, though he did ride out to consult with Hancock on two occasions—once at 9:00 A.M. and another time at 5:25 P.M. At headquarters, according to Adam Badeau, Grant and Meade, "sat or lay on the ground, and discussed the chances, and studied their maps, and read the dispatches when aides-de-camp came breathless in from the front, and listened constantly for the outburst of musketry which should tell that the battle was renewed."[4] Sometimes Grant would pace up and down, but "most of the day he sat upon the stump of a tree, or on the ground, with his back leaning against a tree."[5] The dyspeptic provost marshal Brigadier General Marsena Patrick recalled, "I don't see that Grant does anything but Sit quietly about, whittle, Smoke, and let Genl. Rawlins talk Big—"[6]

Many of the men of the Army of the Potomac wondered about Rawlins, who seemed to be always at Grant's side. Unlike most of the top leadership, Rawlins never received formal military training. And while Grant was reserved and relatively polite to his subordinates, Rawlins was garrulous and untactful. *Because* of these differences, perhaps, the complementary partnership was a successful one for both men. The younger Rawlins, who had dark eyes and jet black hair, worked for Grant since the beginning of the war. According to an observer, who knew both men well, "[Rawlins's] friendship for his chief was of so sacredly intimate a character that he alone could break through the taciturnity into which Grant settled when he found himself in any way out of accord with the thoughts and opinions of those around him. Rawlins could argue, could expostulate, could condemn, could even upbraid, without interrupting for an hour the fraternal confidence and good will of Grant."[7] Lyman said of Rawlins, "He is a man who gives a very disagreeable first impression; loud and profane in talk, fiery and impulsive of temper, and with a general demeanor of the bad 'Western' kind. In truth he is a man of a cool, clear judgment, and well gifted with common sense; despite his temper, too, he is a good hearted man."[8] Gouverneur Warren disagreed and described Rawlins as "a personal coward in danger, but a bold liar and firm believer in the value of a lie."[9]

For Rawlins, Grant, Meade, Washburne, and all the others at headquarters May 6 was a demoralizing and exhausting day. Shortly after the repulse of Lee's troops at the crossroads, Washburne wrote in his diary, "The day will close not so disastrously to us as we apprehended."[10] Sadly, the day was not yet over. Grant's army would soon face another serious crisis. For a brief moment, it appeared that General Sedgwick's entire Sixth Corps might be destroyed.

At 6:45 P.M., C.S.A. Brigadier General John Brown Gordon led an assault against Grant's far right flank. "In less than ten minutes they struck the Union flank and with thrilling yells rushed upon it and along the Union works, shattering regiments and brigades, and throwing them into the wildest confusion and panic," Gordon said of the Georgians and North Carolinians who made the attack, "There was practically no resistance."[11] One Union soldier couldn't forget the audacious assault, "The men in front of us were so much surprised they immediately ran, leaving the pork in the pan and the coffee on the fire and their arms. Some of our boys raise up to run, but under command lay down again until the front line men ran in among us, when we joined them in the stampede."[12]

Brigadier Generals Truman Seymour and Alexander Shaler, along with several hundred soldiers, were captured by the Rebels. Gordon's attack succeeded far beyond anyone's wildest expectations. He wrote, "had not darkness intervened, the Georgia and North Carolina brigades alone would have shattered Sedgwick's entire corps, and the brigades and divisions of Ewell, which confronted those of Sedgwick on the general line, would have marched steadily across to join the Georgians and North Carolinians, instead of rushing across in the darkness, firing as they came, and inflicting more damage upon my men than upon the enemy."[13] Sedgwick's corps was saved by nightfall. In his official report, General Shaler wrote, "The most extraordinary fact was seen that an army of 100,000 men had its right flank in the air with a single line of battle without entrenchments."[14] Humphreys wondered how such a serious error could have occurred, and suspected some sort of neglect was responsible for missing the presence of Gordon nearby.

Lyman and Meade were having supper at around 7:00 P.M. when two officers rode up to tell them that the Sixth Corps was broken and that they "had better look out not to be captured." The two messengers, according to Lyman seemed to be "quite out of their heads." When Meade asked them about the location of the brigades of Colonel Emory Upton and Brigadier General Alexander Shaler, they told him they didn't know their where-abouts. Meade then asked, "Do you mean to tell me that the 6th Corps is not to do any more fighting this campaign?" Lyman sensed Grant was more disturbed by the alarming news than was Meade.[15]

The attack was the brainchild of John Brown Gordon, a thirty-two-year-old brigade commander from Georgia, serving under Ewell. A lawyer and investor before the war, Gordon had served the Army of Northern Virginia with distinction. On the morning of May 6, Gordon discovered Sedgwick's right flank was unprotected, "There was no line guarding this flank. As far as my eye could reach, the Union soldiers were seated on the margin of the rifle-pits, taking their breakfast."[16]

Gordon brought this promising intelligence to his division commander, the acerbic Major General Jubal Early, who initially shot down the idea of a flanking movement. Early wrongly believed Burnside's Ninth Corps was positioned behind Sedgwick and would be able to crush an attack by a smaller Rebel force. In fact, only Ferraro's division of African American soldiers was anywhere near Sedgwick's troops at the time. Ewell backed Early at first, but then appeared to change his mind after a brief meeting with Robert E. Lee in the early afternoon. According to Lee's account years later, he had hoped Ewell would attack sooner, perhaps at the same time as the 4:15 P.M. assault at the Plank Road. After the war, Lee said he "urged Ewell to make the flank attack, made later in the day by Gordon, several times before it was done. He [Lee] intended it to be a full attack in flank, & intended to support it with all Ewell's corps and others if necessary, and to rout the enemy . . . when Gordon did go, it was too late in the day, and he was not supported with sufficient force to accomplish anything decisive." Lee also believed that if Stonewall Jackson had been there, "he would have crushed the enemy."[17] Once again, the ghost of Stonewall loomed over the fighting in the Wilderness.

Gordon expressed bitterness his plan hadn't been adopted sooner by Ewell and Early. He believed an earlier attack "would have resulted in a decided disaster to the whole right wing of General Grant's army, if not in its entire disorganization."[18] Jubal Early, who later became one of the most influential writers on Confederate military history, disputed this belief. In his memoir, Early stated, "It was fortunate, however, that darkness came to close this affair, as the enemy, if he had been able to discover the disorder on our side, might have brought up fresh troops and availed himself of our condition."[19] There was considerable disorganization on the Union side as well. Lyman described the stampede by some of the Sixth Corps men as "disgraceful."

Shortly after the flanking movement, General Patrick rode out to assess the situation and found the Germanna Plank Road still clear. He wondered if the crisis wasn't as bad as it first appeared. Fortunately for the Union, General Sedgwick quickly reestablished his lines, and by midnight, he pulled his lines farther back for greater protection against another possible Confederate flanking maneuver. Grant nevertheless ordered General Ferrero at 9:00 P.M. to bring his division to headquarters, so it wouldn't be cut off by the Rebels. On the following morning, Grant wrote to Major General Henry Halleck, the Union Army's chief of staff in Washington, D.C.,

"Had there been daylight the enemy could have injured us very much in the confusion that prevailed; they, however, instead of getting through the break, attacked General Wright's division of Sedgwick's corps, and were beaten back."[20]

General Ferrero's African American soldiers faced significant danger, if captured. One white Union prisoner, a few days after the flank attack, remembered being greeted by his Rebel captor one morning, "Hey thar you-uns, if you want to see a . . . hang look 'round right smart." The Union prisoner looked out of the opening to the basement and "sure enough they were just pulling up one of Burnside's black heroes in full uniform!" The Northern man told the captor "that the soul of that colored patriot had gone to meet the soul of John Brown, in Heaven." The Rebel then pointed his gun at the prisoner and told him to "shut up."[21]

Grant's staff praised the Union general-in-chief for keeping his head amid the pandemonium at headquarters after Gordon's flank attack. At one point, a nervous general from the Sixth Corps told the Union commander, "General Grant, this is a crisis that cannot be looked upon too seriously. I know Lee's methods well by past experience; he will throw his whole army between us and the Rapidan and cut us off completely from our communications." An exasperated Grant responded, "Oh, I am heartily tired of hearing about what Lee is going to do. Some of you always seem to think he is suddenly going to turn a double somersault, and land in our rear and on both of our flanks at the same time. Go back to your command, and try to think what we are going to do ourselves, instead of what Lee is going to do."[22] This anecdote, told by Horace Porter several decades after the war, might have become embellished over the years, though it perfectly illustrates the tension between Grant's staff and the Army of the Potomac. The former felt the latter was too quick to panic in a crisis.

Porter, Rawlins, Comstock, Badeau, and others on Grant's staff had achieved tremendous success out west and had been skeptical of the Army of the Potomac's fighting abilities before the Overland Campaign. After two days in the Wilderness, Grant's team blamed the Army of the Potomac's culture for the lack of success. That beleaguered army, badly beaten on so many occasions by Lee's men, moved too slowly and was too quick to go on the defensive, according to the western men.

A few weeks later, Grant asked his former aide, Brigadier General James Wilson, who had been with him at Vicksburg and Chattanooga, "Wilson, what is the matter with this army?" Wilson responded, "General, there is a great deal the matter with it, but I can tell you much more easily how to cure it." After Grant asked how, Wilson said, "Send for Parker, the Indian chief, and after giving him a tomahawk, a scalping knife, and a gallon of the worst whiskey the Commissary Department can supply, send him out with orders to bring in the scalps of major generals." Grant smiled and asked, "Whose?" Wilson replied that he had Major General Warren in mind and Grant told him, "Well, I'll take care of Warren anyhow."[23] In the Wilderness, a serious tension emerged between Grant's methods and those of the senior leadership of the Army of the Potomac. This friction would soon get considerably worse.

Turning the tables, Gouverneur Warren would express his own criticism of Grant in the coming weeks. In a letter to his wife, Warren complained that "the popular idea of Genl. Grant" was "very wrong but still it governs all men more or less here." The young Fifth Corps commander believed Grant lacked moral courage, writing, "To sit unconcerned on a log away from the battle field, whittling, to be a man on horseback or smoking a cigar seems to exhaust the admiration of the country, and if this is really just, then Nero fiddling over the burning Rome was sublime . . . And then disregarding the useless slaughter of thousands of noblest soldiers, the country grows jubilant, and watches the smoke wreathes from Grant's cigar as if they saw therefrom a way to propitiate a God."[24]

With the repulse of Gordon's flank attack, the major fighting of the Battle of the Wilderness finally came to a close. In a dispatch to Halleck on May 7, Grant wrote, "At present we can claim no victory over the enemy, neither have they gained a single advantage."[25] Lyman declared "the result of the great Battle of the Wilderness was a drawn fight, but strategically it was a success, because Lee marched out to *stop our advance on Richmond*, which at this point, he did not succeed in doing." Lyman conceded the

Rebels were "more daring and sudden in their movements," and added "I fancy their discipline on essential points is more severe than our own—that is, I fancy they shoot a man when he ought to be shot, and we do not." Lyman also reported that "Grant told Meade that Joe Johnston would have retreated after two such days' punishment. He recognized the difference of the Western Rebel fighting."[26] This grudging concession to the eastern veterans would have pleased Meade and Lyman, who believed Robert E. Lee was a far better general than anyone Grant had faced out west.

General Warren's aide, Washington Roebling, viewed the battle more negatively than Lyman. "The Wilderness was Grant's first great fizzle," Roebling wrote. The young officer, who would later become famous for building the Brooklyn Bridge, blamed Grant's impulsiveness and poor tactical sense for many of the missed opportunities over the two days. In the end, Roebling believed, "the Wilderness was a useless battle, fought with great loss and no result."[27]

The carnage caused by the incessant combat was frightful. "More desperate fighting has not been witnessed on this continent than that of the 5th and 6th of May," Grant later wrote.[28] For the Union, the official casualty number would be 17,666, though the true number may have been much higher. Some regiments suffered losses of more than half their men. Private William Reeves's 76th New York Infantry, for example, lost 54% of its soldiers during the two days. For the Confederacy, who never performed an official accounting, a reasonable estimate of casualties is 11,125.

On the morning after the battle, Grant believed his losses wouldn't exceed 12,000, "of whom an unusually large proportion are but slightly wounded."[29] He was wrong on both counts. According to a member of the medical staff, the Battle of the Wilderness was "one of the most murderous of the war." In his official report, the medical director of the Army of the Potomac noted, "the relative proportion of killed was also large, being nearly one to every five wounded."[30] On May 7, Grant also incorrectly presumed "the loss of the enemy must exceed ours, but this is only a guess based upon the fact that they attacked and were repulsed so often." The ratio of Northern to Southern casualties may have been as high as two to one.

Grant's instant appraisal of the fighting is relevant, given what came next. Immediately after the Battle of the Wilderness, Grant had a far rosier view of the situation than was warranted by the facts. And he may not have fully comprehended the suffering of his soldiers either—many of them had died or were dying, invisible in the dark forest. At Shiloh, Grant was everywhere on the battlefield, and witnessed one location "so covered with dead that it would have been possible to walk across the clearing, in any direction, stepping on dead bodies, without a foot touching the ground."[31] At the Wilderness, he may not have seen as much of the slaughter. Visibility was poor and many of the corpses would have been hidden in the thickets.

At some point after 10:00 P.M. on May 6, an extremely tired Ulysses S. Grant entered his tent to get some sleep. According to Porter, he threw himself down on his cot and fell asleep right away. At one point, he was awakened by a false alarm, but then went back to sleep again. Porter's account differs significantly from that of another close colleague of Grant's. General James Wilson, who wasn't at headquarters at the time, wrote that "both Rawlins and Bowers concurred in the statement that Grant went into his tent, and throwing himself face downward on his cot, gave way to the greatest emotion, but without uttering any word of doubt or discouragement." Rawlins and Bowers, according to Wilson, "had never before seen him so deeply moved as upon that occasion, and that not till it became apparent that the enemy was not pressing his advantage did he entirely recover his perfect composure."[32]

So, who was correct? Porter or Wilson? Based on everything we know about Grant, before and during the Wilderness, it seems more likely Grant went to sleep on his cot without showing much emotion. He had calmly smoked his cigars for two days, while his army had been crippled by deadly fighting under the worst possible conditions. It seems improbable he'd have broken down in tears after an attack he knew couldn't cause too much damage in the darkness. And the victor of Pittsburg Landing may not have been easily shaken by the gruesomeness of a Civil War battlefield. No one who participated in the Battle of Shiloh ever forgot the horror. One Confederate soldier remembered seeing "a large piece of ground literally covered with dead heaped and piled upon each other. I shut my eyes upon the sickening sight . . . Through the dark I heard the sound of hogs quarreling over their carnival feast."[33] Such sights would have hardened all those who witnessed them.

Another false alarm occurred around midnight, according Sylvanus Cadwallader, a journalist at headquarters that evening. After everyone returned to their beds, Cadwallader sat in front of the fire and worried about the fate of the Republic. "We had waged two days of murderous battle and had but little to show for it," he later wrote, "Judged by comparative losses, it had been disastrous to the Union cause . . . We had scarcely gained a rod of the battlefield at the close of a two days' contest." Despite having witnessed firsthand Grant's successes out west, Cadwallader began to have doubts in the darkness about Grant. After giving it more thought, he found his faith in Grant gradually returning, somehow.

And just at that moment, he turned to his right and saw Grant himself, who was also sitting by the fire. Morris Schaff later tried to imagine what Grant might have been thinking as he gazed at the glowing embers of the campfire, "Two days of deadly encounter; every man who could bear a musket had been put in; Hancock and Warren repulsed, Sedgwick routed, and now on the defensive behind breastworks; the cavalry drawn back; the trains seeking safety beyond the Rapidan; thousands and thousands of killed and wounded,—he can almost hear the latter's cries, so hushed is the night—and the air pervaded with a lurking feeling of being face to face with disaster."[34]

Gazing out from under his hat with his blue army coat pulled up around his ears, Grant struck up a friendly conversation with the journalist. After a while, Cadwallader said they should both go back to sleep in order to get some rest for the morning. Recalling that scene, Cadwallader wrote, "He smilingly assented, spoke of the sharp work Gen. Lee had been giving us for a couple of days, and entered into his tent. It was the grandest mental sunburst of my life. I had suddenly emerged from the slough of despond, to the solid bed-rock of unwavering faith."[35]

Whitelaw Reid, another journalist who knew Grant well, believed the lieutenant general had "strong good sense" and a "tremendous unconquerable will." Grant may not have been the smartest commander, but he was "terrible in a determination that was stopped by no question of cost; stolid as to slaughter or famine or fire, so they led to his goal."[36] The Silent General, as Melville called him, was perhaps less sensitive than other generals to the trauma and suffering surrounding him on the battlefield. Despite the chaos and anxiety of the evening of May 6, Grant's overarching strategy remained unchanged. While the Army of the Potomac grappled with Lee, General Sherman would attack Lieutenant General Joseph Johnston in Georgia and Major General Benjamin Butler would move on Richmond. The combined Union armies would "hammer continuously against the armed force of the enemy and his resources, until by mere attrition if in no other way, there should be nothing left to him but an equal submission with the loyal section of the common country to the constitution and the laws of the land."[37]

The heavy casualties in the Wilderness so far didn't alter Grant's calculus, one way or another. He fully expected such a possibility. Referring to his own views of the campaign, he would later write, "whether they might have been better in conception and execution is for the people, who mourn the loss of friends fallen, and who have to pay the pecuniary cost to say. All I can say is, that what I have done has been done conscientiously, to the best of my ability, and what I conceived to be for the best interests of the whole country."[38]

Prior to the Battle of the Wilderness, Grant had struggled within his own professional wilderness for precisely ten years. In the spring of 1854, Captain Grant resigned from the army under a cloud of rumors about his heavy drinking. He then tried farming and later bill collecting in Missouri before reluctantly accepting a position as a clerk at his father's leather shop in Galena, Illinois in 1860. It was in Galena, F. Scott Fitzgerald famously wrote, that Grant was lolling in his general store, "ready to be called to an intricate destiny," when the war came in 1861.

The Fort Humboldt experience in 1854, in which he resigned his commission, must have been a humiliating one for Captain Grant. We still don't know all the details of what happened. His close friend, Rufus Ingalls, said, "Captain Grant, finding himself in dreary surroundings, without his family, and with but little to occupy his attention, fell into dissipated habits, and was found, one day, too much under the influence of liquor to properly perform his duties. For this offense Colonel Buchanan demanded that he should resign or stand trial."[39] Grant resigned. His boat left Fort Humboldt on May 7, 1854, exactly ten years before the Battle of the Wilderness. He returned to Julia and their children, Fred and Buck in Missouri. The difficulty of travel back then meant Grant had yet to meet his son, Buck, who had been born after Grant had gone to the West Coast.

Grant would never shake the perception he had an alcohol problem. Upon meeting Grant before the Wilderness Campaign, Colonel Wainwright wrote in his diary, "it is hard for those who knew him when formerly in the army to believe he is a great man; then he was only distinguished for the mediocrity of his mind, his great good nature, and his insatiable love of whiskey."[40] Around the same time, Major Henry Abbott wrote in a letter, "Uncle John [Sedgwick] said he was very favorably impressed with Grant, for when he last saw him . . . he was drunken & dirty to the last extreme. This was in the Mexican War, & afterwards he had to resign on account of delirium tremens, & used to beg a quarter of a friend, boring them to death."[41] By 1864, Grant seemed to have his drinking under control. He may have been a binge drinker, who would go on the occasional spree when he had too much time on his hands. Insiders believed John Rawlins's role included keeping Grant sober.

From 1855 to 1858, after his bitter experience on the West Coast, Grant struggled as a farmer in Missouri. He even built his own house, humorously called, "Hardscrabble." The historian Edward Gibbon once said of his own brief military service, "The discipline and evolutions of a modern battalion gave me a clearer notion of the phalanx and the legion; and the captain of the Hampshire grenadiers (the reader may smile) has not been useless to the historian of the Roman empire." Similarly, the unforgiving and unprofitable toil of the Missouri dirt farmer, responsible for managing poor laborers and dependent on the vagaries of the weather, had not been useless to the commander of the Union Army. Making a living from the land, without capital to invest in the enterprise, was a frustrating endeavor that frequently ended in failure. Just like a Civil War battle, luck and persistence were essential elements of success. Farming and leading men in battle both required long-range planning and an ability to withstand adversity. Grant's experience as a small farmer would have also allowed him to identify with his recruits, a large number of whom worked the land for a living. Private William Reeves, just one of tens of thousands of examples, was a farm laborer in Upstate New York before his enlistment. Grant may or may not have required too much of his men, but he never asked them to do something he wouldn't have done himself.

Coincidentally, Robert E. Lee also worked in agriculture before the war, managing three estates after his father-in-law died in 1857. Both Lee and Grant used slave labor in their farming efforts. In the case of Lee, he oversaw 200 or so slaves at his various properties. Grant owned at least one slave, while also hiring and overseeing additional slaves held by his father-in-law. His wife Julia owned four slaves that weren't officially freed until 1865. When Grant and Lee met in the Wilderness, one was trying to preserve the Republic, while the other was trying to destroy it. Both men had benefited from slave labor on the eve of the Civil War, however, though neither man was especially successful at farming.

After the war, Adam Badeau told the writer Henry Adams that "neither he nor the rest of the staff knew why Grant succeeded; they believed in him because of his success. For stretches of time, his mind seemed torpid. Rawlins and the others would systematically talk their ideas into it, for weeks, not directly, but by discussion among themselves, in his presence. In the end he would announce the idea as his own, without seeming conscious of the discussion; and would give the orders to carry it out with all the energy that belonged to his nature."[42] For two days in the Wilderness, Grant had been listening to his staff talk, while also following the course of the battle. By the afternoon of May 6, Grant had developed an idea of what he wanted to do next. At 6:30 A.M. on the morning of May 7, he would set his new plan in motion.

At approximately 1:00 P.M. on May 6, with Hancock still reeling from Longstreet's flank attack, Grant decided to move his entire army to Spotsylvania Court House, a small town about ten miles southeast of Wilderness Tavern. "As he lay under the trees, waiting for Burnside's advance, and revolving the news of Hancock's disaster," Adam Badeau recalled, "the idea of a movement still further to the left, thrusting his whole force between Lee and Richmond was presented to his mind."[43] Grant mentioned this idea at the time to General Rawlins and Colonels Porter and Babcock. It made no sense to continue attacking Lee in the Wilderness, Grant believed, especially if the Rebels retreated to their breastworks. By turning Lee's right, Grant would force him to come out into the open to stop his advance on Richmond.

Gordon's attack at dusk had created a panic among some of the Union officers at headquarters, but Grant had never considered retreating, even for a moment. He was up early on May 7 to begin the next stage of the campaign. After having his breakfast around the campfire, Grant wrote an order at 6:30 A.M. to General Meade that began, "Make all preparations during the day for a night march to take position at Spotsylvania C.H."[44] General Warren's Fifth Corps would lead the way going south via Brock Road with General Sedgwick heading to Spotsylvania by a more easterly route. General Hancock's Second Corps would eventually move to Todd's Tavern, thereby protecting the army's newly established right flank.

Shortly after the order was issued, General Wilson rode over to headquarters. When Grant saw him, he shouted, "It's all right, Wilson, the army is moving toward Richmond."[45] Grant wanted to reassure the cavalry officer that they were advancing. He planned on fulfilling his promise to President Lincoln that he made in a note to a journalist the previous day, "Well, if you see the President, tell him from me that, whatever happens, there will be no turning back."[46]

A tired Lincoln anxiously awaited good news from the front. A companion of the president's remembered, "During the first week of the battles of the Wilderness, he scarcely slept at all. Passing through the main hall of the domestic apartment on one of these days, I met him, clad in a long morning-wrapper, pacing back and forth a narrow passage leading to one of the windows, his hands behind him, great black rings under his eyes, his head bent forward upon his breast—altogether such a picture of the effects of sorrow, care and anxiety."[47] When Grant learned at 3:00 P.M. in the afternoon of May 7 that Major General Butler, commander of the Army of the James, had successfully landed at City Point, he issued the final order for the night march. He intended to seize the initiative from Lee.

Grant is fondly remembered in American history for his persistence in pressing the Army of Northern Virginia, despite the horrific losses during the Battle of the Wilderness. Unlike General Hooker at Chancellorsville, who had said he lost faith in Joe Hooker, Grant never lost faith in himself or the campaign.

Sadly, General Meade never received the same credit for his fortitude in the face of the enemy, and was even unfairly gossiped about as advocating a retreat after the first or second day of the fighting, depending on who was telling the tale. This rumor began during the battle, but didn't become public until a month later when the journalist Edward Crapsey wrote an article in the *Philadelphia Inquirer*, which said, "History will record, but newspapers cannot, that on one eventful night during the present campaign Grant's presence saved the army, and the nation too; not that General Meade was on the point to commit a blunder unwittingly, but his devotion to his country made him loth to risk her last army on what he deemed a chance. Grant assumed the responsibility and we are still on to Richmond."

This malicious story about Meade was false. Soon after its publication in June 1864, Meade confronted Crapsey, who said he had heard the story about Meade advocating a retreat across the Rapidan from ordinary soldiers in camp. Meade then "told him it was a base and wicked lie." As a punishment, Meade sent Crapsey beyond the lines and prevented him from returning to camp. General Patrick wrote in his diary that Crapsey "was placed on a horse, with breast & back boards Marked 'Libeler, of the Press'—& marched in rear of my flag, thro' the Army, after which he was sent to White House & thence North—He was completely cut down—It will be a warning to his Tribe." It was an understandable, though extreme and unwise, punishment by Meade. The press never forgot it, and treated Meade ungenerously for the remainder of the war. [48]

In a letter to his wife, Meade wrote that he had discovered the lie may have originated with Congressman Washburne, who possibly spread it throughout Washington, D.C., upon his return from the Wilderness. If Meade found evidence to support that charge, he vowed to "show Mr. Washburne no quarter and will make him my enemy." This rumor may have been designed to make Grant look heroic, when compared to the commander of the Army of the Potomac, an army that had retreated on so many previous occasions. To Grant's credit, he disavowed the rumor and told the authorities in Washington that "Gen. Meade on no occasion advised or considered falling back to, much less across, the Rapidan." Nonetheless, Meade's anger seemed justified. In letters to his wife, he often expressed disappointment that Grant would ultimately receive all the credit for success, while he worked in relative obscurity. [49] Meade might have also been especially sensitive to the accusation of wishing to retire in the face of the Rebels. On the eve of the Wilderness Campaign, he was still trying to defend himself against the false charge of favoring a retreat from Gettysburg at a council of war after the second day of battle. Meade was a courageous and honest commander, whose reputation seemed to wane as Grant's continued to rise. The resulting tension between the two men, which was subtle and mostly unspoken, would never be adequately resolved.

At 8:30 P.M. on May 7, Warren's Fifth Corps, led by Wadsworth's division, now commanded by General Cutler, began moving south down Brock Road. "At intervals, darkness would be made visible on the right by a blazing brand dropping from some distant tree-trunk," a Fifth Corps veteran remembered, "still aglow in the depth of the Wilderness, like a signal-light of goblins. The low, damp air, reeked with the pungent, acrid snuff of horse and human slaughter." [50] They passed the rear of Hancock's men, who remained in position to guard against a possible attack. Small fires lit up the woods, while the troops of the Second Corps leaned against the scorched parapets. Schaff recalled "here comes the head of Warren's corps with banners afloat. What calm serenity, what unquenchable spirit, are in the battle-flags! On they go. Good—by, old fields, deep woods, and lonesome roads." He was also struck by the "thousands of whippoorwills uttering their desolate notes unceasingly" in the "dismal pine woods."[51]

Generals Grant and Meade, along with their staffs, headed south on the Brock Road after dark. They planned on stopping at Hancock's headquarters at the crossroads to wait for the remainder of Warren's men. While Grant and Meade rode in the rear of Hancock's troops, Porter observed a "memorable scene." Some of the men recognized Grant and noticed he was riding south. Soon, word passed from soldier to soldier that "Grant is moving to Richmond." The tired and dirty troops gathered around the commander of the Union Army. "Wild cheers echoed through the forest," Porter wrote, "and glad shouts of triumph rent the air. Men swung their hats, tossed up their arms, and pressed forward to within touch of their chief, clapping their hands, and speaking to him with the familiarity of comrades."

With their cheers and enthusiasm, the ordinary soldiers endorsed Grant's decision to continue pressing the enemy. "The night march," Porter declared, "had become a triumphal procession for the new commander. The demonstration was the emphatic verdict pronounced by the troops upon his first battle in the East."[52] No one could possibly know it at the time, but this moment was a crucial turning point of the war. The Union soldiers had just experienced one of the most terrible battles in human history. But, undaunted, they were still headed to Richmond.

"Afterwards, in hours of disappointment, anxiety, and doubt," Adam Badeau later said, "when the country seemed distrustful and success far distant, those nearest the chief were wont to recall this midnight ride in the Wilderness."[53] As the Union Army left the dark forest that evening, Schaff perhaps best commemorated those hellish two days of fighting, "Notwithstanding this frightful record, I think I can hear the Wilderness exclaim with holy exultation, 'Deep as the horrors were, the battles that were fought in my gloom were made glorious by the principles at stake: and I cherish every drop of the gallant blood that was shed.'"[54]

◆

Private William Reeves, who had been resting at a Fifth Corps field hospital for two days, would not be joining the Union Army on its way to Spotsylvania Court House. Earlier in the day, Meade issued orders for the wounded to be taken across the Rapidan River to Rappahannock Station, where they would be transported by rail to Alexandria, Virginia. This convoy—consisting of an escort of 1,300 cavalry, 325 wagons, and 488 ambulances, along with 7,000 wounded men—didn't depart until late in the evening on May 7. Private Reeves was finally headed north again, at long last. With any luck, he'd soon be treated at a general hospital in Washington, D.C., before going home to Victor, New York.

TWELVE

"The Great Army of the Wounded"

By midday on May 7, Private William Reeves had mixed feelings about leaving his Fifth Corps field hospital. At this time, almost all of the Union wounded—between eight and nine thousand soldiers—had been carried to the army's eleven field hospitals that were scattered behind the lines. Over the course of the previous two days, Union surgeons had performed 560 amputations and 108 excisions under impossible working conditions. Uncomfortable at his overcrowded field hospital, Reeves was eager to get additional treatment at a fully equipped general hospital in the nation's capital. Not only that, but the smoke and unseasonably hot temperatures made conditions unpleasant in the woods. And the cries of the wounded were unbearable. On the other side of the ledger, the long journey to Washington, D.C., would be an arduous one. Reeves's broken cheekbones were highly sensitive to even the slightest movements. A journey by wagon over dirt roads would be extremely painful for the young private.

The hard work of loading the wagons and ambulances with the wounded began during the evening of May 7.[1] The injured soldiers were separated into three groups: those who could walk; those who could ride in wagons; and the severely wounded, who would have to be carried in ambulances. Private Reeves, who remained too weak for a long march, was probably assigned to a wagon, which would have been "bedded with straw and small evergreen boughs covered with blankets and shelter-tents."[2] Two to four men joined him in the wagon, which was equipped with "hard-bread boxes" as seats for those who were able to sit. The ambulances were loaded up with the most severely wounded and then sent off first, accompanied by those who would be marching by foot. Ultimately, slightly more than seven thousand wounded Union soldiers were part of the procession toward Washington, D.C. One thousand sufferers, sadly, who were considered too severely wounded for transport, were left behind. Some of these soldiers were eventually rescued. But many of them were captured, and some died. It was a bitter and cruel fate for these loyal men who bravely fought for their country.

Private Peter Chase, from the 2nd Vermont Infantry Regiment, remembered the shock of discovering that not all the wounded could be moved. He had been shot in the leg on May 5, and became "very anxious to undertake the journey for there was a report that those left behind would be taken prisoners." Just before dark, he learned there were only thirteen ambulances left, and that many men would be left in the woods. Chase wrote, "It was not until the 12th one drove in that my long watched for chance came. I rode all that night over a very rough road and did not get any sleep or rest."[3]

The train of over 7,000 distressed soldiers and 813 vehicles was over seven miles long as it approached Ely's Ford during the early morning hours of May 8. As the head of the procession crossed Ely's Ford, there were reports of Rebel cavalry in the vicinity. The train was ordered to turn back and head to Fredericksburg via the Fredericksburg Pike instead. A military escort was provided and the train began entering Fredericksburg at around 1:00 A.M. on May 9—the men had been on the road for over thirty hours.

All that time on the road felt like torture to Private Reeves. Given the nature of his injury, sleep was impossible during the bumpy wagon ride.

The jostling caused pain and may have reopened his wounds. If his tongue had been badly injured, it's also likely Reeves wouldn't have been able to talk with the medical staff or his comrades. Private Chase provided details of the dreadful journey, "There were hundreds who followed on foot. Many a brave soldier walked the whole distance with an amputated hand or forearm in a sling. Those having two good legs did not stay behind. The suffering which men endured in those two days will never be told."[4]

Theodore Lyman expressed anger at the Union officer whose report of Rebel activity near Ely's Ford led to the turning back of the procession of wounded. Lyman later learned the Confederate force had been a small one that could have been easily driven off. "Alas, for the poor wounded!" Lyman wrote in his diary. "The train of them was already far on its way, when Gen. Meade had to send word to halt, and subsequently to face it toward Fredericksburg. What delay & suffering! How many men whose vital force was just sufficient to have brought them safely to Washington, were killed by this protraction of their trials."[5]

Meade's initial plan had been for the wounded to be transported by train to Alexandria, Virginia, after crossing the Rapidan River. Now, the wounded would have to be treated in Fredericksburg before eventually being sent to Washington, D.C., by boat. This last-minute change of plan led to increased agony for the wounded, as Lyman correctly pointed out. The change may have also negatively affected the prognosis for some of the injured troops by delaying their admittance to general hospitals with trained surgeons and abundant medical supplies. Many of the wounded men noted the pain they experienced during the wagon ride to Fredericksburg. "The sufferings of these men cannot in any degree be realized," one observer said. "The road—an old plank-road—was in a wretched condition, and the groans and shrieks of the sufferers were truly heartrending."[6]

With the changing of the route, the city of Fredericksburg soon became one vast hospital. The evacuation of the wounded men from Fredericksburg to Washington would begin at once, with the most difficult cases going first. The suffering men would have to undergo yet another wagon ride from Fredericksburg to Belle Plain, a small landing point on the

Potomac River, before heading up to Washington, D.C., by boat. Those men awaiting evacuation in Fredericksburg were grouped around the town according to their respective corps.

Private Reeves's 76th New York Infantry Regiment experienced the second most casualties of any Union regiment during the Battle of the Wilderness with 282 total casualties. Peter Chase's 2nd Vermont Infantry had the most with a total of 348. The 2nd Vermont, which had been in the thick of the fighting at the crossroads on both days, appeared to have had more men killed than the 76th New York—forty-nine compared to twenty-seven, but that latter figure is incomplete. The 76th New York, which had three whole companies taken captive, listed 186 men as captured or missing compared with just 14 for the 2nd Vermont. Many of these captured men were sent to Andersonville Prison and eventually died. It's safe to say that the 76th New York had far more deaths as a result of the Battle of the Wilderness than any other Union regiment. The 76th also sustained more casualties at the Wilderness than it did at the Battle of Gettysburg—282 to 234. With 498 soldiers available for combat on May 4, the 76th New York experienced a casualty rate of 57% at the Wilderness. The likelihood of being killed or wounded for an ordinary soldier like Reeves had been shockingly high.

The casualty rate for Grant's army as a whole during the battle wasn't anywhere near as grim. Of the 101,895 soldiers who engaged, 17,666 became casualties, for a rate of 17%. Of all the divisions, Getty's was the hardest hit with 2,994 total casualties. Of Getty's casualties, Colonel Lewis Grant's Vermont brigade accounted for 1,269 of the total. Birney's division suffered 2,242 casualties and Wadsworth's division had 2,008 men killed, wounded, or missing. Getty's, Birney's, and Wadsworth's divisions accounted for 41% of all Union casualties during the battle. Getty, severely wounded on the morning of May 6, was widely praised for his heroic leadership at the Wilderness. No one doubted Wadsworth's personal bravery, though the performance of his troops was open to debate.[7]

Private Reeves remained in Fredericksburg from the early morning of May 9 until May 11, when he was finally admitted to Stanton U.S. Army General Hospital in Washington, D.C. While in Fredericksburg, he was treated at the Washington Woolen Mill that had been converted into a hospital for the Fifth Corps. While there, he obtained much needed rest, though there might not yet have been enough food for all the men. Reeves couldn't eat solid foods at this time. An assistant surgeon cleaned his wounds, and a nurse applied fresh bandages. His medical report does not indicate that he received any surgical procedures at the hospital in Fredericksburg.

Overall, the quality of the medical care seems to have been mixed. Civilian surgeons answered the call and assisted in the treating of the wounded. But some of the doctors and nurses lacked knowledge and experience and perhaps became overwhelmed by the amount of work that needed to be done. The nursing pioneer Clara Barton, after witnessing these conditions, wrote, "The surgeons do all they can but no provision had been made for such a wholesale slaughter on the part of anyone, and I believe it would be impossible to comprehend the magnitude of the necessity without witnessing it."[8] Of his initial treatment in Fredericksburg Peter Chase recalled, "On the morning of the 10th a surgeon with two helpers came into the room to dress the wounds. The worst treatment I received in all my army service was from that man that called himself an army surgeon. He seemed to be void of all feeling for humanity and seemed to delight in torturing wounded men as much as a savage."[9] At the time, the doctors were trying to decide whether to amputate Chase's leg. He spent the night of May 11 in tremendous pain, while struggling for his life. In the end, the doctors decided not to amputate his leg, thinking he "might pull through with good care." Chase later wrote, "I took the one chance that youth afforded me and now 59 years after I tell my own story."[10]

The trip to Belle Plain and then on to Washington wasn't an easy one. In a letter to his mother, Walt Whitman, who worked in the Washington hospitals during this time, wrote, "The journey from the field till they get aboard the boats at Belle Plain is horrible."[11] Clara Barton agreed, writing in her diary, "The poor, mutilated starving sufferers of the Wilderness were pouring into Fredericksburg by thousands—all to be taken away in army wagons across ten miles of alternate hills, and hollows, stumps, roots and mud!"[12]

Belle Plain, the closest spot on the Potomac River to the Wilderness, was thirteen hard miles away from Fredericksburg. Confederate raiders monitored the road and the Union wounded, along with their military escorts, faced the possibility of being captured during the relatively short journey. The boat ride from Belle Plain to Washington took about eight hours or so. Each boat was overcrowded with several hundred injured soldiers on deck. Upon arrival in D.C., the men disembarked from the steamers at one of the capital's bustling wharves. After the arrival of 3,000 severely wounded men at the Sixth Street wharf, the journalist Noah Brooks described the tragic scene, "The long, ghastly procession of shattered wrecks; the groups of tearful, sympathetic spectators; the rigid shapes of those who are bulletined as 'since dead;' the smoothly flowing river and the solemn hush in foreground and on distant evening shores—all form a picture which must some day perpetuate for the nation the saddest sight of the war."[13]

Gouverneur Warren's aide, Washington Roebling, traveled aboard the steamer *Daniel Webster* along with 400 wounded men from the Battle of the Wilderness. "We carried every man on board ourselves," he remembered, "and it was the hardest work that I have done for many years." The wounded soldiers, according to Roebling, were in rough shape. Many hadn't eaten for four days and some hadn't had their wounds dressed since they had first been treated in the field hospitals. Roebling recalled, "We managed to make a few bucketsful of gruel and gave our own crackers in to pass around the wounded. They devoured it like wolves and seemed to be contented after that to lie in the filth and waste straw that we have them lying on. The stench of their wounds is horrible, and the whole thing disgusting in the extreme."[14]

Private William Reeves arrived in Washington on May 11—the same day as Roebling and possibly via the same boat. Upon arriving in the nation's capital, members of the Sanitary Commission offered him, "hot coffee, milk-punch, lemonade, crackers." At this time, someone from the Sanitary Commission wrote down some personal details about Private Reeves on a piece of paper and placed it in his pocket. The private was then transported to Stanton General Hospital, a complex containing 420 beds, where he was admitted. Stanton, one of the newly constructed hospitals after the early battles of the war, was just north of the Capitol and east of the White House. In operation from December 1862 to October 1865, Stanton provided high quality care for thousands of soldiers. The chief surgeon there, Dr. John Lidell, was an expert on gunshot wounds, who wrote widely on that topic.

As wounded soldiers from the Battle of the Wilderness began arriving in Washington, a newspaper reporter described Douglas Hospital, a facility adjacent to Stanton Hospital, "The walls are hung with pictures and biblical placards. Harpers Weekly is being hawked around in muffled voice, by a newsboy. Soldiers more or less convalescent are grouped together at the open door." Not surprisingly, the injured men were idealized for sympathetic and patriotic readers. They were portrayed as "the purest defenders of the purest system of government which has existed from the creation of the world; they are the expositors of that noble destiny which as Unionists we feel awaits us in the shrouded hereafter." A brief description of one of the wounded men at the hospital was perhaps representative of all of them, including Private Reeves. The young man "is sitting with his hands clasped upon his knees, looking silently through the glowing atmosphere which bathes the young green leaves, and longing, it is likely, for his friends and home."[15]

The poet Walt Whitman was a frequent visitor to the Washington general hospitals at the time that Reeves was admitted to Stanton. In a letter to his mother, Whitman mentions that the first group of wounded soldiers arrived from the Wilderness on May 9, 1864. "I have seen 300 wounded," he wrote, "These 300 men were not badly wounded, mostly in arms, hands, trunk of body, etc. They could all walk, though some had an awful time of it."[16] Later, Whitman's assessment of the aftermath of the Battle of the Wilderness became bleaker, "The arrivals, the numbers, and the severity of the wounds outviewed anything that we have seen before. For days and weeks a melancholy tide set in upon us. The weather was very hot. The wounded had been delayed in coming and much neglected. Very many of the wounds had worms in them. An unusual proportion mortified."[17]

Whitman also noticed that some of the young men had become "crazy"—he told his mother, "Every ward has some in it that are wandering. They have suffered too much, and it is perhaps a privilege that they are out of their senses."[18]

Walt Whitman first went to Washington in December 1862, after the Battle of Fredericksburg. He'd heard distressing news about his brother, so he came down to D.C. from Brooklyn, New York, to learn more. After heading to the site of the battle, Whitman discovered his brother escaped the carnage with a minor wound. Accompanying some wounded soldiers from Fredericksburg to Washington, Whitman decided to remain and help at the capital's general hospitals. For the remainder of the war, Whitman estimated he made over 600 hospital visits and went "among from eighty thousand to one hundred thousand of the wounded and sick, as sustainer of spirit and body in some degree in time of need."[19] Years later, he'd write, "Those three years I consider the greatest privilege and satisfaction (with all their feverish excitements and physical deprivations and lamentable sights) and, of course, the most profound lesson of my life."[20]

His hospital visits might last for a couple of hours or for an entire day and night. "Sometimes I took up my quarters in the hospital," he recalled, "and slept or watched there for several nights in succession." It was impossibly difficult and taxing work. In one of his many letters to his mother, he wrote, "I see such awful things. I expect one of these days, if I live, I shall have awful thoughts and dreams—but it is such a great thing to be able to do some real good." Toward the end of the summer of 1864, Whitman had to take a break from his hospital visits because they were beginning to take a toll on his own health.

Written after the war, Whitman's poem, "The Wound Dresser," described his haunting work with the wounded,

> From the stump of the arm, the amputated hand,
> I undo the clotted lint, remove the slough, wash off the matter
> and blood,

Back on his pillow the soldier bends with curv'd neck and side
falling head,
His eyes are closed, his face is pale, he dares not look on the
bloody stump,
And has not yet look'd on it.
I dress a wound in the side, deep, deep,
But a day or two more, for see the frame all wasted and sinking,
And the yellow-blue countenance see.
I dress the perforated shoulder, the foot with the bullet-wound,
Cleanse the one with a gnawing and putrid gangrene, so sick-
ening, so offensive,
While the attendant stands behind aside me holding the tray
and pail.
I am faithful, I do not give out,
The fractur'd thigh, the knee, the wound in the abdomen,
These and more I dress with impassive hand, (yet deep in my
breast a fire, a burning flame.)

In the final stanza, Whitman laments the suffering of young boys like
Private Reeves,

Thus in silence in dreams' projections,
Returning, resuming, I thread my way through the hospitals,
The hurt and wounded I pacify with soothing hand,
I sit by the restless all the dark night, some are so young,
Some suffer so much, I recall the experience sweet and sad.

The stoicism and bravery of these men who had experienced the horror
of combat and the pain of fearful wounds inspired Whitman. In a letter
to Ralph Waldo Emerson, Whitman wrote, "I find the best expression of
American character I have ever seen or conceived—practically here in these
ranks of sick and dying young men . . . I find the masses fully justified by
closest contact, never vulgar, ever calm, without greediness, no flummery,

no frivolity—responding electric and without fail to affection, yet no whining—not the first unmanly whimper have I yet seen or heard."[21]

On May 12, just one day after having been admitted to Stanton Hospital, Private Reeves experienced severe complications. A profuse secondary hemorrhage occurred from his lingual and inferior dental arteries causing him to lose twenty-four ounces of blood. This was major bleeding, which accounted for roughly 14% of all his blood. Dr. John Lidell, the chief surgeon at Stanton, wrote that a "secondary hemorrhage not unfrequently occurs in consequence of the imperfect closure of the breaches in wounded arteries. At first the bleeding is arrested spontaneously, but afterwards the adhesive process fails to close the traumatic orifice completely and permanently."[22] It's also possible that the failure to remove all the bone splinters from the wound in Reeves's face may have led to the severing of the artery that resulted in the secondary hemorrhage. Regardless of the origin of the hemorrhage, the young private was in mortal danger.

Arterial ligation surgery was immediately performed by Assistant Surgeon George Mursick of the U.S. Volunteers. This is a delicate procedure that required threads being used to stop the blood flow by closing the artery. In this case, his left common carotid artery was tied. According to Reeves's medical records, no anesthetic was administered during this surgery underscoring the emergency nature of the procedure. Ordinarily, chloroform would've been applied to alleviate the pain. Without it, Reeves would have been in agony during the surgery.

It proved to be more than he could bear. Reeves suffered "a good deal of shock, and he did not rally afterwards." He had lost too much blood, and died of exhaustion at 4:00 A.M. on Friday, May 13, 1864, eight days after he had been shot in the Wilderness.[23] He was nineteen years old, and left behind his wife, Anna, who was only eighteen years old. A surgeon from Stanton Hospital later reported that information on Reeves's regiment, company, and wounding in the Wilderness "appeared from a Document of a member of the Sanitary Commission found on his person."[24]

On the day that Private Reeves died, his wife and family back in Victor, New York, didn't even know that he was in the hospital. The name of William Reeves wouldn't appear on a list of wounded soldiers until May 14, when it was published in the *Daily Morning Chronicle*, a Washington, D.C., newspaper. His name appeared on another casualty list in the *New York Times* on May 15. It may have been several days before his loved ones received the news of his passing.

Reeves likely faced his death with the same courage that he faced the enemy in the woods south of the Orange Turnpike. Walt Whitman wrote of the wounded soldiers he treated, "Of the many I have seen die, or known of, the past year, I have not seen or heard of one who met death with any terror." [25]

In perhaps Whitman's greatest war poem, "When Lilacs Last in the Dooryard Bloom'd," a young man's noble bravery was surpassed only by the suffering of his fellow soldiers, friends, and family left behind.

> I saw battle-corpses, myriads of them.
> And the white skeletons of young men, I saw them,
> I saw the debris and debris of all the slain soldiers of the war,
> But I saw they were not as was thought,
> They themselves were fully at rest, they suffer'd not,
> The living remain'd and suffer'd, the mother suffer'd,
> And the wife and the child and the musing comrade suffer'd,
> And the armies that remain'd suffer'd.

THIRTEEN

The Bloody Angle

The soldiers of the 76th New York had little time to mourn their fallen comrades in the immediate aftermath of the Battle of the Wilderness. The regiment, alongside Grant's entire army, faced ceaseless and deadly combat as it moved south toward Spotsylvania Court House. Both Federals and Rebels relied more and more on digging entrenchments to protect themselves, during this period. Eventually, being ordered to assault a well-fortified position began to feel like receiving a death sentence.

As they unsuccessfully tried to occupy Spotsylvania Court House, the exhausted New Yorkers of the 76th fought engagements on May 8, 10, and 12, losing another fifty-two men in addition to the 282 they had already lost in the Wilderness. After the murderous fighting on May 12, only 150 or so troops remained in the 76th, which had lost two thirds of its manpower in just a week. The 76th played a prominent role in Grant's campaign from May 5 until May 12. It had kicked off the fighting in the woods near the Turnpike during the early afternoon of May 5. Later that afternoon it followed General Wadsworth to the Plank Road, where it fought all day on May 6. The regiment then led the way during the night march of May 7 and fought the heavily entrenched enemy at Laurel Hill on May 8 and 10. On May 12, it battled the Rebels in two different locations during one of the most horrific days of combat in American military history.

The 76th New York was attached to the brigade of General James Rice, a courageous officer whose entire force experienced horrific casualties during the opening days of the campaign. On the afternoon of May 10, Rice heroically led his brigade in an unsuccessful assault of the Rebel works at Laurel Hill, a short distance northwest of Spotsylvania Court House. A minié ball ripped through one of Rice's thighbones resulting in the amputation of that leg. Rice lost too much blood, however, and died two hours after the surgery. Private Reeves lay resting in a Fredericksburg hospital at the time his brigade commander died.

One soldier remembered Rice, a splendid looking officer riding a beautiful charger, heading toward the front during his final assault. A few minutes later, the witness saw "four men running with a man in a blanket, while behind them trotted the black horse belonging to General Rice . . . The spectacle of that riderless horse told plainer than words the fate of his owner." Rice was only thirty-four years old and left behind his beloved wife, Josephine. Right before dying, Rice asked his faithful drummer boys, who were present, "Turn me over, boys—let me die with my face to the enemy."[1] These defiant final words would later become the basis of a popular patriotic song called, "Let me die with my face to the foe." The song began,

> Let me die with my face to the foe, boys,
> On the field by the brave made gory,
> Tis sweet thus to die and to know, boys,
> That the Old Flag waves in glory . . .

In his final moments, Rice yelled to General Meade, "Don't give up this fight! I am willing to lose my life, if it is to be, but don't you give up this fight!" One of his soldiers wrote of Rice, "He had been a faithful officer since the opening of the struggle, brave to rashness, generous to a fault, kind and even fatherly to his men."[2] James Clay Rice, a passionate antislavery man, never wavered in his commitment to the Union cause. Before crossing the Rapidan, he told his brother, "I enter upon this campaign cheerful and happy, for I love my country more than my life, and my entire hope whether living or dying, is in Christ, my Savior and Redeemer. Again, good-bye, my dear brother; and if we meet not again on this earth, may we meet in Heaven."[3] Meade said of the loss of Rice, a devoted Christian: "Would that all had done it as faithfully, and were as well prepared."[4]

In our more secular age, it may be difficult to appreciate the passion and sincerity of Rice's faith in Christ. He believed that God was an active agent in this world and that He had taken the emancipation of the slaves upon Himself. In a speech before a women's organization in Albany, New York, Rice declared, "I believe that it is God's divine purpose, having used the wrath of the South to commence this war, to cause that wrath to praise Him by the freedom of every slave."[5]

Rice's unwavering belief in God also allowed him to be calm in the face of danger. Before the Battle of the Wilderness, he wrote his mother, "I trust that God may again graciously spare my life, as he has in the past; and yet we cannot fall too early, if, loving Christ, one dies for his country."[6] Similarly, he told a minister, "This is God's war; everything that is holy and good on earth is at stake in it; we are fighting for law, for free government, for the liberty and equality of all men; we are fighting to maintain all that ever or can keep this Nation pure and happy and prosperous; not only our laws and our liberties, and those of our children, but even the religion of Christ would be corrupted if the enemies of the Union could triumph." Rice viewed himself as a "virtuous soldier of God."[7]

No doubt it was Rice's faith in God that allowed him to take big risks on the battlefield. Lyman described him as "very daring" and many of his men felt he was exceedingly brave and always willing to be in the middle of the fighting. The nature of the combat during the opening of Grant's spring campaign made it only a matter of time, however, before a courageous brigade commander like Rice would be struck down. Casualty rates among those officers who led at the front of their troops were especially high during the Battles of the Wilderness and Spotsylvania. After several weeks of the campaign, Washington Roebling wrote, "I tell you we are becoming very callous as regards human life; about the only remarks made were, 'I wonder whose turn it will be to go to the devil next.'"[8]

❖

Gouverneur Warren, who oversaw the movements the 76th New York Infantry along with the rest of the Fifth Corps, continued to struggle to conform to Grant's aggressive fighting style that often involved attacking heavily fortified Confederate works. The rift between Warren and his superiors—Grant and Meade—only widened as the Battle of Spotsylvania Court House unfolded. On May 8, 10, and 12, Warren launched unsuccessful assaults at impregnable Rebel positions at Laurel Hill. The heavy casualties stood in inverse proportion to the negligible results.

After the Battle of the Wilderness, Grant attempted to arrive at Spotsylvania Court House before Lee. Warren's Fifth Corps led the way, but was unfortunately delayed by the presence of Sheridan's cavalry on the Brock Road after midnight on May 8. Commenting on the slow progress of the corps, Colonel Wainwright wrote, "I certainly thought then that both Warren and Meade were not pushing matters as much as they ought."[9] From his perspective, Warren believed he didn't have the power to issue orders to Sheridan's troopers. "In the movement from the Wilderness to Spotsylvania on the night of May 7, 1864," Warren recalled in a letter in 1870, "I was delayed seven hours by our own mounted force, not under my command. Who can tell the different results that might have followed a proper use of this arm of the service in our war?"[10]

Warren engaged the enemy shortly after dawn on May 8. At first, he believed he was only facing cavalry units, but soon discovered that Long-street's First Corps, now commanded by Major General Richard Anderson, had arrived earlier than expected. Warren's men failed to clear the road of the Rebels. They were exhausted by two days of hard fighting in the

Wilderness followed by a night march on May 7. Roebling said the men were "very much hurried and excited . . . the tendency to stampede was so great that Gen. Warren himself had to go to the front of the leading brigade."[11] At 12:30 P.M., Warren wrote Meade, "I have again suffered heavily, especially stragglers . . . I have done my best, but with the force I now have I cannot attack again." Later, he added, "I cannot gain Spotsylvania Court House with what force I have."[12]

By all accounts, Warren did not perform well on May 8, though his men noted his personal bravery on the field.[13] Perhaps the best explanation is that both Warren and his men were too exhausted for the demanding task at hand. In addition, they initially believed they only faced a relatively smaller force of cavalry, instead of an entrenched infantry corps. The most damning criticism of Warren, however, is that he fed his men into the battle as they arrived instead of waiting to concentrate all his forces. When the fighting was finally over on May 8, Warren wrote Meade at 9:00 P.M., "I am so sleepy I can hardly write intelligently."[14]

On May 10, Warren, who may have been overeager to please Grant, convinced Meade that he should attack the Rebel works at Laurel Hill before another coordinated effort that had been planned for later that day. This assault, unfortunately, was "repulsed with heavy loss; the enemy were well-entrenched with plenty of Artillery in position, enfilading both Cutler's and Crawford's line."[15] It was this attack that resulted in the death of Rice. Commenting on Warren, Wainwright wrote, "The little general looked gallant enough at any rate mounted on a great tall white horse, in full uniform, sash and all, and with the flag in his hand."[16]

Over twenty years later, Ulysses S. Grant criticized Warren's performance during the Battle of Spotsylvania Court House. Regarding the assaults on May 8, Grant wrote, "Warren led the last assault, one division at a time, and of course it failed." Grant believed Warren was capable of giving intelligent instructions to his division commanders, but would then "go in with one division, holding the others in reserve until he could superintend their movements in person also, forgetting that division commanders could execute an order without his presence."[17]

Poor General Warren. On May 5 at the Wilderness, Grant grew impatient as Warren tried to align all his divisions and connect with the Sixth Corps in order to crush Ewell on the Turnpike. The Union commander-in-chief had urged Warren *at that time* to attack right away "without giving time for disposition." On May 8, Warren, recognizing the urgency of getting to Spotsylvania Court House first, ordered his troops forward as they arrived without waiting for all of them to be in place at the same time. It appears Grant was a demanding boss for the young corps commander. Ultimately, Grant believed Warren "was an officer of superior ability, quick perceptions, and personal courage to accomplish anything that could be done with a small command."[18] For his part, Warren believed Grant was too willing to send thousands of noble soldiers to their death in fruitless assaults of fortified positions.

The bloodiest fighting of the Battle of Spotsylvania Court House took place on May 12. While much of Grant's army was engaged in a desperate struggle at what would be remembered as the Bloody Angle, Warren was ordered to launch yet another assault at Laurel Hill to prevent Lee from moving troops from that area to the angle where the fighting was most intense. Presciently, Warren knew the Rebel works at Laurel Hill were too strong and that another assault would only result in the unnecessary slaughter of his troops. Nevertheless, he ordered his men forward during the early morning of May 12, but the initial assault was easily repulsed. Warren then called off the attack. Meade's chief of staff, Andrew Humphreys, wrote to Warren at 9:15 A.M., "The order of the major-general commanding is peremptory that you attack at once at all hazards with your whole force if necessary."[19]

Both Meade and Grant were losing their patience with Warren. They believed he was jeopardizing their chance at winning a stunning victory that day. Humphreys, who was also Warren's friend, sent him another note at 9:30 A.M., "Don't hesitate to attack with the bayonet. Meade has assumed responsibility, and will take the consequences."[20] Resigned, Warren told his division commanders to attack again at once. "Do it. Don't mind consequences," he wrote.[21] Just as predicted, the assault failed, resulting in even more casualties. Humphreys, who had been sent by Meade to oversee Warren, witnessed the failed attack. He agreed with Warren that future assaults would be suicidal, and canceled them.

An angry and irritable Meade blamed Warren for the lack of success at Laurel Hill, writing to Grant, "Warren seems reluctant to assault." An equally exasperated Grant replied to Meade, "If Warren fails to attack promptly, send Humphreys to command his corps, and relieve him."[22] Eventually, Meade came to the realization that nothing more could be done on Warren's front, and he decided to move two of Warren's divisions to the center of the line. Warren's job would be safe for the time being.

Of his threat to relieve Warren of his command, Grant told Porter on May 12, "I feel sorry to be obliged to send such an order in regard to Warren. He is an officer for whom I had conceived very high regard. His quickness of perception, personal gallantry, and soldierly bearing pleased me, and a few days ago I should have been inclined to place him in command of the Army of the Potomac in case Meade had been killed; but I began to feel, after his want of vigor in assaulting on the 8th, that he was not as efficient as I believed, and his delay in attacking and the feeble character of his assaults today confirm me in my apprehensions."[23]

A month later outside Petersburg, Virginia, in late June 1864, Meade also proposed relieving Warren of his command in a letter to Rawlins. Among the various criticisms of Warren was his behavior on May 12 outside Spotsylvania Court House. Meade argued that Warren had no right to delay acting on a direct order without offering reasons why, though he also added, "Such is my opinion of Genl Warren's judgment that in nine cases out of ten, I would have yielded my judgment." Meade concluded his missive by saying, "If he could be assigned to some independent and separate command he would do very well, for he is full of resources, of great coolness and firmness—It is only the difficulty he labors under of yielding his judgment to that of his superior officer, which impairs his efficiency."[24] Despite Meade's letter, Warren retained his command of Fifth Corps at that time as well. His standing with Grant and Meade, however, had been forever altered by the opening days of the Wilderness Campaign.

◆

At 4:30 A.M. on May 12, Grant launched his main assault against the center of Lee's line. The deployment of Lee's forces at this location jutted outwards, resembling a "mule shoe," a feature also referred to as the "salient." The fighting there on May 12 would last almost continuously for nearly twenty-four hours. At the western angle of Lee's fortifications—forever remembered as the "Bloody Angle"—the fighting was especially murderous. On the morning after the slaughter at the Bloody Angle, a reporter for the *New York Times* wrote, "The scene of the conflict, from which I have just come, presents a spectacle of horror that curdles the blood of the boldest. The angle of the works at which Hancock entered, and for the possession of which the savage fight of the day was made, is a perfect Golgotha. In this angle of death the dead and wounded rebels lie, this morning, literally in piles—men in the agonies of death groaning beneath the dead bodies of comrades." The reporter concluded, "The one exclamation of every man who looks on the spectacle is, 'God forbid that I should ever gaze upon such a sight again.'"[25]

Many of the soldiers on both sides reported that the fighting at the Bloody Angle was the most horrific of the entire war. Visiting the angle on the day after the battle, Colonel Lewis Grant of the Vermont Brigade observed, "The sight was terrible and sickening, much worse than at Bloody Lane, Antietam. There a great many dead men were lying in the road and across the rails of the torn down fences, and out in the cornfield, but they were not piled up several deep and their flesh was not so torn and mangled as at the 'angle.'"[26]

At times, the fighting had descended into hand-to-hand combat. Christian boys from small hamlets and big cities from all across America bashed each other's brains out with their rifle butts. Sometimes, they stabbed one another with bayonets at close quarters. "The storm of war burst upon us," one Union soldier remarked. "It seemed as though instead of being human we were turned into fiends and brutes, seeking to kill all in our way."[27] A South Carolinian wrote, "On the 12th we fought behind breastworks, &

nearly every man that was killed or wounded on our side was shot through the head. . . . I fought almost ankle deep in the blood & brains of our killed & wounded . . . Sergt Force of our Co was killed just by me & his blood & Brains poured out on my right leg & Shoe. Such, is war *in reality*."[28]

After eight days of almost continuous fighting at the Wilderness and Spotsylvania Court House, the violence reached a crescendo at the Bloody Angle on May 12. As a Maine recruit eloquently put it, "All around that salient was a seething, bubbling, roaring hell of hate and murder. In that baleful glare men didn't look like men. Some had lost or thrown away hats and coats. Some were gashed and cut, and looked like tigers hunted to cover. Darkness alone brought an end to the carnage."[29] In a letter home, a Confederate private wrote, "I know it to be the hottest and the hardest fought battle that has ever been on this continent."[30]

Brigadier General Francis Barlow, a Harvard graduate who had risen from private to divisional commander, called the Union attack on the salient "undoubtedly the most brilliant thing of its kind during the war." Roughly 19,000 men from Hancock's command had assembled during the wee hours of May 12 in the rain and the fog for an assault on the Rebel works at the salient. Barlow, who was nicknamed the "boy general" due to his youthful appearance, recalled that he had no idea as to the position or strength of the enemy when he led his forces across the muddy field at 4:30 A.M. Before marching, Barlow said to a staff officer, "For Heaven's sake, at least, face us in the right direction, so that we shall not march away from the enemy, and have to go round the world and come up in their rear."[31]

The Federals, utilizing tactics developed by Colonel Upton only two days previously, didn't stop to fire their rifles as they approached the Rebel works. Initially, the attack caught the Rebels by surprise, and Hancock's men captured roughly 3,000 prisoners, along with two senior Confederate officers, Major General Edward Johnson and Brigadier General George Steuart. At long last, the Union had achieved a break in Lee's line. When Rawlins heard the news at headquarters, he shouted, "By God! They are done!—Hancock will just drive them to Hell!"[32]

Barlow, who referred to the breakthrough as a "lucky accident," later recalled, "It was an accident that we struck this angle, always a weak point in a line; an accident that the morning was misty to an unusual degree; an accident that we found a space for our rush so free from obstacles; an accident that we escaped the observation of the enemy's outposts and pickets that we were upon them before they could make any substantial resistances."[33] Unfortunately, Grant would be unable to exploit this initial breakthrough.

Lee rallied his forces and was eventually able to bring back and straighten out his line during the early hours of May 13. During the moment of crisis on the morning of May 12, Lee became involved in another "Lee to the Rear" incident. While Lee tried to lead his men into battle, he was stopped by General Gordon who said, "These men have never failed! They never will! Will you, boys?" From the troops came shouts of: "No! no!" "Gen. Lee to the rear." "Go back. Go back." "General Lee to the rear!"[34] Describing Lee at that moment, a Richmond reporter wrote, "As he sat on his charger I never saw a man look so noble, or a spectacle so impressive."[35]

Assessing the struggle at the salient, Barlow wrote, "Except for the first assault, the operations for the day were a failure. At its close we had made no substantial advance beyond the ground won by the first attack. A great opportunity had been lost. The reason of this, in my opinion, was that no one had foreseen the magnitude of the success which was coming, and hence no one was prepared for it."[36] The initial breakthrough led to too many Union men rushing into the first line of works. The subsequent confusion allowed the Rebels to regroup and launch counterattacks. At one point amid the chaos, Barlow yelled to Hancock, "For God's sake, Hancock, do not send any more troops in here." Barlow later confessed he had been so agitated he forgot to call him *General* Hancock.[37]

In retrospect, the fighting on May 12 was a bloody stalemate and the Union's meager gains seemed unworthy of the heavy sacrifice. Perhaps unsurprisingly, the Union high command chose to view the results in a somewhat flattering light. In his diary, Lyman wrote of the angle, "The result was damaging to the enemy—very—but the army of Lee was not cut in two, an issue clearly looked for by Rawlins and some others of Grant's staff, but not so confidently assumed by those who knew a little more."[38] Grant seemed upbeat when he wrote Halleck at 6:30 P.M. on May 12, "The eighth day of the battle closes, leaving between three and four thousand prisoners in our hands for the day's work, including two general officers, and over thirty pieces of artillery. The enemy are obstinate, and seem to have found their last ditch."[39] On the morning of May 13, Meade decided to send a congratulatory message to the troops,

> For eight days and nights, almost without intermission, in rain and sunshine, you have been gallantly fighting a desperate foe, in positions naturally strong and rendered doubly so by intrenchments; you have compelled him to abandon his fortifications on the Rapidan to retire and attempt to stop your onward progress and now he has abandoned the last intrenched position, so tenaciously held, suffering in all a loss of 18 guns, 22 colors, and 8,000 prisoners [Meade is referring to prisoners captured since the beginning of the campaign], including 2 general officers.[40]

Even though the Army of the Potomac had lost roughly one third of its manpower during the opening eight days of the campaign, Meade concluded his message on an optimistic note, "Let us determine then to continue vigorously the work so well begun, and, under God's blessing, in a short time the object of our labors will be accomplished."

The brutal fighting at the angle was exceedingly terrible even to hardened Civil War veterans. "No language can describe the hand to hand fight," wrote a Union officer, "The drenching, chilling rain that fell during the day had no effect on the incessant fire . . . Men fired into each other's faces, were shot through the crevices of logs, bayoneted over the top of the works . . . The dead and dying were in piles on both sides of the works, and several times during the day the dead had to be tossed out of the trenches that the living might have the chance to stand."[41] Another participant said, "I think it is no exaggeration to say the dead lay as thick as pumpkins in a cornfield in autumn."[42] A Union colonel succinctly summarized May 12, "History will record the fight as the longest, the most obstinate, fierce and bloody single engagement of the whole war."[43]

Almost every soldier recalled the impact of the constant gunfire on nearby trees. In his diary, Lyman noted, "For 14 hours the troops were at close quarters, and the amount of bullets fired may be known from the fact, that a red oak, 23 inches in diameter was reduced about 6 feet from the ground, to a fibrous structure and blew down that night!"[44] One soldier described how it happened, "The leaden storm searching ceaselessly in the darkness completed an astounding process at about midnight: it chipped through, one tiny nip at a time, a towering, 22-inch-thick oak tree."[45] When Robert E. Lee was told of the oak stump, he didn't believe it until he saw it with his own eyes.

The destruction of the large oak tree, along with the gruesome combat in the mud and rain, seemed to foreshadow the slaughter on the Western Front in France and Belgium, fifty years later. During the Battle of Verdun in 1916, an American aviator, who flew over the battlefield, remembered looking down at "red-roofed Verdun" that had "spots in it where no red shows and you know what happened there." The pilot added "there is only that sinister brown belt, a strip of murdered nature. It seems to belong to another world. Every sign of humanity has been swept away. The woods and roads have vanished like chalk wiped from a blackboard; of the villages nothing remains but grey smears."[46]

What seemed remarkable in the Virginia woods in 1864 would become commonplace in France from 1914 to 1918. The fighting on May 12 may have marked a turning point in the history of warfare. A private from Pennsylvania found himself incapable of describing the horror in his diary, "I have seen so much that I can't nor will put it in this book. I will seal this in my memory by myself. God, have mercy on those who started this cruel war."[47] A frustrated officer from North Carolina wrote in a letter home, "I am heartily sick of blood & the sound of artillery & small arms & the ghastly, pale face of death and all the horrible sights and sounds of war."[48]

The casualties on May 12 were similar to each of the days at the Battle of the Wilderness. The Union lost about 9,000 men compared with 8,000 or so for the Confederates. Barlow's division of the Second Corps was the hardest hit, losing 1,430 soldiers. The grim tally for Union casualties during the first eight days of the campaign came to over 30,000, making it the costliest stretch of the entire war. Later that summer, Gouverneur Warren expressed concern about this bloody arithmetic, "If there was no limit to the number of men we could continually waste in battle I might be more hopeful. But we have been so senselessly ordered to assault intrenchments that the enemy suffer little in comparison with us and may outlast us."[49] Immediately after the fighting at the angle, Warren's aide, Washington Roebling, wrote his wife (and Warren's sister), "Our corps has only 12,000 left out of 27,000. Uncle Robert Lee isn't licked yet by a long shot, and if we are not mighty careful he will beat us. I think we have done very well to avoid that fate so far. Our fighting is very severe and everyone is played out, including your humble admirer. G. K. [Warren] has a heavy disgust on."[50]

Lieutenant Uberto Burnham of the 76th New York, in a letter to his parents after the Bloody Angle, summarized the first eight days of the campaign for his regiment,

> We have fought one of the greatest battles ever fought. Neither party has been yet badly beaten, though I think the 'Johnnies' (Rebels) have had the worst of it. The number killed is fearful. The 76th has lost heavily. The 1st day seven of the nine col-orguard were shot. Our Col. is wounded. Our maj a prisoner. The Adjt was wounded. We don't know whether he is dead or a prisoner. I have only a very incomplete list of the losses.

Burnham then told his parents about his visit to the angle on the morning of May 13. He surveyed the ground occupied by the Rebels before they fell back, "Their bodies by hundreds still lay on the ground. The rifle pits were literally choked with them. Some of them were still breathing. You could hardly believe that oak trees one foot in diameter were cut down by musket balls alone. Yet such is the fact."

Burnham concluded his letter by sharing his impressions on letters he found on the ground beside some fallen Rebel soldiers. He sent the letters to his parents, and wrote:

> One you will notice is stained with blood. The writer it seems is a conscript officer in Mississippi and acknowledges that he had been engaged in hanging Union men in the state. Two are from wives to their husbands. Oh! How many thousand will have never again a chance to write to their husbands. My feelings while looking at the bodies of our dead enemies were not of joy alone. I thought how many hopes were bound up in the lives of those men whose broken bloody bodies were lying hopeless on that muddy field. I had not enmity toward those men, not any even for their living companions who from the woods beyond were even then occasionally sending a whistling bullet after us. They are brave and believe in the cause they fight for.[51]

These were remarkably noble sentiments from a Union officer less than forty-eight hours after the barbarous combat of the Bloody Angle.

The fighting at the salient ended around 3:00 A.M. in the morning on May 13. A mere one hour later, Private William Reeves died at 4:00 A.M. On the same day, Friday the 13th, the first two Union soldiers were buried at Robert E. Lee's former estate at Arlington, Virginia. On Saturday, May 14, Private Reeves became the fourth soldier to be interred at what would be later known as Arlington National Cemetery. Reeves was only the second *battlefield* casualty to be buried on this sacred ground.

FOURTEEN

Arlington

"The biggest heroes in this war are the privates in the line—the man with the musket."

—Washington Roebling

On the day that Private Reeves died, the *New York Times* coincidentally published on its front page an account of the fighting that had resulted in his wounding. It had been eight days since Warren's Fifth Corps attacked Ewell at the Orange Turnpike during the early afternoon of May 5. Summarizing the initial encounter of Grant's Overland Campaign, the reporter for the *Times* wrote, "This was not done without severe loss, especially on the part of Warren, two of whose divisions, namely, those of Wadsworth and Griffin, lost each a third of its numbers."[1]

The day before Reeves died—the same day as the fighting at the Bloody Angle—Secretary of War Edwin Stanton wrote favorably of the Army of the Potomac's recent accomplishments in a letter to Meade, "This Department congratulates you and your heroic army and returns its cordial thanks for their gallant achievements during the last seven days, and hope that the valor and skill thus far manifested will be crowned with the fruits of ultimate and decisive Victory."[2] Private Reeves died the following day on that unlucky Friday the 13th, but had bravely played his part in trying to bring the war to a successful conclusion—sometime in the near future, hopefully. Perhaps mistakenly, most Northerners, along with senior members of the Lincoln administration, believed the spring campaign had gotten off to a promising start.

Reeves left behind few possessions at Stanton General Hospital after his death. The only personal effects in his possession, according to records, were his uniform and boots. The United States government still owed him $75 from a government bounty, which was in addition to the $300 he had already received as Hiram Humphrey's substitute. The government also owed Reeves $22.68 in back pay, though Reeves had an outstanding debit of $22.59 for "extra clothing drawn." In the end, the government owed Reeves $80.41, which it would pay to his widow, Anna. She applied for a widow's pension on May 21, 1864, exactly a week after his burial, and eventually received $8 per month, which was backdated to begin on May 13, 1864.[3]

Shortly after Reeves's death, an orderly from Stanton General Hospital took his body to the "dead house," once all the required paperwork was completed. Each of the large general hospitals had a dead house where corpses were stored. In some cases, the body would be embalmed and then transported up north to the family of the fallen soldier. In most instances, however, embalming was considered too expensive and the bodies were buried soon after the soldier's death.

The process of embalming required chemicals being injected into the body's arteries. A Washington reporter described the process in detail, "The body is placed on an inclined platform, the mouth, ears, nose, &c., are stopped with cotton; if wounded, cotton is put in the wound, and a plaster is put on; an incision is made in the wrist, the attachment is made from an air pump, and fluid is injected into the arteries. The wound is then sewed up and the body is hoisted up to dry."[4] Most of the Union dead were not embalmed. On average, the procedure cost $7 for enlisted men and $13 for officers.

At the Armory Square Hospital in Washington, D.C., Dr. D. Willard Bliss embalmed every soldier who died at his hospital "requested or not." The families that could afford it would pay him and he'd arrange to have the bodies transported to the various locations. Bliss billed $3 for materials and $10 for the "embalming package and encasing the body." For families that couldn't afford it, the bodies would be buried locally. Stanton General Hospital, located only a couple of miles away from Armory Square Hospital, didn't have a similar policy. In the case of Reeves, he wasn't embalmed and it seems unlikely his wife, Anna, or his father, Theophilus, were contacted by the hospital on the day of his death to see if they were interested in the procedure. The hospital staff likely assumed the family of a lowly substitute, with few personal possessions, could not afford to have his corpse embalmed and transported to Upstate New York. Instead, it would be necessary to bury Private Reeves on the following day in a nearby cemetery.

The most logical burial location normally would have been the cemetery at the Old Soldiers' Home, a site three miles north of the White House in Washington, D.C. By May 1864, roughly 8,000 soldiers had been buried at the asylum. President Lincoln had access to a cottage on the grounds of the Old Soldiers' Home, and spent considerable time there from 1862 to 1864. On May 13, 1864, however, the cemetery at the Old Soldiers' Home had reached capacity and "the Secretary of War directed that a new site be selected on Lee's farm, at Arlington, Va."[5]

Secretary of War Stanton and Quartermaster General Montgomery Meigs previously agreed that Arlington—an 1,100-acre estate that was the home of Robert E. Lee before the war—would become the New National Military Cemetery, where soldiers who died in Washington area hospitals would be buried in the aftermath of the Wilderness Campaign. A graduate of West Point, Montgomery C. Meigs had worked and socialized with Lee before the war. The efficient and talented quartermaster general became a bitter foe of all secessionists once the fighting began, however. The first two burials at Arlington took place on May 13, 1864, the exact day the Soldiers' Home cemetery had filled up, according to an official report. There would be six more burials on May 14 and four on May 15. By the end of June 1864, there were 2,600 Union soldiers interred at Arlington.[6]

Robert E. Lee, his family, and sixty-seven slaves lived at Arlington before the war. The United States government believed General Lee personally owned the estate, though legally, that wasn't true. The beautiful property originally had been owned by George Washington's adopted son, George Washington Parke Custis, who died in 1857. He bequeathed it to his daughter—Lee's wife—Mary Anna Custis Lee for the remainder of her life. It would then pass on to Robert and Mary's eldest son, George Washington Custis Lee, after Mary's death. The Lee mansion still stands today, and sits on a hill overlooking the Potomac River, offering glorious views of the nation's capital. It was (and is) one of the most beautiful locations in the Washington, D.C., area.

The strategic location of the estate on the south bank of the Potomac River required that it be seized immediately after the outbreak of hostilities in 1861. When Lee and his wife were later unable to pay *in person* a tax of $92.07 on the Arlington property, local commissioners sold the estate to the federal government for $26,800. By 1864, the United States government considered the estate federal property. Union soldiers were stationed at Arlington throughout the war and the army created a model community there in 1863 for freed slaves, which became known as Freedman's Village. Lee and his family were distraught at what had happened to their beloved home. During the war, Lee wrote to one of his daughters, "I should have preferred it to have been wiped from the earth, its beautiful hill sunk, and its sacred trees buried, rather than to have been degraded by the presence of those who revel in the ill they do for their own selfish purposes."[7]

Quartermaster General Meigs chose Arlington as the site for the New National Military Cemetery to penalize Robert E. Lee for his treason. He believed Lee and the other Rebel leaders should be prosecuted and punished "by the government which they have betrayed [and] attacked."[8] By burying the bodies of heroic Union soldiers as close to the Lee mansion as possible, Meigs ensured that the Lees would never be able to return to their family home. Referring to Freedmen's Village and the new cemetery at Arlington, a newspaper columnist wrote, "How appropriate that Lee's land should be appropriated to two such noble purposes—the free living black man whom Lee would enslave, and the bodies of the dead whom Lee had killed in a wicked cause!"[9]

Many years after the war, a member of the Meigs family reported that President Lincoln had asked his quartermaster general what should be done with Arlington in the spring of 1864. Meigs replied, "Why not make it a field of honor? The ancients filled their enemies' fields with salt and made them useless forever but we are a Christian nation, why not make it a field of honor." Lincoln agreed with his idea, according to this source.[10]

An even more detailed story of the founding of Arlington emerged in the decades following Appomattox. On May 13, 1864, one day after the horror at the Bloody Angle, Meigs was supposedly walking by the White House portico when Lincoln called out, "Step in here, Meigs, and take a drive with me. You look tired and worn out; you need a rest." They drove for a while and ended up at the Lee estate in Arlington. After each man attended to some business, they reconvened to drive back to Washington. Meigs looked around at the beauty of the estate and became angry about Lee's betrayal of his country. He turned to the president and said, "Lee shall never return to Arlington. No matter what the issue of the war may be, the arch-rebel shall never again enjoy the possession of these estates."

Lincoln smiled, as some soldiers carried stretchers of dead bodies past the two leaders. Meigs then said to the soldiers transporting the bodies, "Set down the stretchers. Captain, order out a burial squad and see that all the bodies at Arlington are buried on the place at once." The quartermaster general then walked toward Mrs. Lee's garden near the mansion and said, "Bury them here." After that, Lincoln and Meigs rode away. According to this tale, it was in this way that "the first interment of Union dead had been made at Arlington."[11]

The fanciful story of Meigs, after an excursion with the president, deciding on the spot to bury Union soldiers at Arlington is almost certainly untrue. We know that the first soldiers to be buried at the new cemetery had recently died in area hospitals. They weren't already present on the property. We also know that the first burials took place—against Meigs's expressed wishes—at the northeastern corner of the estate, which is about a half mile from Lee's mansion and Mrs. Lee's garden. Perhaps Arlington Cemetery, like the founding of Rome by Romulus and Remus, required a compelling creation myth. Surprisingly, the actual creation story, though unknown to most Americans, is even more compelling. On the morning after one of the bloodiest days in American military history, the first bodies of loyal Union men consecrated the ground of what would become our preeminent national cemetery on the former estate of the man who remained the single biggest threat to the future of the Republic.

The first burial at Arlington, on May 13, 1864, was of Private William Christman of the 67th Pennsylvania Infantry. Christman, a farm laborer during peacetime like William Reeves, was just twenty years old. He had enlisted on March 25, 1864, but never saw combat. On May 1, he was diagnosed with the measles; he died on May 11 at Lincoln General Hospital in Washington, D.C. While Christman had been in the hospital, his regiment, the 67th Pennsylvania, had been outflanked on the early evening of May 6 in the Wilderness, while serving as part of General Seymour's brigade.

It's not surprising that the first man to be buried at Arlington died of sickness. Soldiers were two times more likely to die of an illness than from a battlefield wound, during the Civil War.[12] Just being in the army represented a huge risk for young men at the time. The second burial on May 13, Private William McKinney, also died of illness. McKinney had been admitted to an Alexandria, Virginia, hospital with a diagnosis of pneumonia, and died on May 12, 1864. A former sawmill worker, McKinney joined the 17th Pennsylvania Cavalry on March 16, 1864. He was only seventeen years old. All the first graves at Arlington were dug by one of Lee's former slaves, Jim Parks, who would later recall the spot where, as Grant's campaign continued, "coffins had been piled in long rows like cordwood."[13] Parks was also a young man at the time just like the soldiers he buried. Each of the early graves received a pine headboard, painted white with black writing. Later the wooden headboards would be replaced with marble gravestones.

The new National Military Cemetery at Arlington was officially sanctioned by Stanton one month after the first burials in a letter to Meigs on June 15, 1864. The Secretary of War ordered his quartermaster general to set aside 200 acres "to be immediately surveyed, laid out, and enclosed" for the cemetery. "The bodies of all soldiers," Stanton wrote, "dying in the Hospitals of the vicinity of Washington and Alexandria will be interred at this Cemetery." On the same day, Meigs wrote Stanton recommending that the interments at the northeast corner of the estate "be discontinued and that the land surrounding the Arlington Mansion now understood to be the property of the United States, be appropriated to the National Military Cemetery." Meigs added—in a sentence that would have angered Robert and Mary Lee—"the grounds about the Mansion are admirably adapted to such a use."[14]

Meigs clearly wanted the initial burials to be closer to the main house. After the war, he said, "it was my intention to have begun the interments nearer the mansion." Senior Union officers, who were living in Lee's house in May and June 1864, opposed his decision, however. They "did not like to have the dead buried near them" and "caused the interment to be begun in the Northeast quarter of the grounds near the Alexandria road." When Meigs discovered that his order was being disobeyed, he once again gave "special instructions to make the burials near the mansion."[15]

Later, when Meigs learned these men were still ignoring his command, he directly intervened to make sure Union officers were buried near Mrs. Lee's garden. Meigs's insistence that the burials be close to the main house shows how determined he was that the Lees should not be able to return to Arlington. He knew that patriotic Northerners would never allow the bodies of their heroes to be disinterred from their final resting place after the war. He was proven correct about that.

On Saturday, May 14, the weather improved in the Washington, D.C., area after forty-eight hours of rain. A local newspaper, the *Daily Morning Chronicle*, ran several encouraging headlines on its front page: GRANT'S BRILLIANT VICTORIES; LEE IN FULL RETREAT; SEVEN THOUSAND PRISONERS AND FORTY-TWO CANNON TAKEN ON THURSDAY. With spring in full bloom in the nation's capital, there was a new optimism about the war effort after what was thought to have been a great victory at the Bloody Angle.

On that same Saturday, the body of Private William Reeves was put in a pine coffin along with a written form of identification. His coffin was then placed in the back of a hearse—a covered ambulance that had been painted black. A military escort accompanied the hearse as it moved slowly through the muddy streets of Washington, D.C. The hearse crossed the Long Bridge toward Arlington, and eventually made its way up the hill to the New National Military Cemetery at Robert E. Lee's former home.

Jim Parks had already dug several graves when Reeves's casket finally made it to the northeastern corner of the grounds. Private William Reeves was buried with full honors that day. It had been nine days since his fateful wound in the Wilderness. A band may have played "Taps," which was becoming more and more common at the time. A chaplain then said a few appropriate words for the occasion. After these brief comments, a firing party gave a three-volley salute to their fallen comrade. Sadly, unlike Private William McKinney, the young cavalryman buried on the previous day, no one from Reeves's family could be there for his burial. His final resting place was hundreds of miles from his home in Victor, New York.[16]

Reeves's blood would now forever link the Wilderness with Arlington National Cemetery. His peaceful grave overlooking Washington contrasted with the smoke and horror of the woods, where he had been shot. Today, his grave is adjacent to a large maple tree on a gentle hill about a ten-minute walk from the Lee mansion. In 1912, a local reporter wrote of this particular location, "The field of graves lies between the Seneca sandstone north wall and a little stream on the south side that trickles down through the impressive wood—woodland yet untouched by the grave digger's spade and which covers the rough terrain north of the mansion . . . The hard rolled gravel road that runs through these woods show few wheel tracks, and days and days pass without anybody moving there, except a watchman going his lonely round."[17]

Immediately before the burial of Reeves, Private William Blatt received a similar interment ceremony. Blatt had been mortally wounded during the Battle of Spotsylvania Court House. In the middle of Upton's famous assault on May 10, Blatt was shot in the head. He died while being taken from the wharf to Armory Square Hospital in Washington. More than half of Private Blatt's regiment suffered casualties during the attack on May 10. Blatt became the third burial at Arlington; Reeves was the fourth. Today, Blatt is remembered as the first battlefield casualty to be interred at our national cemetery. Private Reeves, who was wounded five days before Blatt, was the second.

The burial rites for Union soldiers had some similarities with those of the Ancient Greeks. Thucydides wrote of the fallen Athenians during the Peloponnesian War, "They bury them in the public tomb, which is in the most beautiful suburb of the city, and in which they always bury those killed in war . . . After they cover them with earth, a man chosen by the state, known for wise judgment and of high reputation makes an appropriate speech of praise, and after this they depart." The most famous oration in Ancient Greece was given by Pericles. His comments on the Athenian war dead would have also been applicable to the Union departed, "For in giving their lives in common cause, they individually gained imperishable praise and the most distinctive tomb, not the one where they are buried but the one where on every occasion for word and deed their glory is left after them eternally . . . Emulate them now, judge that happiness is freedom and freedom courage, and do not stand aside from the dangers of war."[18]

Abraham Lincoln, of course, gave an oration at Gettysburg that rivaled that of Pericles. Several months after the battle, Lincoln said, "it is rather for us to be here dedicated to the great task remaining before us that from these honored dead we take increased devotion to that cause for which they gave the last full measure of devotion that we here highly resolve that these dead shall not have died in vain; that this nation shall have a new birth of freedom." Eleven months after the Emancipation Proclamation, Lincoln had made the abolition of slavery a war aim.

We don't know Private Reeves's personal view of slavery. He was a Methodist, a sect with many notable abolitionists. But he was also a poor farm laborer, who may have shared many of the prejudices of his day.

Regardless, by bravely fighting for the Union cause, he helped save the Union *and* free the slaves. In 1871, the great orator and abolitionist Frederick Douglass, in an address at Arlington National Cemetery, honored the sacrifice of Reeves and his fellow Union soldiers,

> We must never forget that the loyal soldiers who rest beneath this sod flung themselves between the nation and the nation's destroyers. If today we have a country not boiling in an agony of blood, like France, if now we have a united country, no longer cursed by the hell-black system of human bondage, if the American name is no longer a by-word and a hissing to a mocking earth, if the star-spangled banner floats only over free American citizens in every quarter of the land, and our country has before it a long and glorious career of justice, liberty, and civilization, we are indebted to the unselfish devotion of the noble army who rest in these honored graves all around us. [19]

It's fitting that the location of Reeves's grave at Arlington—in what became known as Section 27—would soon become the site where African American civilians and soldiers were buried. Once Meigs's orders were followed, white soldiers were buried closer to the mansion in the future. By mid-1867, there were 3,450 African Americans buried in Section 27. [20] Only a relative handful of white soldiers—Reeves, Blatt, McKinney, Christman, and several others—remained alongside them.

FIFTEEN

Gen. Wadsworth's Body

After having been shot in the head around midday on May 6, James Wadsworth had been left on the ground behind enemy lines. Later that afternoon, the Rebels transported Wadsworth to a hellish field hospital that served Brigadier General Richard Anderson's division, part of A. P. Hill's Corps. Wadsworth, whose name was familiar to many Americans, was placed in an officer's tent, which had been put up "for his especial benefit." The squire of Geneseo, New York, appeared to be conscious, though incommunicative, and still fiddled with various objects with his left hand. Robert E. Lee reported to Richmond later that evening at 8:00 P.M. that Wadsworth had been among the dead and wounded left "in our hands."

On the following morning, Saturday, May 7, Captain Zabdiel Boylston Adams of the 56th Massachusetts Infantry awakened to find himself on a stretcher next to Wadsworth. Adams recalled seeing the general leading his troops on the Orange Plank Road on the previous day. Adams raised himself up on his elbow and tried to speak to Wadsworth, who made no reply. "He was rather tall," the Union captain wrote of Wadsworth, "an eminently handsome man of commanding presence, but showing gentle breeding." Adams, an experienced surgeon, discovered that Wadsworth's right arm was paralyzed. Taking a closer look, he learned, "that a musket ball had entered the top of his head a little to the left of the median line. In his left hand, which lay quietly upon the breast of his buttoned coat, he held a scrap of paper, on which was written, 'Gen. James S. Wadsworth.'"[1]

Adams, an eighth-generation descendant of Henry Adams—an Englishman who first settled in Massachusetts in the early 17th century—belonged to a prominent New England family. An ardent abolitionist, he graduated from Harvard Medical School and practiced as a surgeon before Fort Sumter. Earlier in the war, Adams became the head surgeon for the 32nd Massachusetts Infantry. He became ill, however, from working tirelessly at the Battle of Gettysburg. Shortly after being mustered out of the service, he tried to return, but was unable to secure a spot with the Surgical Corps. The resourceful Adams decided in the end to join the 56th Massachusetts as an infantry captain. His dedication to the Union cause was extraordinary.

On the morning of May 6 in the Wilderness, Adams led his regiment amid the bloody fighting on the Orange Plank Road. He recalled the Rebels overwhelming his men, and wrote, "The woods seemed to be full of smoke, and shots came in almost every direction except from behind us. Presently, I felt a crack on my leg as though it had been struck by a bar of red-hot iron, a blow which shook me all over." Unable to walk or retreat, he was soon captured by the Confederates and eventually taken to the same field hospital as Wadsworth. At one point, he examined his own wound, "I found that the ball had entered above the top of my buttoned boot and had not come out on the opposite side, and must, therefore, be still inside the leg; that both bones were fractured, but worst of all that I had bled so profusely that my boot was completely filled with blood."[2] He later learned that the woods were on fire in that area and many of the wounded had been burned to death.

At some point on May 7, two Confederate surgeons, who smelled strongly of whiskey, examined Adams's wounds. Later, numerous Confederate officers began peeking into his tent asking questions along the lines of, "Do you mean to say that this is James S. Wadsworth of New York, the proprietor of vast estates in the Geneseo valley, the candidate for governor in 1862? etc." Some of the Rebels also exclaimed, "I'd never believe that they had such men as that in their army." When the officers would read Wadsworth's name from his paper on his chest, "he would frown and show restlessness."[3]

One drunken Confederate soldier got extremely agitated and swore at Adams, calling him a liar for saying the wounded man was James S. Wadsworth, "declaring that he knew our officers were crazy abolitionists, mercenaries, low politicians, hirelings from foreign armies, etc." The situation deteriorated and the drunken Rebel got even angrier when he learned Adams was from Massachusetts, boasting that he'd call the roll of his slaves on Bunker Hill in the future. The enraged Confederate soldier then lost control completely. Adams recalled the Rebel "drew his revolver from his belt, cocked it, and was about to shoot me, when his friends caught hold of the weapon and pushed him out of the tent."[4]

Later, on the evening of May 7, a couple of surgeons arrived to examine Wadsworth's wound. They removed a piece of his skull and then probed for the ball, which struck Adams "as bad surgery." Watching the procedure, Adams noticed "the ball had entered near the top of the head, had gone forward, and was lodged in the anterior lobe of the left side of the brain." He subsequently learned that Wadsworth's horse was shot first. As they both went down, Wadsworth was hit as he fell forward. According to Adams's notes, Wadsworth "seemed to be unable to swallow, for if more than a teaspoonful was put into his lips it ran out of the corners of his mouth upon his beard. Occasionally he heaved a deep sigh, but otherwise lay in calm slumber."[5]

Shortly after dark on that eventful Saturday, May 7, Wadsworth and Adams were visited by a local farmer named Patrick McCracken. The forty-three-year-old farmer, an Irish immigrant, slipped through the back fly of the tent, and said to Adams, "My name is Patrick McCracken and I have a little farm a few miles out. I have heard that General Wadsworth is here wounded, and I want to do something for him." McCracken then told the story of how he had been accused of being a Rebel spy and spent nine weeks in the Old Capitol prison in Washington, D.C., in 1862. Wadsworth, the military governor of the nation's capital at the time, intervened and released McCracken "on his promise that, if allowed to return home, he would not assist in any way the cause of the Confederacy."[6]

McCracken now lived just seven miles west on the Plank Road toward Orange Court House, and wished to repay Wadsworth for his earlier kindness. He told Adams he'd be happy if he "would take some milk or anything he could supply, and give it to the general." Adams told him that he didn't think Wadsworth could swallow anything, but McCracken nevertheless left some milk and food. McCracken returned on Sunday morning, May 8, around 9:00 A.M., noting "I had carried some sweet milk to the hospital, and wet his lips several times, and let a little go down his mouth."[7]

The Irish American farmer returned to the field hospital later that same afternoon, around 3:00 P.M., to discover Wadsworth had died about an hour earlier. Adams observed that Wadsworth had become comatose, "with rising and falling respiration, and ceased to breathe finally at near 2:00 P.M., having lived about forty-eight hours since his wounding." That gallant statesman died "in the midst of that lonesome wild of woods and swamp and thicket, and in the hands of his enemies." Adams remembered the sadness of Wadsworth dying without his friends or kindred at his side, and later remarked, "Here was one whose sacrifices in the Union cause equaled, if they did not now surpass in greatness those of any man in our whole country. A character of the finest mold and coming of the noblest strain. Gentle as he was brave, modest as he was rich; one who despised luxury of living, was a plain man, abstemious in habits and tastes, and pure in his life." Adams cut a lock of hair from the general's head, which he eventually gave to Wadsworth's widow, Mary Craig Wadsworth. He then gave the body to McCracken, who agreed to bury it at his farm. Many years later, Adams would recall, "The incident of the death of General Wadsworth by my side upon the battlefield of the Wilderness will ever remain to me as one of the most memorable of my experiences in the army.

What could be more inspiring and uplifting than the life and example of this heroic character!"[8]

On the following day, May 9, McCracken wrote a very heartfelt letter to Mary Craig Wadsworth. He told her he saw her husband on Saturday, May 7, though the general "could not speak or take any notice of anything." He also assured her that he made a coffin for the general—"as good as any could be made in the country"—and "had a large plank planed and marked for a headstone, and placed at the head of the grave." McCracken said he'd await arrangements by the government to have the body eventually moved through the lines to be taken north to New York. Finally, he wanted her to know that the general "received all the attention and kindness at the hands of the Confederate authorities that could be bestowed upon him."[9]

On that same day, Wadsworth's son-in-law, Captain Montgomery Ritchie, sent a telegram to a firm in Geneseo that managed his father-in-law's business matters, "Gen Wadsworth was killed at the head of his troops. His body in our possession." Sadly, the body was not actually in the Union Army's possession at that time. It would be another nine days before it entered Union lines. Ritchie, who had married Wadsworth's eldest daughter, Cornelia, would be responsible for bringing the body home to Geneseo, New York. He had been formerly a part of the 1st Massachusetts Cavalry, but had resigned his commission on May 6, 1864—the second day of the Battle of the Wilderness.[10]

Abraham Lincoln was particularly distressed by the sad news about Wadsworth. "I have not known the President so affected by a personal loss since the death of Baker, as by the death of General Wadsworth," recalled John Hay, Lincoln's personal secretary. On May 14, 1864, Hay recorded in his diary, "While deeply regretting the loss of Sedgwick, Lincoln added, 'Sedgwick's devotion and earnestness were professional. But no man has given himself up to the war with such self-sacrificing patriotism as Genl. Wadsworth. He went into the service not wishing or expecting great success or distinction in his military career & profoundly indifferent to popular applause, actuated only by a sense of duty which he neither evaded nor sought to evade.'"[11] When Grant heard the news about his division commander, he said "that he would rather have lost an entire infantry brigade rather than this brave and wise man."[12] Hancock called the death of Wadsworth "one of the greatest losses the army has met with," and believed the general "behaved nobly on the morning of the 6th of May in the Wilderness . . . On that day he exposed himself, individually, more than any other soldier."[13]

Obtaining Wadsworth's body proved to be more difficult than anticipated. An initial party sent out to the Wilderness to receive it from the Rebels under a flag of truce was unsuccessful. Fortunately, a second mission led by Arthur K. St. Clair, an assistant surgeon for a Michigan cavalry unit, was eventually able to take possession of the body on May 17.

At 10:00 A.M. that morning, Wadsworth's coffin was delivered to the Depot Field Hospital at Fredericksburg, Virginia. An embalmer named Dr. John Ross from Washington, D.C., was already there waiting for the arrival of the general's body. Unfortunately, the corpse was in an advanced state of decomposition, and couldn't be embalmed. Dr. Ross did what he could and then placed the body in a metallic coffin for its trip to Geneseo for the funeral and burial that was scheduled for Saturday, May 21. The first leg of the journey would be to Washington, D.C. On the evening of May 17, Wadsworth's body was put aboard the steamer *Mary Rapley*, and it arrived in the nation's capital on the morning of May 18.

On the whole, General Wadsworth was treated with great respect by friends and foes alike in the immediate aftermath of his wounding and death. Robert E. Lee and George Gordon Meade had corresponded about bringing the body from Confederate to Union lines. And individuals like Captain Adams, Patrick McCracken, and Dr. St. Clair did everything they could for the famous general.[14] On the debit side of the ledger, sadly, one soldier from a Virginia regiment stole a pocketbook and $90 in cash from Wadsworth. Another Virginian stole his gold watch. Wadsworth also had possessed an expensive pair of field glasses that may have been confiscated as well. The field glasses were so extraordinary that they were mentioned twice in Virginia newspapers during the summer of 1864. On May 27, 1864, they were described in the *Richmond Examiner*: "They are of the most unique, elaborate and expensive kind, being adapted either for the sea or field service. The power of the lens upon actual test, was found to be very great."[15]

Wadsworth's body arrived in New York City at 6:00 P.M. on May 19. On the following day, it arrived at City Hall in a hearse. According to a newspaper reporter, "The box was then taken out of the hearse, while the military gave a solemn salute and the drums beat a mournful accompaniment. The box was conveyed by eight sergeants up the stairs of the City Hall to the Governor's room, where it was laid on benches in the usual place."[16] The only inscription on the coffin was "Body of Brigadier General James S. Wadsworth." Among the pallbearers at the various ceremonies that day were Hamilton Fish—a former governor and senator for New York—and Horace Greeley, the publisher of the *New-York Tribune*. At 3:00 P.M.on May 20, Wadsworth's body then headed north to Rochester, New York.

His coffin, draped in an American flag, finally arrived in Geneseo at 11:00 A.M. on Saturday morning, May 21, fifteen days after he had been wounded at the Battle of the Wilderness. The funeral was held later that day at 2:00 P.M. at St. Michael's, an Episcopal Church regularly attended by the Wadsworth family. In the afternoon, the body was finally buried at Temple Hill Cemetery just outside the village limits, amid the graves of Wadsworth's ancestors and relatives. The village was profoundly moved by the loss of its beloved son, "Every place of business is closed, and funeral wreaths are hung upon the doors, balconies and windows, and the people fill the streets and doorsteps and every standpoint from which the long and solemn procession can be viewed as it passes on its way to the humble village church and to the modest rural cemetery."[17] The Wadsworth family paid $75 for the funeral, with the American flag that draped the coffin costing $12. It cost the estate $240 to transport Wadsworth's body from the Wilderness to Geneseo.[18]

In the weeks after the funeral, Mary Wadsworth received warm condolences from some of the most preeminent citizens from across America. In one letter, John Lothrop Motley, a diplomat and historian who had known Wadsworth at Harvard, told Mary, "A nation is mourning with you—a whole great people in these dark, but most honorable days of our history is weeping for the loss of the great and good Wadsworth." Motley emphasized that Wadsworth fought for the Union and against slavery, "I had long known that he detested negro slavery, both because of the wrong committed on an unhappy deeply injured race, but because the very name was a perpetual satire on our boasted freedom and because the slaveholders, with few honorable exceptions, were the deadly enemies of our great Republic."[19] An obituary in the *New York Times* mentioned Wadsworth's zeal for abolition as well, "Amid the guarded words of most Northern leaders at the outburst of the war, it was refreshing to hear one loyal man who did not hesitate to avow that he *hated* the rebellion and Slavery, and meant to fight them wherever he could."[20]

Perhaps the most thoughtful letter to Mary came from Gouverneur Warren, Wadsworth's commanding officer. In four pages written in his own hand, Warren began by highlighting the great legacy Wadsworth had left to his children and countrymen. After recounting Wadsworth's exploits during the Battle of the Wilderness, Warren wrote, "Nobly did he perform his whole duty. The love and admiration of his comrades cling to his memory and the gallant Rice and a host of others of his command emulating his heroism on the battlefield, have followed in the path of glory." Warren identified an important component of Wadsworth's success as a leader. Though he appeared to take unnecessary risks at times, he inspired his men with his courage to fight against long odds. His efforts weren't always successful during the Battle of the Wilderness—his division suffered extraordinarily high casualties—but his example seemed to contradict those critics who felt the Army of the Potomac was lacking in aggression.

Warren concluded his letter with a beautiful tribute to the man, "With him, his country stood first, and in the maintenance of her honor and perpetuity he surrendered the companionship of friends, the comforts and joys of a happy home, and the highest civil honors, and went to meet her foes. With the men of his command he shared all the privations and toils and dangers of a soldier's life. His thoughts were ever for the comfort and efficiency of his troops. It was his nature to lead, and when the shock of battle was heaviest, there was General Wadsworth."[21]

Unlike Private Reeves, General Wadsworth received the type of burial he would have always hoped for. His noble sacrifice was commemorated in Washington, New York, Rochester, and his hometown of Geneseo. His dearest friends and family members attended his funeral and laid him to rest in his family burial ground. A nation mourned for this courageous and selfless citizen. Heartfelt tributes came in from across the country. James Samuel Wadsworth represented many of the nation's highest ideals. His sacrifice had struck a chord with his fellow Americans.

Despite their class differences, Reeves and Wadsworth weren't entirely dissimilar. Victor, New York, and Geneseo are only thirty miles or so apart. Both Upstate New Yorkers volunteered for the army, despite the extreme risks involved. Wadsworth, a tremendously wealthy landowner with a wife and five children, had much to lose. But so too did Reeves. The young newlywed had hopes, perhaps, of starting his own family and buying some land near his father, Theophilus. Both Wadsworth and Reeves had risked and lost *everything* on behalf of their country. In 1864, Wadsworth's burial at his home among his loved ones would've been the preferred death by most soldiers. Today, a resting place at Arlington is considered one of our nation's highest honors. Wadsworth's name is still known, though not widely. The name of William Reeves has been ignored for over one hundred and fifty-five years. Visitors to Section 27 at Arlington National Cemetery surely see his name, but almost no one knows his story. Yet, his sacrifice is worth celebrating, too.

SIXTEEN

Fathers and Sons

S everal decades after the Civil War, a sad story circulated about Private
William Reeves's father, Theophilus Reeves. Reportedly, Theophilus
never received notification of William's death, so he joined Company H
of the 140th New York Infantry Regiment to look for his missing son in
the woods of Virginia. In *A History of Ontario County, New York and Its
People*, published in 1911, the local historian Charles Milliken wrote that
Theophilus "was a soldier in the Civil War, enlisting in order to search
for his son, William Reeves, who had entered the service at the age of 16,
who served a term of three years and then reenlisted, and was killed in the
Battle of the Wilderness."[1] Unsuccessful in his quest, the bereft Theophilus
eventually died on July 7, 1881 in East Victor, New York. He was buried
alongside his wife Louise at the Victor Village Cemetery. Today, there's
still a GAR symbol—the letters are an acronym for "Grand Army of the
Republic"—next to Theophilus's gravestone, indicating his service during
the Civil War.

The story of Theophilus is a heartbreaking tale. It's also not true. The
wounding of Private William Reeves at the Wilderness was listed in the *Daily*

Morning Chronicle, a Washington, D.C., newspaper, on May 14 and the *New York Times* on May 15, so Theophilus, who was able to read, would've known his son was injured. And we know that Anna Reeves applied for a widow's pension on May 21, 1864, a mere week after William's death. At some point between May 14 and May 21, the United States government notified Anna of the death of her husband and his burial at Arlington. It's a certainty she'd have relayed this information to her father-in-law, who lived in the same village. Also, a review of the roster of the 140th New York Infantry Regiment reveals there is a "Theopilus [sic] Reeves" listed but it's clearly not the same person. He's twenty years younger than William's father, and he was discharged in 1863, well before the Battle of the Wilderness. Finally, William was nineteen not sixteen when he enlisted, and he never had the opportunity to reenlist.

It's also safe to assume that Theophilus didn't join the army. Instead, he remained at home in Victor, where he grieved alongside his daughter-in-law, who resided in the household of her father, Thomas Barnett. Anna never spent more than a few days under the same roof as her husband. She remarried on December 26, 1865, and had a child in 1869 whom she named William. One wonders if Anna and Theophilus ever took a long trip together to Arlington Cemetery to visit William's grave. They must have missed him terribly.

Hiram Humphrey, who hired William as a substitute, married Sarah Abigail Miller on November 7, 1866. They had a daughter named Stella Miller Humphrey in 1869. In a very tangible way, William's sacrifice had made it possible for Hiram to start a family. It reminds us of the line from *The Great Gatsby*, "The Carraways are something of a clan and we have a tradition that we're descended from the Dukes of Buccleuch, but the actual founder of my line was my grandfather's brother who came here in fifty-one, sent a substitute to the Civil War and started the wholesale hardware business that my father carries on today."[2]

It's not all that surprising that a story took root about a grieving father, who took extreme measures to look for his missing son on the battlefields of Virginia. During the Civil War, more than 40% of the dead soldiers remained unidentified and the casualty lists were often highly inaccurate.

Among African American soldiers, roughly 66% of the dead were never identified. In the midst of Grant's Overland Campaign, desperate families seeking news overwhelmed departmental offices in the nation's capital. Many of the missing soldiers were held in Confederate prisons: the Rebels held 194,743 Union prisoners during the war, and 30,218 of them died in captivity. At the Battle of the Wilderness alone, 3,383 Union soldiers were either captured or missing. Some of those men eventually returned home. Some died and were identified. Many others died and remained unidentified, an incredibly sad outcome for their loving friends and family members.

Shortly after the war, one heartsick mother wrote a letter seeking information about her son from Clara Barton, who was organizing efforts to identify missing soldiers. Mrs. T. B. Hurlbut from Illinois told Barton her son was reported killed during the Battle of the Wilderness on May 6, 1864. His body hadn't been found and an exhaustive search didn't turn up any information about him. She added, "My son was twenty-two years old. Wore no moustache or beard. Was about six feet in height. When in College he was rather spare, but the outdoor life of the army had given him a robust appearance." He had black hair and dark hazel eyes. Mrs. Hurlbut concluded, "It may be well to add my son's name to the many missing ones, and could you by any means give me any knowledge of the last resting place of my darling one you would confer such a favor as none less desolate than myself can appreciate."[3] Sadly, the body of Captain Wilbur Lovejoy Hurlbut was never identified. It may have been moved to Fredericksburg National Cemetery to be buried along with other unknown Union soldiers.

Clara Barton may have been unsuccessful in this case, but her overall efforts on behalf of the families of missing soldiers were truly astonishing. After the war, she set up a department called Friends of the Missing Men of the U.S. Army that sought to help identify the tens of thousands of young men who had disappeared. Over the course of three years, her new office received 63,182 letters from distraught family members, and identified 22,000 previously missing soldiers. Of that number, Barton assisted in identifying 13,000 men that died at the infernal Andersonville Prison in Georgia.[4] Among those dead, who were given wooden headboards that identified them by name, were at least forty-six men from Private William Reeves's 76th New York Infantry Regiment.

Very few Americans avoided the trauma of losing a loved one during the Civil War. Like Theophilus Reeves, Abraham Lincoln lost his own "William" during the war. Willie Lincoln, his father's favorite, died of typhoid fever in February 1862. Just twelve years old, young Willie never experienced the unique ordeals of a Civil War soldier. Nonetheless, Abraham Lincoln's devastating loss caused him to identify with his fellow citizens, who grieved for their fallen husbands, sons, brothers, and friends. After losing his beloved Willie, Lincoln still had to manage the war that wasn't going particularly well at the time. Meanwhile, his wife Mary Lincoln became incapacitated by grief.

Willie got sick during the first days of February 1862 and died a few weeks later on February 20. After Willie's last breath, Lincoln walked out of his son's room and told his secretary, "Well, Nicolay, my boy is gone—he is actually gone!" Later, Lincoln could be heard murmuring, "My poor boy, he was too good for this earth. God has called him home. I know that he is much better off in heaven, but then we loved him so."[5] Elizabeth Keckley, Mary Lincoln's dressmaker, said of the president, "I never saw a man so bowed down with grief."[6]

Several prominent doctors embalmed Willie on February 21. A local reporter wrote, "The embalmment was a complete success, and gave great satisfaction to all present." The funeral was held on February 24 at 2:00 P.M. in the East Room of the White House. Mary Lincoln was too distraught to attend. Keckley recalled, "the White House was draped in mourning. Black crape everywhere met the eye, contrasting strangely with the gay and brilliant colors of a few days before." Willie was buried at Oak Hill Cemetery in Georgetown. After Lincoln's assassination in 1865, Willie's coffin was taken from Georgetown and placed on the same funeral train as his father. Both Willie and Abraham are now buried at Oak Ridge Cemetery in Springfield, Illinois.[7]

Montgomery C. Meigs, the creator of Arlington Cemetery, also tragically lost a son during the war. John Rodgers Meigs was killed at Swift Run

Gap, Virginia, in October 1864. Initially, the circumstances surrounding John's death were unclear. Montgomery Meigs believed his son had been murdered by Rebels and not killed in a fair fight between soldiers. Sadly, Meigs wrote of his son's killing, "And so has perished my first born a noble boy—gallant generous gifted—who had already made himself a name in the land. A martyr in the cause of liberty."[8] Like Willie Lincoln, John Rodgers Meigs was initially buried at Oak Hill Cemetery in Georgetown.

Meigs, who said of his son, "I never did know an equal and I never shall find one other like him," struggled to deal with his terrible loss.[9] His wife Louisa Meigs wrote, "Dear Mont grieves for him most deeply and tenderly, but has so much pride in remembering what he *was* and so much patriotism which encourages him to remember that holy cause, in which our happiness was sacrificed that he does not give way to despondency."[10] In 1880, John Rodgers Meigs's body was moved to a family plot at Arlington National Cemetery, where it remains today. Montgomery Meigs commissioned a bronze sculpture for his tomb, depicting the scene of John's killing.

◈

Just shy of a year after the Battle of the Wilderness, General Philip Sheridan relieved Gouverneur Warren of his command of the Fifth Corps after the Union victory at Five Forks on April 1, 1865. Grant had given Sheridan the authority to do so beforehand. The disgraced Warren spent the remainder of his life trying to clear his name. Friends and other observers believed the stress of trying to restore his honor resulted in his early death at fifty-two years old. The hero of Little Round Top, who also led his corps at the Wilderness, Spotsylvania Court House, Cold Harbor, and many other engagements, was unceremoniously cashiered eight days before the Army of the Potomac's final victory at Appomattox Court House.

Grant expressed displeasure in Warren's performance during the beginning of the Virginia Campaign of 1864. Nevertheless, he continued to give Warren important assignments during the closing months of the war. In the spring campaign of 1865, Grant expected Warren's corps to play a leading role. Yet, on the day of Five Forks, Grant's earlier doubts about Warren led him to have one of his aides send a message to Sheridan: "General Grant directs me to say to you if, in your judgement, the Fifth Corps would do better under one of its division commanders, you are authorized to relieve General Warren and order him to report to him [General Grant] at headquarters."[11]

During the battle, the ill-tempered Sheridan felt Warren failed to provide the necessary leadership to his men. As the Fifth Corps was rounding up Confederate prisoners, an aide to Sheridan provided Warren with a message, "Major General Warren, you are relieved of command of the V Corps and will report for orders to General Grant." Warren, who believed there must have been a mistake, rode to Sheridan asking for a reconsideration of the order. Sheridan responded, "Reconsider, Hell! I don't reconsider my decisions. Obey the order!"[12]

The Union captured 4,500 Rebel prisoners at Five Forks and the victory was a death blow to Lee's Army of Northern Virginia, which surrendered on April 9, 1865. Despite the Fifth Corps' prominent role in the victory, Sheridan accused Warren of being slow and negligent in his actions on the battlefield. Most damning of all, Sheridan indirectly accused Warren of cowardice. Widely regarded by friends and foes alike of extraordinary bravery in combat, Warren couldn't allow such a disparaging charge to stand. Immediately after the battle, the sketch artist Alfred Waud wrote in pencil on the back of one of his drawings, "Here Warren made his last charge, his horse shot under him . . . Sheridan came up and relieved Gen. Warren from command. Of course if this had not been done, Warren would have had the credit of the victory he had justly won. Sheridan and the ring he belongs to intends to grab all laurels no matter the cost of what injustice."[13]

Many years later, at a court of inquiry, Grant didn't seem to remember any of the important facts relating to the battle. Brigadier General Joshua Chamberlain, who led a brigade at Five Forks, wrote that the details of the battle provided by Grant "are so erroneous as to movements, their time and place and bearing on the result, that they would not be recognized as pertaining to that battle by anyone who was there."[14] For Grant, Warren's dismissal seemed to be more about what had happened in the past than anything that happened at Five Forks. Grant told a newspaper reporter, "I should have relieved Warren then [after the Crater fiasco in August 1864], but I did not like to injure an officer of so high rank for what was an error of judgment. But at Five Forks it was different. There was not time to think of rank or persons' feelings, and I told Sheridan to relieve Warren if he at all failed him. Sheridan did so, and no one regretted the necessity more than I did."[15]

Chamberlain believed "there was a variety of antagonism towards General Warren stored up and accumulating in General Sheridan's mind, and the tension of a heated moment brought the catastrophe."[16] Washington Roebling dated the conflict between Warren and Sheridan to the night march to Spotsylvania Court House. The logjam caused by Sheridan's troopers had prevented Warren's men from arriving at Spotsylvania Court House before Lee's troops. This led to a heated argument between Meade and Sheridan, who may have continued to hold a grudge against Warren. Roebling believed Grant behaved dishonorably toward Warren after Five Forks, "Grant himself has often acknowledged in private that it was all wrong, but never had the manhood to right the wrong."[17]

Warren never forgave Grant, who he believed had deliberately tried to disgrace him. During the court proceedings to clear his name, Warren wrote his wife, "The action of Grant and Sheridan wonderfully affected me. For the first time I realized the devil on earth. There is something dreadful in the realization when you find him in the highest places."[18] The Warren Court of Inquiry eventually absolved Warren of the worst of Sheridan's charges. Unfortunately, the court published its report after Warren's death.

At 6:00 P.M. on August 8, 1882, Gouverneur Warren died of complications associated with diabetes. His final words to his family were, "Convey me quietly to my grave without pageant or show. I die a disgraced soldier."[19] The loyal officer Carswell McClellan, who believed Grant had behaved horribly toward Warren, wrote of his death, "There was no waiting world without the door—only a weeping family gathered round—when Warren, the savior of Gettysburg, the hero of Mine Run, the victor of Five Forks, lay down to die, slain in the house of his friends!"[20] Warren's fellow corps commander Winfield Scott Hancock attended his funeral in Newport, Rhode Island. Congress eventually gave Warren's widow a generous pension of $50 per month. The bill was introduced by Congressman James "Jimmy" Wadsworth—James Samuel Wadsworth's youngest son, who served on Warren's staff at Five Forks. Warren had taken him on as a favor to Wadsworth's widow, who had expressed concerns to him about Jimmy joining the army after the death of his father.

❖

Ulysses S. Grant suffered dreadfully during the last year of his life. On June 2, 1884, while at his summer home at Long Branch, New Jersey, Grant bit into a peach, and experienced severe pain in his throat. He finally saw a doctor about it in October 1884, and learned he had cancer of the tongue. His excellent team of medical professionals could do little for him, besides treating his pain. They knew their famous patient had less than a year to live.

While stoically facing this grim prognosis, Grant began writing his memoirs. After his presidency, Grant had been a silent partner in a financial firm that went bust. One of his doctors stated that Grant's motives in writing his memoirs were "his desire to lift his family above the financial distress resulting from the failure of Grant and Ward."[21] In March 1885, Grant began the second volume of his memoirs that included the chapters on the Wilderness and Spotsylvania Court House. On some days, he could write an astonishing 10,000 words even though he had severe pain in his throat. On other days, he needed to take medication that made writing difficult or impossible. Grant wrote the section on the Battle of the Wilderness under extremely trying circumstances to say the least.

Grant's account of the battle was muddled at times. He stated that Warren's initial assault on May 5 met "with favorable though not decisive results." This clearly wasn't true. Grant had ordered Warren to attack before he was ready and the results were disastrous. Grant provided a disordered and inaccurate depiction of the fighting at the Plank Road on the second day at the Wilderness. At one point, he writes, "Hancock followed Hill's retreating forces, in the morning, a mile or more. He maintained this position until, along in the afternoon, Longstreet came upon him." Longstreet's men arrived, of course, at 6:00 A.M., and began pushing Hancock's troops back at that time. Later, Longstreet rolled up Hancock's left shortly after 11:00 A.M. Finally, Grant writes, "Our losses in the Wilderness were very severe. Those of the Confederates must have been even more so."[22] The Union actually suffered almost twice as many casualties as the Rebels during the battle. This is just a sample of Grant's somewhat loose command of the facts relating to the Wilderness. Most likely, Grant wrote his account of the Wilderness too quickly. His illness may have prevented him from examining all of the available source materials.

Grant rightly said that "More desperate fighting has not been witnessed on this continent than that of the 5th and 6th of May." But then he claimed it was a Union "victory" since he had been able to successfully cross the Rapidan River. It's difficult to maintain that the Battle of the Wilderness was a Union victory in any meaningful sense, though it did represent the beginning of almost constant hard fighting that ultimately defeated Lee's army in April 1865.

In Carswell McClellan's book *The Personal Memoirs and Military History of U.S. Grant versus the Record of the Army of the Potomac*, published in 1887, he challenged Grant's facts and interpretation of events during the final year of the war. He believed Grant and Sheridan tried to take all the credit for success in Virginia. Both men, McClellan believed, failed to understand the Army of the Potomac and its leaders. "The haunted jungle of the Wilderness, the hideous 'angle' at Spotsylvania, and the death-filled trenches at Cold Harbor," McClellan wrote, "attest that duty could ask no effort they would shrink from."[23]

Ulysses S. Grant died at Mount McGregor in Upstate New York at 8:08 A.M. on July 23, 1885, just days after putting the finishing touches on his memoirs. During his final weeks, he had lost his voice and weighed slightly over 100 pounds, down from roughly 200 pounds before his illness. President Grover Cleveland appointed Major General Winfield Scott Hancock, who played such a crucial role in the Wilderness, to oversee Grant's funeral in New York City. Sherman and Sheridan, along with Confederate Generals Joseph Johnston and Simon Buckner, were among the pallbearers at the funeral.

According to his doctor, Grant's mental and physical suffering during the final nine months of his life "could scarcely be imagined, and his fortitude in enduring the infliction could hardly be over-estimated."[24] Grant's suffering perhaps mirrored that of his men across the many Civil War battlefields from Fort Donelson to Shiloh to the Wilderness and later at Five Forks. The Union general-in-chief's military reputation has ebbed and flowed over the past 156 years. In the Wilderness, he made many mistakes. There was even a danger at midday on May 6 that his army would be routed. Hancock's men fell back and regrouped, however. And on the following evening, Major General Gouverneur Warren's Fifth Corps led the night march to Spotsylvania Court House. Grant and the Army of the Potomac didn't turn back until Lee's Army of Northern Virginia was defeated at Appomattox Court House eleven months later.

The Wilderness didn't result in a dramatic outcome like Zama or Waterloo,[25] but it did mark the beginning of the end of the Confederate States of America. It ended up taking even longer than "a long summer day," but Grant eventually triumphed over Lee.

ACKNOWLEDGEMENTS

Midway through the journey of our life, I found
myself in a dark wood, for I had strayed
from the straight pathway to this tangled ground.

So begins Dante's *The Divine Comedy*, the classic medieval poem that was often alluded to by the more literary soldiers during and after the Battle of the Wilderness. "Death scarce could be more bitter," Dante said of his journey through the *Inferno*. He nonetheless felt obligated to describe what he saw in order to draw "lessons of the good" that eventually came his way.

Dante's fiery Hell was a place of unimaginable horror and suffering. Just like the Wilderness.

The Battle of the Wilderness was one of the most traumatic events in American history. Fires broke out in the deep woods during the fighting and some wounded soldiers were burned alive. Many young men died alone in the forest.

In writing this book, I wanted to comprehend this trauma and discover what it meant to our country. Is it possible for a nation to forget something so horrific? My sense is that it is not, and I believe the ghosts of the Wilderness are still with us today, as our divided nation grapples with the legacy of the Civil War.

The Battle of the Wilderness interests me for other reasons as well. This was the first time Ulysses S. Grant faced Robert E. Lee in the field. It was one of those historic confrontations like the Duke of Wellington vs. Napoleon or Hannibal vs. Scipio Africanus. Later myths surrounding both Lee and Grant were partly rooted in the woods of the Wilderness. Grant would forever be remembered for heading south and continuing his march on Richmond despite the heavy losses during the battle. And the "Lee to the Rear" episode on day two of the fighting resonated with acolytes of the Confederate general in the decades after the war.

I've long been astonished and disturbed by the utter brutality of the Overland Campaign. The fighting descended into barbarism at times and the odds of surviving intact were very slim indeed. Yet, ordinary Union soldiers faced the danger and went about saving the Republic. Victory wasn't a foregone conclusion either. The Duke of Wellington's assessment of Waterloo seemed to apply equally to the Wilderness, it was "the nearest run thing you ever saw." I felt compelled to learn more about this pivotal event, and took from it more than I anticipated.

But I did not set out to write a purely military history of the battle. I wanted to also consider politics and medicine and how we commemorate fallen soldiers. Most of all, my aim was to closely examine the sacrifices and suffering of Civil War soldiers. Frederick Douglass's words—quoted in Chapter 14—inspired me from the very beginning, "We must never forget that victory to the rebellion meant death to the republic. We must never forget that the loyal soldiers who rest beneath this sod flung themselves between the nation and the nation's destroyers." This view is often ignored, but its importance cannot be overstated.

I am not related to Private William Reeves—at least, not that I know of. His humble, yet heroic story represented the experiences of tens of thousands of young men from all across America, who served in the Army of the Potomac at the beginning of the spring campaign in 1864. His tragic death epitomized the steep price that was paid for saving the Union.

Morris Schaff—a staff officer, who wrote *The Battle of the Wilderness* in 1910—served as my "Virgil" as I tried to learn what exactly happened in the woods. His account, along with narratives by Theodore Lyman, Andrew Humphreys, Edward Porter Alexander, and Moxley Sorrel, were extraordinarily helpful in providing me with accurate, first-hand descriptions of the fighting. Gordon Rhea's more recent book, *The Battle of the Wilderness, May 5-6, 1864*, was also invaluable for understanding "a confused tale about confusion."

As I began doing research for this project, I was lucky to be invited to participate in a staff ride at the Wilderness battlefield by retired U.S. Army Colonels Robert B. Killebrew and Greg Gardner. I quickly discovered it is essential to consider the battle from the perspective of professional soldiers, who understand the challenges of moving and supplying tens of thousands of troops through enemy territory. The staff ride was both an incredible learning experience and a fun outing. I'm glad they let me join them.

I'd also like to thank the archivists and librarians at the Library of Congress, National Archives, Historical Society of Pennsylvania, New York State Library, and the Fredericksburg and Spotsylvania National Military Park. I'm in awe of the generous and thoughtful assistance everyone provided me along the way.

For this book, I've been fortunate to have careful readers at every step of the way. My friend—and former English teacher—Andy Leddy cheerfully provided feedback on countless drafts of various chapters. And my old friend, Chris Solimine, assisted me with the storytelling, particularly at the beginning of the project. My brother-in-law, Dr. Christopher Veale, provided essential guidance on medical topics. Notably, I'm indebted to his advice on Private Reeves's injury.

I'm also exceedingly grateful for Pat Brady's thorough critique of a rough draft of the book. I met Pat during a talk I gave at the Puget Sound Civil War Roundtable and was impressed by his detailed knowledge of Civil War military history.

I'm very thankful for all of the assistance provided by my agent, Max Sinsheimer of Sinsheimer Literary. He believed in the project and helped make it better. It's been nice collaborating with someone who is passionate about books and understands the marketplace.

Working with Claiborne Hancock and his team at Pegasus Books has also been a pleasure. They are outstanding at what they do and I've appreciated their close attention to all of the details of the publishing process.

Writing a book is hard and I could never have completed this one without the love and support of my family. My children, Maxim and Sophie, patiently put up with my frequent monologues about the battle and what it all meant. Best of all, they have accepted the tradeoffs that come with having a writer for a father. I am especially thankful to my wife, Justine Kalas Reeves, who encouraged me to write this book. As a professional psychoanalyst, she recognized the importance of trying to come to terms with all the loss and trauma in those woods. I couldn't be more grateful for her understanding and advice.

Finally, I'd like to thank the late William Greider. I've been inspired by his extraordinarily successful writing career and his dedication to intellectual integrity. His interest in my own work meant a lot to me.

SELECTED BIBLIOGRAPHY

MANUSCRIPTS

Archives at Fredericksburg and Spotsylvania National Military Park
John Warwick Daniel family papers
Porter Farley typescripts
Theodore Lyman family papers
Washington Roebling journal

Historical Society of Pennsylvania
Andrew Atkinson Humphreys papers
George C. Meade collection

Library of Congress
Custis-Lee family papers
DeButts-Ely collection of Lee family papers
Montgomery C. Meigs papers
James Wadsworth family papers

National Archives and Records Administration, Washington, D.C.
Civil War and Later Veteran's Pension Index (1861–1934)
Records of the Adjutant General's Office (RG 94)
Records of the Office of the Quartermaster General (RG 92)

New York State Library
Uberto Adelbert Burnham papers, 1853–1928
Gouverneur Kemble Warren papers, 1848–1882

Yale University Library
Diary of Elihu Washburne

PERIODICALS

The Annals of War
The Century Illustrated Monthly Magazine
Daily Morning Chronicle
Harper's Weekly
New York Herald
The New York Times
New-York Tribune
Papers of the Military Historical Society of Massachusetts
Philadelphia Inquirer
Richmond Dispatch
Richmond Enquirer
Southern Historical Society Papers

PRINTED PRIMARY SOURCES

Agassiz, George, ed. *Meade's Headquarters, 1863–1865: Letters of Theodore Lyman from the Wilderness to Appomattox.* Boston: Atlantic Monthly Press, 1922.

Aldridge, Katherine, ed. *No Freedom Shrieker: The Civil War Letters of Union Soldier Charles Biddlecom.* Rochester, N.Y.: Paramount Books, 2011.

Alexander, E. P. *Military Memoirs of a Confederate.* New York: Charles Scribner's Sons, 1907.

Anderson, Captain John. *The Fifty-Seventh Regiment of Massachusetts Volunteers.* Boston: E. B. Stillings & Co., 1896.

Atkinson, Charles Francis. *Grant's Campaigns of 1864 and 1865.* London: Hugh Rees, 1908.

Battles and Leaders of the Civil War, Volume Four. New York: Century Company, 1884.

Benedict, G. G. *Vermont in the Civil War: A History, Volume 1.* Burlington, Vt.: The Free Press Association, 1886.

Brainard, Mary Genevie Green. *Campaigns of The One Hundred and Forty-Sixth Regiment.* New York: G. P. Putnam's Sons, 1915.

Brooks, Noah. *Washington in Lincoln's Time.* New York: The Century Co., 1895.

Badeau, Adam. *Grant in Peace from Appomattox to Mount McGregor.* Hartford, Conn.: S. S. Scranton, 1887.

———. *Military History of Ulysses S. Grant,* vol. 3. New York: D. Appleton and Co., 1867.

Burlingame, Michael, ed. *Civil War Dispatches of Noah Brooks.* Baltimore: The Johns Hopkins University Press, 1998.

Cadwallader, Sylvanus. *Three Years with Grant.* Benjamin Thomas, ed. Lincoln: University of Nebraska Press, 1955.

Caldwell, James Fitz James. *The History of a Brigade of South Carolinians.* Bedford, Mass.: Applewood Books, 1866.

Chamberlain, Joshua Lawrence. *The Passing of the Armies.* New York: G. P. Putnam's Sons, 1915.

Chamberlin, Thomas. *History of the One Hundred and Fiftieth Regiment.* Philadelphia: F. McManus Jr. & Co., 1905.

Clark, Rufus. *Heroes of Albany.* Albany, N.Y.: S. R. Gray, 1871.

Conover, George. *History of Ontario County.* Syracuse, N.Y.: D. Mason & Co., 1893.

Craft, David. *History of the One Hundred and Forty-First.* Towanda, Penn.: Reporter-Journal Printing Company, 1885.

Crotty, D. G. *Four Years Campaigning in the Army of the Potomac.* Grand Rapids, Mich.: Dygert Bros. & Co., 1874.

Dame, William Meade. *From the Rapidan to Richmond and the Spotsylvania Campaign.* Baltimore: Green-Lucas Company, 1920.

Dawes, Rufus. *Service with The Sixth Wisconsin Volunteers.* Marietta, Ohio: E. R. Alderman & Sons, 1890.

Dowdey, Clifford, and Louis H. Manarin, eds. *The Wartime Papers of R. E. Lee.* Boston: Little, Brown, 1961.

Early, Jubal Anderson. *Autobiographical Sketch and Narrative of the War Between the States.* Philadelphia: J. B. Lippincott, 1912.

Gallagher, Gary, ed. *Fighting for the Confederacy: The Personal Recollections of General Edward Porter Alexander.* Chapel Hill: The University of North Carolina Press, 1989.

Gordon, John Brown. *Reminiscences of the Civil War*. New York: Charles Scribner's Sons, 1904.

Grant, Ulysses S. *Personal Memoirs of U. S. Grant*. New York: Da Capo Press, 1982.

Hancock, Almira. *Reminiscences of Winfield Scott Hancock*. New York: Charles L. Webster & Company, 1887.

Hennessey, John J., ed. *Fighting with the Eighteenth Massachusetts: The Civil War Memoir of Thomas H. Mann*. Baton Rouge: Louisiana State University Press, 2000.

History of the 118th Pennsylvania Volunteers. Philadelphia: J. L. Smith, 1905.

History of the 121st Regiment Pennsylvania Volunteers. Philadelphia: Catholic Standard Times, 1906.

Houghton, Edwin B. *The Campaigns of the Seventeenth Maine*. Portland, Me.: Short & Loring, 1866.

Humphreys, Andrew. *The Virginia Campaign of '64 and '65*. Edison, N.J.: Castle Books, 1883.

Jones, J. William, ed. *Army of Northern Virginia Memorial Volume*. Richmond, Va.: J. W. Randolph & English, 1880.

———, ed. *Life and Letters of Robert E. Lee: Soldier and Man*. New York: Neale Publishing Company, 1906.

———, ed. *Personal Reminiscences, Anecdotes, and Letters of Gen. Robert E. Lee*. New York: D. Appleton and Company, 1867.

Judson, A. M. *History of the Eighty-Third Regiment Pennsylvania Volunteers*. Erie, Penn.: B.F.H. Lynn, 1881.

Keckley, Elizabeth. *Behind the Scenes, Or, Thirty Years a Slave and Four Years in the White House*. New York: G. W. Carleton & Co., 1868.

Longstreet, James. *From Manassas to Appomattox: Memoirs of the Civil War in America*. New York: J. B. Lippincott Company, 1896.

Lyman, Theodore. *Meade's Army: The Private Notebooks of Lt. Col. Theodore Lyman*. Kent, Ohio: Kent State University Press, 2007.

Marbaker, Thomas. *History of the Eleventh New Jersey Volunteers*. Trenton, N.J.: MacCrellish & Quigley, 1898.

McClellan, Carswell. *The Personal Memoirs and Military History of U. S. Grant versus The Record of the Army of the Potomac*. Boston: Houghton, Mifflin and Company, 1887.

Meade, George. *The Life and Letters of George Gordon Meade*, vol. 2. New York: Charles Scribner's Sons, 1913.

Miers, Earl Schenck, ed. *Wash Roebling's War*. Newark, Del.: The Curtis Paper Company, 1961.

Morrison, James, ed. *The Memoirs of Henry Heth*. Westport, Conn.: Greenwood Press, 1974.

Mulholland, St. Clair A. *The Story of the 116th Regiment Pennsylvania Infantry*. Philadelphia: F. McManus Jr. & Co., 1899.

Nash, Eugene. *A History of the Forty-Fourth Regiment*. Chicago: R. R. Donnelly & Sons Company, 1911.

Nevins, Allan, ed. *A Diary of a Battle: The Personal Journals of Colonel Charles S. Wainwright, 1861–1865*. New York: Harcourt & World, 1962.

Northrop, John Worrell. *Chronicles from the Diary of a War Prisoner in 1864*. Wichita, Kan.: Wining Printery, 1904.

Porter, Horace. *Campaigning with Grant*. Lincoln: University of Nebraska Press, 2000.

Powell, William. *The Fifth Army Corps*. New York: G. P. Putnam's Sons, 1896.

Reid, Whitelaw. *Ohio in the War, Volume 1*. Cincinnati: The Robert Clarke Company, 1895.

Robertson, James, ed. *The Civil War Letters of General Robert McAllister*. Baton Rouge: Louisiana State University Press, 1965.

Royall, William. *Some Reminiscences*. New York: The Neale Publishing Company, 1909.

Schaff, Morris. *The Battle of the Wilderness*. London: Forgotten Books, 1910.

Scott, Robert Garth. *Fallen Leaves: The Civil War Letters of Major Henry Livermore Abbott*. Kent, Ohio: The Kent University Press, 1991.

Simon, John Y. ed. *The Papers of Ulysses S. Grant*, vol. 15. Carbondale: Southern Illinois Press, 1967.

Smith, A. P. *History of the Seventy-Sixth Regiment New York Volunteers*. New York: J. P. Davis & Speer, 1867.

Sparks, David, ed. *Inside Lincoln's Army: The Diary of Marsena Rudolph Patrick*. London: T. Yossloff, 1964.

Sorrel, Gen. G. Moxley. *Recollections of a Confederate Staff Officer*. New York: The Neale Publishing Company, 1905.

Swinton, William. *Campaigns of the Army of the Potomac*. New York: Charles Scribner's Sons, 1882.

U.S. War Department. *War of the Rebellion, A Compilation of the Official Records of the Union and Confederate Armies*. 127 vols. Washington: Government Printing Office, 1880–1901.

U.S. Surgeon's Office. *The Medical and Surgical History of the War of the Rebellion.* 2 vols. Washington: Government Printing Office, 1870–1888.

Walker, Francis. *General Hancock.* New York: D. Appleton and Company, 1894.

———. *History of the Second Army Corps in the Army of the Potomac.* New York: Charles Scribner's Sons, 1886.

Weygant, Charles. *History of the One Hundred and Twenty-Fourth Regiment.* Newburgh, N.Y.: Journal Printing House, 1877.

Wilkeson, Frank. *Recollections of a Private Soldier in the Army of the Potomac.* New York: G. P. Putnam's Sons, 1897.

Wilson, James Harrison. *The Life of John Rawlins.* New York: The Neale Publishing Company, 1916.

———. *Under the Old Flag.* New York: D. Appleton, 1912.

Whitman, Walt. *The Wound Dresser.* Richard Bucke, ed. Boston: Small, Maynard & Company, 1898.

Youker, J. Clayton, ed. *The Military Memoirs of Captain Henry Cribben of the 140th Volunteers.* 1911.

SECONDARY WORKS

Adams, George Worthington. *Doctors in Blue: The Medical History of the Union Army in the Civil War.* Baton Rouge: Louisiana State University, 1980.

Carmichael, Peter. *The War for the Common Soldier.* Chapel Hill: The University of North Carolina Press, 2018.

Casdorph, Paul. *Confederate General R. S. Ewell: Robert E. Lee's Hesitant Commander.* Lexington: University Press of Kentucky, 2014.

Chernow, Ron. *Grant.* New York: Penguin Books, 2017.

———. *Washington: A Life.* New York: Penguin Books, 2010.

Decker, Karl, and Angus McSween. *Historic Arlington.* Washington: Decker & McSween, 1892.

Dowdey, Clifford. (1960) *Lee's Last Campaign.* Reprint. New York: Skyhorse Publishing, 2011.

Epler, Percy. *The Life of Clara Barton.* New York: The MacMillan Company, 1915.

Faust, Drew Gilpin. *This Republic of Suffering.* New York: Vintage, 2009.

Fellman, Michael. *The Making of Robert E. Lee.* New York: Random House, 2000.

Freeman, Douglas Southall. *R. E. Lee,* 4 vols. New York: Charles Scribner's Sons, 1934–37.

Furgurson, Ernest. *Chancellorsville 1863.* New York: Vintage Books, 1992.

Gallagher, Gary, ed. *The Spotsylvania Campaign*. Chapel Hill: University of North Carolina Press, 1998.

———, ed. *The Wilderness Campaign*. Chapel Hill: University of North Carolina Press, 1997.

Gallagher, Gary and Alan Nolan, eds. *The Myth of the Lost Cause and Civil War History*. Bloomington: Indiana University Press, 2010.

Garland, Hamlin. *Ulysses S. Grant: His Life and Character*. New York: Doubleday & McClure Co., 1898.

Geary, James. *We Need Men: The Union Draft in the Civil War*. DeKalb: Northern Illinois University Press, 1991.

Groeling, Meg. *The Aftermath of Battle*. El Dorado Hills, Calif.: Savas Beattie, 2015.

Hess, Earl. *The Rifle Musket in Civil War Combat*. Lawrence: University of Kansas Press, 2008.

Jordan, David. *"Happiness Is Not My Companion": The Life of General G. K. Warren*. Bloomington: Indiana University Press, 2001.

———. *Winfield Scott Hancock*. Bloomington: Indiana University Press, 1996.

Laderman, Gary. *The Sacred Remains: American Attitudes Toward Death, 1799–1883*. New Haven, Conn.: Yale University Press, 1996.

Mackowski, Chris. *Hell Itself: The Battle of the Wilderness, May 5–7, 1864*. El Dorado Hills, Calif.: Savas Beatie, 2016.

Mahood, Wayne. *General Wadsworth: The Life and Wars of Brevet Major General James S. Wadsworth*. New York: Hachette Books, 2009.

Marvel, William. *Burnside*. Chapel Hill: University of North Carolina Press, 1991.

Matthews, Richard. *The 149th Pennsylvania Volunteer Infantry Unit in the Civil War*. Jefferson, N.C.: McFarland Company, 1994.

McCarthy, Michael J. *Confederate Waterloo: The Battle of Five Forks, April 1, 1865*. El Dorado, Calif.: Savas Beatie, 2017.

McElya, Micki. *The Politics of Mourning: Death and Honor in Arlington National Cemetery*. Cambridge, Mass.: Harvard University Press, 2016.

McFeely, William. *Grant: A Biography*. New York: W. W. Norton, 1981.

McGaugh, Scott. *Surgeon in Blue: Jonathan Letterman, the Civil War Doctor Who Pioneered Battlefield Care*. New York: Arcade Publishing, 2013.

Melville, Herman. *The Battle-Pieces of Herman Melville*. Hennig Cohen, ed. New York: Thomas Yoseloff, 1963.

Miller, Richard. *Harvard's Civil War: A History of the Twentieth Massachusetts Volunteer Infantry*. Hanover, N. H.: University Press of New England, 2005.

Milliken, Charles. *A History of Ontario County, New York and Its People, Volume 2.* New York: Lewis Historical Publishing Co., 1911.

Murdock, Eugene Converse. *One Million Men: The Civil War Draft in the North.* Westport, Conn.: Greenwood Press, 1980.

Nelligan, Murray. "Old Arlington." PhD dissertation, Columbia University, 1954.

Nolan, Alan. *Lee Considered.* Chapel Hill: University of North Carolina Press, 1991.

Nolan, Alan and Sharon Eggleston Vipond. *Giants in Their Tall Black Hats.* Bloomington: Indiana University Press, 1998.

O'Harrow, Robert. *The Quartermaster: Montgomery C. Meigs, Lincoln's General, Master Builder.* New York: Simon & Schuster, 2016.

Pearson, Henry Greenleaf. *James Wadsworth of Geneseo.* New York: Charles Scribner Sons, 1913.

Poole, Robert. *On Hallowed Ground: The Story of Arlington National Cemetery.* New York: Walker & Company, 2009.

Power, J. Tracy. *Lee's Miserables: Life in the Army of Northern Virginia from the Wilderness to Appomattox.* Chapel Hill: University of North Carolina Press, 1998.

Pryor, Elizabeth Brown. *Reading the Man: A Portrait of Robert E. Lee Through His Private Letters.* New York: Penguin, 2007.

Ray, Frederic, ed. *Our Special Artist: Alfred R. Waud's Civil War.* London: Stackpole Books, 1994.

Reeves, John. *The Lost Indictment of Robert E. Lee.* Lanham, Md.: Rowman & Littlefield, 2018.

Rhea, Gordon. *The Battle for Spotsylvania Court House and the Road to Yellow Tavern.* Baton Rouge: Louisiana State University Press, 1997.

———. *The Battle of the Wilderness, May 5–6, 1864.* Baton Rouge: Louisiana State University Press, 1994.

Robertson, James. *General A. P. Hill: The Story of a Confederate Warrior.* New York: Vantage Books, 1992.

Scott, Robert Garth, ed. *Fallen Leaves: The Civil War Letters of Major Henry Livermore Abbott.* Kent, Ohio: The Kent University Press, 1991.

Sears, Stephen. *Chancellorsville.* New York: Houghton Mifflin, 1996.

———. *Gettysburg.* New York: HMH Books, 2004.

———. *Lincoln's Lieutenants: The High Command of the Army of the Potomac.* New York: Houghton Mifflin, 2017.

Simpson, Brooks. *Let Us Have Peace*. Chapel Hill: University of North Carolina Press, 1997.

———. *Ulysses S. Grant: Triumph Over Adversity*. New York: Houghton Mifflin, 2000.

Smith, Diane Monroe. *Command Conflicts in Grant's Overland Campaign*. Jefferson, N.C.: McFarland & Company, 2013.

Steere, Edward. *The Wilderness Campaign: The Meeting Between Grant and Lee*. Mechanicsburg, Penn.: Stackpole Books, 1960.

Stocker, Jeffrey, ed. *From Huntsville to Appomattox*. Knoxville: The University of Tennessee Press, 1996.

Thomas, Emory. *Robert E. Lee*. New York: W. W. Norton, 1995.

Trudeau, Noah Andre. *Bloody Roads South*. Baton Rouge: Louisiana State University Press, 2000.

Wert, Jeffry. *General James Longstreet*. New York: Simon & Schuster, 1993.

Young, Alfred. *Lee's Army During the Overland Campaign: A Numerical Study*. Baton Rouge: Louisiana State University Press, 2013.

Young, John Russell. *Around the World with General Grant, Volume Two*. New York: Subscription Book Department, 1879.

Zeller, Paul. *The Second Vermont Volunteer Infantry Regiment, 1861–1865*. Jefferson, N.C.: McFarland & Company, 2002.

ENDNOTES

ONE: THE GHOST OF STONEWALL JACKSON

1   Uberto Burnham to mother, April 21, 1864, *Uberto Burnham Papers*, New York State Library.

2   James Rice quoted in Rufus Clark, *Heroes of Albany* (Albany, N.Y.: S.R. Gray, 1867), 71.

3   Robert Garth Scott, ed., *Fallen Leaves: The Civil War Letters of Major Henry Livermore Abbott* (Kent, Ohio: The Kent State University Press, 1991), 241.

4   Katherine Aldridge, ed., *No Freedom Shrieker: The Civil War Letters of Union Soldier Charles Biddlecom* (Rochester, N.Y.: Paramount Books, 2011), 150.

5   Robert E. Lee to William Henry Fitzhugh Lee, April 24, 1864, *Papers of the Lee Family*, Lee Family Digital Archive.

6   Ulysses S. Grant, *Personal Memoirs of U. S. Grant* (New York: Da Capo Press, 1982), 391.

7   Ulysses S. Grant to Maj. Gen. H. W. Halleck, July 22, 1865, *U.S. War Department, The War of the Rebellion: Official Record of the Union and Confederate Armies* [hereinafter, *OR*], (Washington: U.S. Government Printing Office, 1880–1901), ser. I, vol. 36, part 1, 12.

8   *OR*, I, 36, (1), 13.

9   Horace Porter, *Campaigning with Grant* (Lincoln: University of Nebraska Press, 2000), 36–37.

10 Ulysses S. Grant to Julia Grant, May 2, 1864, John Simon, ed., *The Papers of Ulysses S. Grant*, vol. 10 (Carbondale: Southern Illinois Press, 1982), 394.

11 Abraham Lincoln to Ulysses S. Grant, April 30, 1864, *Collected Works of Abraham Lincoln*, vol. 7 (Ann Arbor: University of Michigan Digital Library, 2001), 325.

12 Whitelaw Reid, *Ohio in the War*, vol. 1 (Cincinnati, Ohio: The Robert Clarke Company, 1895), 354.

13 Porter, *Campaigning with Grant*, 14–15.

14   Porter, *Campaigning with Grant*, 14–15.

15   Richard Dana quoted in James Ford Rhodes, *History of the United States*, vol. 4 (New York: The MacMillan Company, 1906), 438.

16   William S. McFeely, *Grant: A Biography* (New York: W. W. Norton & Company, 1982), 159.

17   Joseph Allan Frank and George Reaves, *Raw Recruits and the Battle of Shiloh* (Carbondale: University of Illinois Press, 1989), 143.

18   Reid, *Ohio in the War*, 377–378.

19   Grant, *Personal Memoirs*, 186.

20   Andrew Humphreys, *The Virginia Campaign of '64 and '65* (Edison, N.J.: Castle Books, 1883), 14; see also *OR*, I, 33, 1036.

21   Allan Nevins, ed., *A Diary of Battle: The Personal Journals of Colonel Charles S. Wainwright, 1861–1865* (New York: Harcourt, Brace & World, 1962), 47.

22   *OR*, I, 36, (1), 277.

23   Noah Brooks, *Washington in Lincoln's Time* (New York: The Century Co., 1895), 57–58.

24   Morris Schaff, *The Battle of the Wilderness* (London: Forgotten Books, 1910), 84.

25   Porter, *Campaigning with Grant*, 42.

26   Schaff, *Wilderness*, 84.

27   Herman Melville, *The Armies of the Wilderness*, https://poets.org/poem/armies -wilderness.

28   John Worrell Northrop, *Chronicles from the Diary of a War Prisoner in 1864* (Wichita, Kan.: Wining Printery, 1904), 24.

29   Gouverneur Warren to Emily Warren, May 4, 1864, *Gouverneur Kemble Warren Papers*, New York State Library.

30   In a letter to Emily on May 1, 1864, he complained of not feeling well in late April, "having some neuralgic symptoms." *Warren Papers*.

31   Porter, *Campaigning with Grant*, 41–43.

32   Porter, *Campaigning with Grant*, 43.

33   Porter, *Campaigning with Grant*, 43–44.

34   Grant to Halleck, May 4, 1864, *OR*, I 36, (1), 1.

35   Porter, *Campaigning with Grant*, 44.

36   Grant to Burnside, May 4, 1864, *OR*, I, 36, (2), 380.

37   Lee quoted in J. Tracy Power, *Lee's Miserables: Life in the Army of Northern Virginia from the Wilderness to Appomattox* (Chapel Hill: The University of North Carolina Press, 1998), 7.

38   *Power, Lee's Miserables*, 2.

39   For an excellent discussion of Grant's and Meade's thinking on Lee's likely movements, see Gordon Rhea, *The Battle of the Wilderness, May 5–6, 1864* (Baton Rouge: Louisiana State University Press, 1994), 51–59.

40   Chris Mackowski, *Hell Itself: The Battle of the Wilderness, May 5–7, 1864* (Eldorado Hills, Calif.: Savas Beatie, 2016), 11.

41   Schaff, *Wilderness*, 58.

42   For the history and development of the Wilderness, see *Iron from the Wilderness: The History of Virginia's Catharine Furnace*, National Park Service, Human Resource Study, June 2011.

43   David Jordan, *"Happiness Is Not My Companion": The Life of General G. K. Warren* (Bloomington: Indiana University Press, 2001), 81.

44   Don Fehrenbacher and Virginia Fehrenbacher, eds., *Recollected Words of Abraham Lincoln* (Stanford, Calif.: Stanford University Press, 1996), 274.

45   Edwin B. Houghton, *The Campaigns of the Seventeenth Maine* (Portland, Me.: Short & Loring, 1866), 164–165.

46   James Robertson, ed., *The Civil War Letters of General Robert McAllister* (Baton Rouge: Louisiana State University Press, 1965), 415.

47   Robertson, *Civil War Letters*, 76.

48   Thomas Marbaker, *History of the Eleventh New Jersey Volunteers* (Trenton, N.J.: MacCrellish & Quigley, 1898), 70.

49   Schaff, *Wilderness*, 119–120.

50   Frank Wilkeson, *Recollections of a Private Soldier in the Army of the Potomac* (New York: G. P. Putnam's Sons, 1897), 30–31. Wilkeson purported to offer a firsthand account of the Battle of the Wilderness, though the historian William Marvel has challenged the accuracy of some of his claims.

51   Stephen Sears, *Chancellorsville* (New York: Houghton Mifflin, 1996), 120.

52   Stephen Sears, *Lincoln's Lieutenants: The High Command of the Army of the Potomac* (New York: Houghton Mifflin Harcourt, 2017), 506.

53   Ernest Furgurson, *Chancellorsville 1863* (New York: Vintage Books, 1992), 23.

54   Sears, *Lieutenants*, 522.

55   Jordan, *Life of Warren*, 330.

56   Sears, *Chancellorsville*, 504.

57   Robert E. Lee to his wife, May 11, 1863, Rev. J. William Jones, ed., *Personal Reminiscences of General Robert E. Lee*, (New York: Tom Doherty Associates, 2003), 139.

58   Power, *Lee's Miserables*, 9.

59   Charles Richardson, *Southern Generals: Who They Are and What They Have Done* (London: Sampson Low, Son & Marston, 1865), 149.

60   Michael Fellman, *The Making of Robert E. Lee* (Baltimore: The Johns Hopkins University Press, 2000), 11.

61   Gary Gallagher, ed., *Fighting for the Confederacy: The Personal Recollections of General Edward Porter Alexander* (Chapel Hill: The University of North Carolina Press, 1989), 91.

62   Clifford Dowdey, (1960) *Lee's Last Campaign* (Reprint, New York: Skyhorse Publishing, 2011), 62.

63   Nevins, *Diary of Battle*, 339.

64   Schaff, *Wilderness*, 48.

65   George Agassiz, ed., *Meade's Headquarters, 1863–1865. Letters of Theodore Lyman from The Wilderness to Appomattox* (Boston: Atlantic Monthly Press, 1922), 81.

66   Porter, *Campaigning*, 47.

67   Rhea, *Wilderness*, 26.

68   For an excellent discussion of the challenges faced by Lee, see Rhea, *Wilderness*, 25–29.

TWO: PRIVATE WILLIAM REEVES

1   A. P. Smith, *History of the Seventy-Sixth Regiment New York Volunteers* (New York: J. P. Davis & Speer, 1867), 248.

2   For casualties suffered by the 76th New York, see New York State Military Museum, April 6, 2007, https://dmna.ny.gov/historic/reghist/civil/infantry/76thInf/76thInfTable.htm.

3   We don't have any correspondence or journal entries relating to Private William Reeves. The details of his life and military service were obtained from various records at the National Archives. See Military Records for Private William Reeves, Record Group 94: Records of the Adjutant General's Office, Compiled Military Service Records for the 76th New York Infantry Regiment, National Archives. Also, Pension Application Files, Private William Reeves, Company C, 76th New York Infantry, National Archives.

4   Wilkeson, *Recollections*, 19–20.

5   Kati Singel "Mine Run Campaign," *Encyclopedia Virginia*, May 12, 2012, https://www.encyclopediavirginia.org/mine_run_campaign#start_entry.

6   Smith, *Seventy-Sixth*, 271.

7   George Conover, *History of Ontario Country* (Syracuse, N.Y.: D. Mason & Co., 1893), 122.

8   Stephen Crane, *The Red Badge of Courage* (New York: D. Appleton and Company, 1896), 30.

9   Aldridge, *Biddlecom*, 132.

10   Court-martial Order of Thomas Barton, Co. F, December 19, 1863, https://www.76nysv.us/76bartont.html.

11   Nevins, *Diary of Battle*, 279.

12   Eugene Converse Murdock, *One Million Men: The Civil War Draft in the North* (Westport, Conn.: Greenwood Press, 1980), 186.

13   Murdock, *One Million Men*, 187.

14   Wilkeson, *Recollections*, 11.

15   George Beniski, 76th NY Roster, https://76nysv.us/roster-b.html.

16   Beniski, 76th NY Roster.

17   See Murdock, *One Million Men*, 203–207.

18   Nevins, *Diary of Battle*, 266.

19   John J. Hennessey, ed., *Fighting with the Eighteenth Massachusetts: The Civil War Memoir of Thomas H. Mann* (Baton Rouge: Louisiana State University Press, 2000), 192.

20   James Geary, *We Need Men: The Union Draft in the Civil War* (DeKalb: Northern Illinois University Press, 1991), 67.

21   Murdock, *One Million Men*, 356.

22 For more on exemptions, see James Fry, *New York and the Conscription of 1863* (New York: G. P. Putnam's Sons, 1885), 71; Murdoch, *One Million Men*, 5.

23 "The Draft for Yates, Livingston and Ontario Counties," *New York Times*, August 1, 1863.

24 "Report on Deserters," *George G. Meade collection*, Historical Society of Pennsylvania.

25 "The Execution of Deserters," *Harper's Weekly*, September 26, 1863; Peter Carmichael, *The War for the Common Soldier* (Chapel Hill: The University of North Carolina Press, 2018), 198.

26 Wilkeson, *Recollections*, 21.

27 *New York Times*, August 29, 1863.

28 D. G. Crotty, *Four Years Campaigning in the Army of the Potomac* (Grand Rapids, Mich.: Dygert Bros. & Co., 1874), 123.

29 Abraham Lincoln to General Meade, August 27, 1863, John Nicolay and John Hay, eds., *Complete Works of Abraham Lincoln*, vol. 2 (The De Vienne Press, 1894), 401.

30 *New York Times*, August 29, 1863.

31 *Harper's Weekly*, September 26, 1863.

32 Crotty, *Four Years*, 123.

33 Smith, *Seventy-Sixth*, 261.

34 Smith, *Seventy-Sixth*, 261.

35 Aldridge, *Biddlecom*, 59.

36 Earl Schenck Miers, ed., *Wash Roebling's War* (Newark, Del.: The Curtis Paper Company, 1961), 29.

37 Grant, *Memoirs*, 414–415.

38 Smith, *Seventy-Sixth*, 281.

39 Northrop, *Chronicles*, 24.

40 *New York Times*, May 13, 1864.

THREE: CONFEDERATES ON THE TURNPIKE

1   Schaff, *Wilderness*, 125.

2   Rhea, *Wilderness*, 94–97.

3   Schaff, *Wilderness*, 126.

4   Schaff, *Wilderness*, 126; Rhea, *Wilderness*, 100.

5   Gouverneur Warren to Andrew Humphreys, May 5, 1864, *OR*, I, 36, (2), 413.

6   For an excellent account of the opening of the Battle of the Wilderness by a participant, see Lieutenant-Colonel William Swan, "Battle of the Wilderness," *Papers of The Military Historical Society of Massachusetts*, vol. 4. (Boston: The Military Historical Society of Massachusetts, 1905), 117–163.

7   Schaff, *Wilderness*, 146.

8   Rhea, *Wilderness*, 123–125.

9   Theodore Lyman quoted in Henry Greenleaf Pearson, *James Wadsworth of Geneseo* (New York: Charles Scribner Sons, 1913), 255.

10 Schaff, *Wilderness*, 128.

11   Grant to Meade, May 5, 1864, *OR*, I, 36 (2), 403.

12   Rhea, *Wilderness*, 131.

13   "Orders for May 5, 1864," *OR*, I, 36 (2), 371.

14   Schaff, *Wilderness*, 129.

15   Nevins, *Diary of Battle*, 339.

16   Schaff, *Wilderness*, 30.

17   Emerson Gifford Taylor, *Gouverneur Kemble Warren: The Life and Letters of an American Soldier, 1830–1882* (Boston: Houghton Mifflin Company, 1932), 141.

18   Gouverneur Warren to Emily Warren, December 25, 1862, *Warren Papers*.

19   Taylor, *Warren*, 90–91.

20   Taylor, *Warren*, 116.

21   Harry Pfanz, *Gettysburg: The Second Day* (Chapel Hill: The University of North Carolina Press, 1987), 201.

22   Josiah Granville Leach, ed., *The Journal of the Reverend Silas Constant* (Philadelphia: J. B. Lippincott Company, 1903), 457.

23   Taylor, *Warren*, 155.

24   General Alexander Hays to John B. McFadden, October 23, 1863, George Thornton Fleming, ed., *Life and Letters of General Alexander Hays* (Pittsburgh, Penn.: University of Pittsburgh, 1919), 506.

25   Aldridge, *Biddlecom*, 144.

26   Agassiz, *Meade's Headquarters*, 56.

27   George Gordon Meade, ed., *Life and Letters of General Meade*, vol. 2 (New York: Charles Scribner's Sons, 1913), 158.

28   Jordan, *Warren*, 116.

29   Taylor, *Warren*, 164.

30   Lieutenant Colonel John Gates, "Evolution of Entrenchments During the American Civil War" (Carlisle, Penn.: U.S. Army War College, 1991), 4.

31   Taylor, *Warren*, 164.

32   Meade to Grant, May 5, 1864, *OR*, I, 36 (2), 404.

33   Rhea makes a persuasive case that Grant exerted his authority over events at this time, *Wilderness*, 132.

34   *OR*, I, 36 (2), 420.

35   Mary Genevie Green Brainard, *Campaigns of The One Hundred and Forty-Sixth Regiment* (New York: G. P. Putnam's Sons, 1915), 187–188.

36   Rufus Dawes, *Service with The Sixth Wisconsin Volunteers* (Marietta, Ohio: E. R. Alderman & Sons, 1890), 259.

37   Warren to Charles H. Porter, November 21, 1875, *Warren Papers*.

38   Colonel Thomas Livermore, "Grant's Campaign Against Lee," *Papers of The Military Historical Society of Massachusetts*, vol. 4, 420.

39   William Swinton, *Campaigns of the Army of the Potomac* (New York: Charles Scribner's Sons, 1882), 440.

40   Swan, *Papers*, 129–130.

41   Roebling, *Roebling's War*, 23.

42   Schaff, *Wilderness*, 142.

43   Swan, *Papers*, 130.

44   Rhea, *Wilderness*, 150.

45   Earl Hess, *The Rifle Musket in Civil War Combat* (Lawrence: University of Kansas Press, 2008), 159.

46   Wilkeson, *Recollections*, 18.

47   In the language of the Civil War soldier, "seeing the elephant" meant experiencing combat.

FOUR: THE ELEPHANT APPEARS

1   Unsurprisingly, the documentation for the wounding of an obscure private like William Reeves is fragmentary and inconsistent. According to his military and medical records, two different dates—May 5 and 6—are given for when he was shot. Records kept by the 76th New York Infantry Regiment list May 5, 1864 as the date Reeves was wounded. The hospital, where Reeves arrived a week after his injury, recorded May 6 as the date. The evidence overwhelmingly supports the view he was wounded on the initial march into the woods during the early afternoon of May 5. His company suffered tremendously high casualties at that time and the survivors would have been able to receive timely medical treatment.

2   Surgeon General Joseph K. Barnes, United States Army, *The Medical and Surgical History of the War of the Rebellion.* (1861–65), Part 1, vol. 2 (Washington: Government Printing Office, 1870), 353.

3   For the medical topics in this chapter, I consulted with Dr. Christopher Veale, a retired physician with more than forty years of experience.

4   Wilkeson, *Recollections*, 100.

5   Report of Colonel J. William Hofmann, *OR*, I (1), 623.

6   Edward Steere, *The Wilderness Campaign: The Meeting Between Grant and Lee* (Mechanicsburg, Penn.: Stackpole Books, 1960), 170–171.

7   "Roebling's Report," *Warren Papers*; Rhea, *Wilderness*, 165.

8   See Wilkeson, *Recollections*, 33–44.

9   Wayne Mahood, *General Wadsworth: The Life and Wars of Brevet General James S. Wadsworth* (New York: Hachette Books, 2009), 231.

10   Agassiz, *Meade's Headquarters*, 101.

11   For an excellent account of the medical services at the Battle of the Wilderness, see Captain Louis Duncan, "The Medical Department of the Army in the Civil War, The Battle of the Wilderness," *The Military Surgeon*, vol. 30, April 1912, 370–396.

12   George Worthington Adams, *Doctors in Blue: The Medical History of the Union Army in the Civil War* (Baton Rouge: Louisiana State University, 1980), 73–76.

13   Captain Louis Duncan, "Pope's Virginia Campaign," *The Military Surgeon*, vol. 32, 23.

14   Duncan, "Pope's Virginia Campaign," 13.

15   See Scott McGaugh, *Surgeon in Blue: Jonathan Letterman, the Civil War Doctor Who Pioneered Battlefield Care* (New York: Arcade Publishing, 2013), passim; Adams, *Doctors in Blue*, passim.

16   Adams, *Doctors*, 111.

17   "Condition of the Army," *OR*, I, 36 (1), 217.

18   Walt Whitman, *The Wound Dresser*, Richard Bucke, ed. (Boston: Small, Maynard & Company, 1898), 38.

19   Schaff, *Wilderness*, 340.

20   Joseph Warren Keifer, *Slavery and Four Years of War*, vol. 4 (New York: G. P. Putnam's Sons), 86.

21   Schaff, *Wilderness*, 212.

22   "Case LXVIII," *Surgical Memoirs of the War of the Rebellion*, vol. 1 (Washington: Government Printing Office, 1870), 201.

23   Adams, *Doctors in Blue*, 117.

24   Clyde King, ed., *Mobilizing America's Resources for the War*, vol. LXXVIII, July 1918 (Philadelphia: American Academy of Political and Social Science, 1918), 14.

25   Crane, *The Red Badge of Courage*, 56.

26   Schaff, *Wilderness*, 161.

27   Smith, *Seventy-Sixth*, 284–292.

28   Northrop, *Chronicles*, 26–27.

29   Smith, *Seventy-Sixth*, 289.

30   Northrop, *Chronicles*, 30.

31   Northrop, *Chronicles*, 58.

32   This estimate is based on the author's calculations after having reviewed the regimental roster for the 76th New York.

33   Smith, *Seventy-Sixth*, 376.

34   Metcalfe quoted in *Documents of the Assembly of the State of New York*, vol. 10 (Albany, N.Y.: C. Van Benthuysen & Sons, 1867), 549–552.

35   Metcalfe quoted in *Documents of the Assembly*, 552.

FIVE: RAGING FIRE AT SAUNDERS FIELD

1   Theodore Lyman, *Meade's Army: The Private Notebooks of Lt. Col. Theodore Lyman* (Kent, Ohio: Kent State University Press, 2007), 134.

2   *History of the 121st Regiment Pennsylvania Volunteers* (Philadelphia: Catholic Standard and Times, 1906), 77.

3   Prince de Joinville, *The Army of the Potomac* (New York: Doubleday & Company, 1952), 279.

4   "Portrait of a General: General Roy Stone," *Highway History*, June 27, 2017, https://www.fhwa.dot.gov/infrastructure/stone02.cfm.

5   Richard Matthews, *The 149th Pennsylvania Volunteer Infantry Unit in the Civil War* (Jefferson, N.C.: McFarland Company, 1994), 135.

6   Sharon Eggleston Vipond, "A New Kind of Murder," *Giants in Their Tall Black Hats*, Alan T. Nolan and Sharon Eggleston Vipond, eds., (Bloomington: Indiana University Press, 1998), 126.

7   Report of General Cutler, *OR*, I, 36 (1), 611.

8   Pearson, *Wadsworth*, 263.

9   *OR*, I, 36 (1), 610.

10   Lance Herdegen, *How the Iron Brigade Won Its Name* (Bloomington: Indiana University Press, 2005), 37.

11   Vipond, "A New Kind of Murder," 128.

12   Schaff, *Wilderness*, 159.

13   William Powell, *The Fifth Army Corps* (New York: G. P. Putnam's Sons, 1896), 610.

14   Swan, *Wilderness*, 131.

15   Matthews, *The 149th*, 128.

16   Schaff, *Wilderness*, 159.

17   A. M. Judson, *History of the Eighty-Third Regiment Pennsylvania Volunteers* (Erie, Penn.: B.F.H. Lynn, 1881), 94.

18   *History of the 118th Pennsylvania Volunteers* (Philadelphia: J. L. Smith, 1905), 400.

19   *History of the 118th Pennsylvania Volunteers*, 401.

20   Rhea, *Wilderness*, 149–150.

21   Brainard, *Campaigns*, 190.

22   Brainard, *Campaigns*, 191.

23   Brainard, *Campaigns*, 192.

24   Brainard, *Campaigns*, 192.

25   Brainard, *Campaigns*, 194.

26   Brainard, *Campaigns*, 196-197.

27   Brainard, *Campaigns*, 197.

28   Diane Monroe Smith, *Command Conflicts in Grant's Overland Campaign* (Jefferson, N.C.: McFarland & Company, 2013), 112.

29   J. Clayton Youker, ed., *The Military Memoirs of Captain Henry Cribben of the140th Volunteers* (Privately printed, 1911), 60.

30   Agassiz, *Meade's Headquarters*, 91.

31   Lyman, *Private Notebooks*, 134.

32   "Journal of Maj. Gen. Warren," *OR*, I, 36 (1), 539–540.

33   Warren to Charles H. Porter, Nov. 21, 1875, *Warren Papers*; Jordan, *Warren*, 135.

34   Roebling, *Wash Roebling's War*, 23.

35   Grant, *Memoirs*, 403.

36   Swan, *Wilderness*, 130.

37   Swan, *Wilderness*, 134.

38   Brainard, *Campaigns*, 195.

39   Brainard, *Campaigns,* 195.

40   Brainard, *Campaigns,* 195.

41   Brainard, *Campaigns,* 195.

42   Schaff, *Wilderness*, 166.

43   Power, *Lee's Miserables*, 22.

44   Porter, *Campaigning with Grant*, 72–73.

45   Wilkeson, *Recollections*, 30.

46   Frederic Ray, ed., *Our Special Artist: Alfred R. Waud's Civil War* (London: Stackpole Books, 1994), 148.

47   Philip Omi, *Forest Fires* (Santa Barbara, Calif.: ABC-CLIO, 2005), 115.

48   Wilkeson, *Recollections*, 38.

49   Wilkeson, *Recollections*, 38.

50   Porter, *Campaigning with Grant*, 51.

51   Schaff, *Wilderness*, 168.

SIX: CONFEDERATES ON THE ORANGE PLANK ROAD

1   A. L. Long, ed., *Memoirs of Robert E. Lee* (London: Sampson, Low, Marston, Searle, and Rivington, 1886), 327.

2   A. L. Long, ed., *Memoirs of Robert E. Lee*, 327.

3   James Morrison, ed., *The Memoirs of Henry Heth* (Westport, Conn.: Greenwood Press, 1974), 182.

4   James Robertson, *General A. P. Hill: The Story of a Confederate Warrior* (New York: Vantage Books, 1992), 252.

5   Robertson, *General A. P. Hill*, 15.

6   Robertson, *General A. P. Hill*, 240.

7   Robertson, *General A. P. Hill*, 250.

8   Rhea, *Wilderness*, 115–117.

9   William Meade Dame, *From the Rapidan to Richmond and The Spotsylvania Campaign* (Baltimore: Green-Lucas Company, 1920), 78.

10   Pat Sullivan "The World According to Phenie Tapp," *Spotsylvania Memory*, September 27, 2014, http://spotsylvaniamemory.blogspot.com/2014/09/the-world-according-to-phenie-tapp.html.

11   General Hazard Stevens, "The Sixth Corps in the Wilderness," *Papers of The Military Historical Society of Massachusetts*, vol. 4. (Boston: The Military Historical Society of Massachusetts, 1905), 180.

12   Stevens, "The Sixth Corps in the Wilderness," 179.

13   Stevens, "The Sixth Corps in the Wilderness," 194.

14   Stevens, "The Sixth Corps in the Wilderness," 190.

15   Dowdey, *Lee's Last Campaign*, 117; William Royall, *Some Reminiscences* (New York: The Neale Publishing Company, 1909), 28.

16   Morrison, *Heth*, 182–183; Rhea, *Wilderness*, 194–195.

17   Rhea, *Wilderness*, 132.

18   Porter, *Campaigning with Grant*, 50.

19   Humphreys to Major-General Hancock, May 5, 1864, *OR*, I, 36, (2), 407.

20   Rhea, *Wilderness*, 187–193; Edward Steere, *The Wilderness Campaign*, 187–190.

21   Miers, *Wash Roebling's War*, 23.

22   Rhea, *Wilderness*, 190–191; Humphreys, *Virginia Campaign*, 29–33; Steere, *Wilderness*, 188–190.

23   General Francis Walker, *General Hancock* (New York: D. Appleton and Company, 1894), 139.

24   Stephen Sears, *Gettysburg* (New York: HMH Books, 2004), 400.

25   Almira Hancock, *Reminiscences of Winfield Scott Hancock* (New York: Charles L. Webster & Company, 1887), 101.

26   Humphreys to Major-General Hancock, May 5, 1864, *OR*, I, 36, (2), 409.

27   Humphreys to Major-General Hancock, May 5, 1864, *OR*, I, 36, (2), 410.

28   Rhea, *Wilderness*, 204.

29   Schaff, *Wilderness*, 184.

30   St. Clair A. Mulholland, *The Story of the 116th Regiment Pennsylvania Infantry* (Philadelphia: F. McManus, Jr. & Co., 1899), 176.

31   Mulholland, *The Story of the 116th*, 176.

32   "Reports of Maj. Gen. Winfield Scott Hancock," *OR*, I, 36, (1), 325.

33   Carol Reardon, "The Other Grant," *The Wilderness Campaign*, Gary Gallagher, ed., (Chapel Hill: University of North Carolina Press, 1997), 209.

34   Reardon, "The Other Grant," 209.

35   Schaff, *Wilderness*, 196.

36   Agassiz, *Meade's Headquarters*, 92.

37   Fleming, *Life and Letters*, 598.

38   Fleming, *Life and Letters*, 603.

39   Walker, *Hancock*, 166.

40   Alfred Hudson Guernsey and Henry Mills Alden, *Harper's Pictorial History of the Great Rebellion, Part 2* (New York: McDonnell Brothers, 1866), 628.

41   Wayne Mahood, *General Wadsworth: The Life and Times of Brevet Major General James Wadsworth* (New York: Da Capo Press, 2003), 233–234.

42   Mahood, *General Wadsworth*, 257.

43   Mahood, *General Wadsworth*, 3.

44   Mahood, *General Wadsworth*, 35.

45   Mahood, *General Wadsworth*, xii; Judith Hunter, "Abolition as Logical Conclusion: General James Wadsworth as a Case Study in Anti-Southern Sentiment and the Radicalizing Experience of the Civil War," *The Struggle for Equality*, Orville Vernon Burton, Jerald Podair, and Jennifer Weber, eds. (Charlottesville: University of Virginia Press, 2011), 33.

46   Pearson, *Wadsworth*, 154.

47   Pearson, *Wadsworth*, 63.

48   Nevins, *Diary of Battle*, 149.

49   Pearson, *Wadsworth*, 182.

50   Eugene Nash, *A History of the Forty-Fourth Regiment* (Chicago, Ill.: R. R. Donnelley & Sons Company, 1911), 27.

51   Nash, *A History of the Forty-Fourth*, 229.

52   Mahood, *Wadsworth*, 194–195.

53   Nevins, *Diary of Battle*, 260.

54   Mahood, *Wadsworth*, 58.

55   James Wadsworth to his wife, "May 3, 1864," *Wadsworth Family Papers*, Library of Congress.

56   Schaff, *Wilderness*, 198.

57   Matthews, *The 149th Pennsylvania*, 140–143.

58   Matthews, *The 149th Pennsylvania*, 143.

59   "Report of Capt. Frank Cowdrey," *OR*, I, 36, (1) 615.

60   Matthews, *The 149th Pennsylvania*, 143–144, 172; Steere, *Wilderness*, 241–242.

61   Matthews, *The 149th Pennsylvania*, 172.

62   Royall, *Some Reminiscences*, 29.

63   Royall, *Some Reminiscences*, 30.

64   Humphreys, *Virginia Campaign*, 33.

65   "Roebling's Report," *Warren Papers*.

66   Schaff, *Wilderness*, 198–199.

67   Humphreys, *Virginia Campaign*, 34.

68   "Diary of Elihu Washburne," Yale University Library.

69   Pearson, *Wadsworth*, 270.

70   General Wilcox, "Lee and Grant in the Wilderness," *The Annals of War* (Philadelphia: The Times Publishing Company, 1879), 494.

71   Dawes, *Sixth Wisconsin*, 261.

SEVEN: NIGHTTIME IN THE WILDERNESS

1   Power, *Lee's Miserables*, 22.

2   Schaff, *Wilderness*, 215.

3   *History of the Corn Exchange Regiment: 118th Pennsylvania Volunteers* (Philadelphia: J. L. Smith, 1888), 403.

4   G. G. Benedict, *Vermont in the Civil War: A History*, vol. 1 (Burlington, Vt.: The Free Press Association, 1886), 428.

5   Schaff, *Wilderness*, 209–210.

6   Schaff, *Wilderness*, 209–210.

7   Rhea, *Wilderness*, 246.

8   Agassiz, *Meade's Headquarters*, 147.

9   Power, *Lee's Miserables*, 22.

10   Wilkeson, *Recollections*, 34.

11   Walt Whitman, *The Collected Works of Walt Whitman*, Floyd Stovall, ed. (New York: New York University Press, 1963), 114–115.

12   Whitman, *Collected Works*, 49.

13   Whitman, *Collected Works*, 117.

14   Benedict, *Vermont in the Civil War*, 424, 428.

15   *OR*, I, 36, (1), 219.

16   Alexander Gardner, "Incidents of the War: A Harvest of Death," Library of Congress, https://www.loc.gov/static/collections/civil-war-glass-negatives/articles -and-essays/does-the-camera-ever-lie/the-case-of-confused-identity.html.

17   Smith, *Seventy-Sixth*, 290; "Letters of Corporal Albert Hilton," May 12, 2001, https://76nysv.us/76hiltonal.html.

18   A. B. Isham, "The Story of a Gunshot Wound," *Sketches of War History, 1861–1865*, vol. 4, W. H. Chamberlain, ed., (Cincinnati: The Robert Clarke Company, 1896), 434.

19   Schaff, *Wilderness*, 201.

20   Agassiz, *Meade's Headquarters*, 91.

21   Charles Francis Atkinson, *Grant's Campaigns of 1864 and 1865* (London: Hugh Rees, 1908), 164.

22   Gary Gallagher, ed., *Fighting for the Confederacy: The Personal Recollections of General Edward Porter Alexander* (Chapel Hill: The University of North Carolina Press, 1989), 354.

23   Grant, *Memoirs*, 181.

24   OR, I, 36, (2), 415.

25   Porter, *Campaigning*, 55.

26   Schaff, *Wilderness*, 225–226.

27   Meade to Grant, May 5, 1864, *OR*, I, 36, (1), 405.

28   Stevens, "The Sixth Corps in the Wilderness," 184.

29   Agassiz, *Meade's Headquarters*, 240.

30   "Roebling's Report," *Warren Papers*.

31   Schaff, *Wilderness*, 226–227.

32   Michael Burlingame, ed., *Civil War Dispatches of Noah Brooks* (Baltimore: The Johns Hopkins University Press, 1998), 107.

33   Bucke, *Wound Dresser*, 167.

34   Agassiz, *Meade's Headquarters*, 102.

35   *New York Times*, May 5, 1864.

36   *New York Times*, May 5, 1864.

37   James Longstreet, *From Manassas to Appomattox* (Philadelphia: J. B. Lippincott Company, 1903), 557.

38   Bishop O. P. Fitzgerald, *Judge Longstreet* (Nashville, Tenn.: Methodist Episcopal Church, 1891), 19.

39   Jeffry Wert, *General James Longstreet* (New York: Simon & Schuster, 1993), 200.

40   Gen. G. Moxley Sorrel, *Recollections of a Confederate Staff Officer* (New York: The Neale Publishing Company, 1905), 23–24.

41   Wert, *Longstreet*, 206.

42   Wert, *Longstreet*, 283.

43   *The Times Dispatch*, November 12, 1911.

44   Heth, *Memoirs*, 184.

45   Heth, *Memoirs*, 184.

46   Dowdey, *Lee's Last Campaign*, 125.

47 Captain Robert Monteith, "Battle of the Wilderness . . . ," *War Papers read before the Commandery of the State of Wisconsin*, vol. 1 (Milwaukee: Burdick, Armitage & Allen, 1891), 410.

48 Monteith, "Battle of the Wilderness," 413.

49 Warren to Wadsworth, *OR*, I 36, (2), 458.

50 *OR*, I 36, (2), 449.

EIGHT: LEE TO THE REAR

1 For an indispensable account of the "Lee to the Rear" episode, see Robert Krick, "'Lee to the Rear,' the Texans Cried," *The Wilderness Campaign*, 160–200.

2 Krick, "Lee to the Rear," 161.

3 Cadmus Wilcox, "Lee and Grant in the Wilderness," *The Annals of War*, Alexander Kelly McClure, ed., (Philadelphia: The Times Publishing Company, 1879), 494–496.

4 Agassiz, *Meade's Headquarters*, 94.

5 Rhea, *Wilderness*, 287.

6 Rhea, *Wilderness*, 289.

7 Krick, "Lee to the Rear," 168.

8 Krick, "Lee to the Rear," 168.

9 James Fitz James Caldwell, *The History of a Brigade of South Carolinians* (Bedford, Mass.: Applewood Books, 1866), 133.

10 Krick, "Lee to the Rear," 176.

11 Schaff, *Wilderness*, 249.

12 Gallagher, *Fighting for the Confederacy*, 1998.

13 John William Jones, *Army of Northern Virginia Memorial Volume* (Richmond, Va.: J. W. Randolph & English, 1880), 229.

14 Longstreet, *Memoirs*, 571.

15 "Address of Colonel C. S. Venable," *Southern Historical Society Papers*, vol. XIV, January to December, 1886, 525.

16 Dame, *From the Rapidan*, 85.

17 Royall, *Reminiscences*, 33.

18 "Reminiscences of the Campaign of 1864 in Virginia," General William Perry, *Southern Historical Society Papers*, vol. VII, February, 1879, 51.

19 Jeffrey Stocker, ed., *From Huntsville to Appomattox* (Knoxville: The University of Tennessee Press, 1996), 216.

20 Sorrel, *Recollections*, 240.

21 Sorrel, *Recollections*, 240.

22 Krick, "Lee to the Rear," 176.

23 Noah Andre Trudeau, *Bloody Roads South* (Baton Rouge: Louisiana State University Press, 2000), 92.

24 Krick, "Lee to the Rear," 167.

25 Royall, *Reminiscences*, 32.

26   "Address of Colonel C. S. Venable," *Southern Historical Society Papers*, 525.

27   See Krick, "Lee to the Rear," 175–185.

28   Gallagher, *Recollections*, 358.

29   "Narrative of Major-General C. W. Field," *Southern Historical Society Papers*, vol. XIV, January to December, 1886, 544.

30   Dame, *From the Rapidan*, 87.

31   Longstreet, *Memoirs*, 384.

32   Krick, "Lee to the Rear," 175–186.

33   Krick, "Lee to the Rear," 184.

34   *Unveiling and Dedication of Monument to Hood's Texas Brigade* (Houston: F. B. Chilton, 1911), 175.

35   Power, *Lee's Miserables*, 21.

36   Alfred Young, *Lee's Army During the Overland Campaign: A Numerical Study* (Baton Rouge: Louisiana State University Press, 2013), 254.

37   *New York Herald*, April 21, 1865.

38   Ron Chernow, *Washington: A Life* (New York: Penguin Books, 2010), 254.

39   Grant, *Memoirs*, 188–189.

NINE: HIGH NOON ON THE ORANGE PLANK ROAD

1   Schaff, *Wilderness*, 241.

2   Walker, *Second Corps*, 425–426.

3   Grant, *Memoirs*, 405.

4   Grant, *Memoirs*, 408.

5   "Hancock's report," *OR*, I, 36, (1), 325–326.

6   Schaff, *Wilderness*, 232.

7   Nevins, *Diary of Battle*, 352.

8   For a more favorable appraisal of Burnside in the Wilderness, see William Marvel, *Burnside* (Chapel Hill: University of North Carolina Press, 1991), 349–358.

9   Rawlins to Burnside, May 6, 1864, *OR*, I, 36, (2), 461.

10   Captain John Anderson, *The Fifty-Seventh Regiment of Massachusetts Volunteers* (Boston: E. B. Stillings & Co., 1896), 49.

11   Schaff, *Wilderness*, 247.

12   Francis Walker, "General Gibbon in the Second Corps," *Personal Recollections in the War of the Rebellion*, A. Noel Blake, ed., (New York: G. P. Putnam's Sons, 1897), 307–308.

13   *OR*, I, 36, (1), 325.

14   Pearson, *Wadsworth*, 276.

15   Pearson, *Wadsworth*, 276.

16   Schaff, *Wilderness*, 253.

17   Pearson, *Wadsworth*, 276.

18   Matthews, *The 149th Pennsylvania*, 147.

19   *OR*, I, 36, (2), 458.

20   Dame, *From the Rapidan*, 51.

21   Schaff, *Wilderness*, 253.

22   *OR*, I, 36, (1), 611.

23   Schaff, *Wilderness*, 236.

24   Schaff, *Wilderness*, 236.

25   Aldridge, *No Freedom Shrieker*, 150.

26   Cutler to Locke, May 7, 1864, OR, I, (2), 506.

27   David Sparks, ed., *Inside Lincoln's Army: The Diary of Marsena Rudolph Patrick* (London: T. Yossloff, 1964), 368.

28   Schaff, *Wilderness*, 236.

29   *Washburne's Diary*, May 6, 1864.

30   Swan, "The Wilderness Campaign," 146.

31   Swan, "The Wilderness Campaign," 149.

32   Anderson, *Fifty-Seventh Massachusetts*, 42.

33   Schaff, *Wilderness*, 258.

34   Pearson, *Wadsworth*, 281–282; Mahood, *Wadsworth*, 243.

35   Montieth, "Battle of the Wilderness," 414.

36   James Wadsworth to his wife, "May 3, 1864," *Wadsworth Family Papers*, Library of Congress.

37   Alexander Webb, "Through the Wilderness," *Battles and Leaders of the Civil War*, vol. 4 (New York: Century Company, 1884), 160.

38   Webb, "Through the Wilderness," 160.

39   Richard Miller, *Harvard's Civil War: A History of the Twentieth Massachusetts Volunteer Infantry* (Hanover, N.H.: University Press of New England, 2005), 338.

40   Miller, *Harvard's Civil War*, 338.

41   Miller, *Harvard's Civil War*, 340.

42   Lyman, *Meade's Army*, 140–141.

43   There were many conflicting reports surrounding the shooting of James Wadsworth. The narrative presented here is a composite of the varying accounts. Mahood, *Wadsworth*, 248–250; Smith, *Seventy-Sixth*, 291–292; Pearson, *Wadsworth*, 283–284.

44   Schaff, *Wilderness*, 271.

45   Dawes, *Sixth Wisconsin*, 262.

46   Anderson, *Fifty-Seventh Massachusetts*, 41.

47   Mahood, *Wadsworth*, 252.

48   Col. John Cheves Haskell, *The Haskell Memoirs* (New York: G. P. Putnam's Sons, 1960), 64.

49   Dowdey, *Lee's Last Campaign*, 122.

50   *In Memoriam James Samuel Wadsworth, 1807–1864* (Albany, N.Y.: J. B. Lyon, 1916), 117.

51   *New York Times*, July 20, 1864.

52   Lyman, *Meade's Army*, 138.

53   Patrick, *Inside Lincoln's Army*, 368.

54   *Washburne's Diary*, May 6, 1864.

55   Schaff, *Wilderness*, 273–274.

TEN: ROBERT E. LEE'S ENTICING OPPORTUNITY

1   Schaff, *Wilderness*, 273.

2   Sorrel, *Recollections*, 243.

3   Longstreet, *Memoirs*, 563.

4   "Kershaw's Report," *OR*, I, 36, (1), 1062.

5   Douglas Southall Freeman, *R. E. Lee: A Biography*, vol. 3 (Bloomington: Indiana University Press, 1934), 292–293.

6   Robert E. L. Krick, "Like a Duck on a June Bug: James Longstreet's Flank Attack," *The Wilderness Campaign*, 251.

7   E. P. Alexander, *Military Memoirs of a Confederate* (New York: Charles Scribner's Sons, 1907), 505.

8   Schaff, *Wilderness*, 267.

9   Sorrel, *Recollections*, 241–242.

10   "The Battle of the Wilderness," *Southern Historical Society*, vol. 20 (Richmond, Va.: 1892), 81.

11   Steere, *Wilderness*, 398.

12   "The Battle of the Wilderness," *SHS*, vol. 20, 86.

13   Longstreet, *Memoirs*, 564.

14   Trudeau, *Bloody Roads South*, 105.

15   Trudeau, *Bloody Roads South*, 566.

16   Sorrel, *Recollections*, 243.

17   Keith Bohannon, "Longstreet Reeled in his Saddle," *HistoryNet*, June 2017, https://www.historynet.com/longstreet-reeled-in-his-saddle.htm.

18   Schaff, *Wilderness*, 277.

19   Longstreet, *Memoirs*, 566.

20   Wert, *Longstreet*, 388.

21   Rhea, *Wilderness*, 373.

22   Sorrel, *Recollections*, 248.

23   John Turner, "The Battle of the Wilderness," *War Talks of Confederate Veterans* (Petersburg, Va.: Fenn & Owen Publishers, 1892), 104.

24   Schaff, *Wilderness*, 280.

25   Sorrel, *Recollections*, 245.

26   Longstreet, *Memoirs*, 565.

27   Sorrel, *Recollections*, 245.

28   *OR*, I, 36, (1), 323.

29   Schaff, *Wilderness*, 275.

30   Lyman, *Meade's Headquarters*, 96.

31   Porter, *Campaigning*, 61.

32   Lyman, *Meade's Headquarters*, 96.

33   *OR*, I, 36, (1), 324.

34   *OR*, I, 36, (1), 324.

35   *OR*, I, 36, (1), 324.

36   "Capturing the Wilderness's signature horror: fire," *Mysteries & Conundrums*, May 3, 2014, https://npsfrsp.wordpress.com/2014/05/03/capturing-the-wildernesss -signature-horror-fire/.

37   Thomas Chamberlin, *History of the One Hundred and Fiftieth Regiment* (Philadelphia: F. McManus, Jr. & Co., 1905), 212–213.

38   *OR*, I, 36, (1), 624.

39   Humphreys, *Virginia Campaign*, 48.

40   Schaff, *Wilderness*, 294.

41   David Jordan, *Winfield Scott Hancock* (Bloomington: Indiana University Press, 1996), 125; Rhea, *Wilderness*, 433.

42   "Washburne's Diary," May 6, 1864.

43   Lyman, *Meade's Army*, 140.

44   Swan, *Wilderness*, 144–145.

45   Porter Alexander, *Military Memoirs*, 507.

46   Gallagher, *Recollections*, 363.

47   Charles Weygant, *History of the One Hundred and Twenty-Fourth Regiment* (Newburgh, N.Y.: Journal Printing House, 1877), 297.

48   Longstreet, *Memoirs*, 567.

49   Gallagher, *Recollections*, 360.

50   William Swinton, *Campaigns of the Army of the Potomac* (New York: Charles B. Richardson, 1866), 434.

51   Freeman, *Lee*, v. 3, 327.

52   John Russell Young, *Around the World with General Grant*, vol. 2 (New York: The American News, 1879), 459.

53   Lyman, *Meade's Headquarters*, 100.

54   Lyman, *Meade's Headquarters*, 151.

ELEVEN: GRANT'S NIGHT MARCH

1   Porter, *Campaigning*, 71.

2   Porter, *Campaigning*, 59.

3   Porter, *Campaigning*, 63.

4   Adam Badeau, *Military History of Ulysses S. Grant*, vol. 2 (New York: D. Appleton and Company, 1881), 119–120.

5   Porter, *Campaigning*, 64.

6   Patrick, *Lincoln's Army*, 369.

7   James Harrison Wilson, *The Life of John Rawlins* (New York: The Neale Publishing Company, 1916), 378.

8   Lyman, *Meade's Army*, 153.

9   Jordan, *Warren*, 236.

10 "Washburne's Diary," May 6, 1864.

11 John Brown Gordon, *Reminiscences of the Civil War* (New York: Charles Scribner's Sons, 1903), 249.

12 Rhea, *Wilderness*, 417.

13 Gordon, *Reminiscences*, 252.

14 Rhea, *Wilderness*, 411.

15 Lyman, *Meade's Army*, 140.

16 Gordon, *Reminiscences*, 244.

17 "Memoranda of Conversations with General Robert E. Lee," William Allan, *Encyclopedia of Virginia*, January 31, 2018, https://www.encyclopediavirginia.org /Allan_Memoranda_of_Conversations_with_General_Robert_E_Lee_by _William_1868_1870.

18 *OR*, I, 36, (1), 1078.

19 Jubal Anderson Early, *Autobiographical Sketch and Narrative of the War Between the States* (Philadelphia: J. B. Lippincott, 1912), 350.

20 *OR*, I, 36, (2), 480.

21 William Styple, ed., *The Anderson Diaries & Memoirs of Charles Hopkins* (Kearny, N.J.: Belle Grove Publishing Co., 1988), 59.

22 Porter, *Campaigning*, 69–70.

23 James Harrison Wilson, *Under the Old Flag* (New York: D. Appleton, 1912), 399–403.

24 Taylor, *Warren*, 186.

25 *OR*, I, 36, (2), 480.

26 Agassiz, *Meade's Headquarters*, 102.

27 Miers, *Wash Roebling's War*, 23.

28 Grant, *Memoirs*, 408.

29 *OR*, I, 36, (2), 480.

30 *OR*, I, 36, (1), 219.

31 Grant, *Memoirs*, 185.

32 Porter, *Campaigning*, 71; Wilson, *Rawlins*, 216–217.

33 Meg Groeling, *The Aftermath of Battle* (El Dorado Hills, Calif.: Savas Beatie, 2015), 13.

34 Schaff, *Wilderness*, 326.

35 Sylvanus Cadwallader, *Three Years with Grant*, Benjamin P. Thomas, ed. (Lincoln: University of Nebraska Press, 1955), 180–182.

36 Whitelaw Reid, *Ohio in the War*, vol. 1 (Cincinnati: Moore, Wilstach & Baldwin, 1968), 413.

37 *OR*, I, 36, (1), 13.

38 *OR*, I, 36, (1), 13.

39 Hamlin Garland, *Ulysses S. Grant* (New York: The MacMillan Company, 1920), 127.

40 Nevins, *Diary of Battle*, 329.

41 Robert Garth Scott, *Fallen Leaves: The Civil War Letters of Major Henry Livermore Abbott* (Kent, Ohio: The Kent University Press), 241.

42   Henry Adams, *The Education of Henry Adams* (Boston: Houghton Mifflin Company, 1918), 264.

43   Badeau, *Military History*, 123.

44   *OR*, I, 36, (2), 481.

45   Wilson, *Rawlins*, 215.

46   Gordon Rhea, *The Battles for Spotsylvania Court House and the Road to Yellow Tavern* (Baton Rouge: Louisiana State University Press, 1997), 3.

47   Francis Fisher Browne, *The Every-Day Life of Abraham Lincoln* (Chicago, Ill.: Browne & Howell Company, 1913), 320.

48   For the Crapsey affair, see "George Meade collection," *Historical Society of Pennsylvania.*

49   "George Meade collection," *Historical Society of Pennsylvania.*

50   *History and Roster of Maryland Volunteers, War of 1861–5*, vol. 1 (Baltimore: Press of Guggenheimer, Weil & Co., 1898), 270.

51   Schaff, *Wilderness*, 344–345.

52   Porter, *Campaigning*, 79.

53   Badeau, *Military History*, 135.

54   Schaff, *Wilderness*, 341.

Twelve: "The Great Army of the Wounded"

1   Duncan, "Battle of the Wilderness," 20.

2   *OR*, I, 36, (1), 229.

3   Paul Zeller, *The Second Vermont Volunteer Infantry Regiment, 1861–1865* (Jefferson, N.C.: McFarland & Company, 2002), 186.

4   "Peter S. Chase in the Wilderness," *Brattleboro History*, http://brattleborohistory .com/war/peter-s-chase-in-the-wilderness.html.

5   Lyman, *Meade's Army*, 143.

6   *The Soldiers Aid* (Rochester, N.Y.), June 1, 1864.

7   For casualty figures see, *OR*, I, 36, (1), 119–133.

8   "Clara Barton," *Clara Barton: Missing Soldiers Office Museum*, September 18, 2018, https://www.clarabartonmuseum.org/firstaid/.

9   "Peter Chase in the Wilderness," *Brattleboro History*

10   "Peter Chase in the Wilderness," *Brattleboro History*

11   Bucke, *The Wound Dresser*, 187.

12   Percy Epler, *The Life of Clara Barton* (New York: The MacMillan Company, 1915), 93.

13   Gordon Rhea, *To the North Anna River* (Baton Rouge: Louisiana University Press, 2005), 373.

14   D. B. Steinman, *The Builders of the Bridge: The Story of John Roebling and his Son* (New York: Harcourt, Brace and Company, 1945), 262.

15   "Our Hospital Heroes," *Daily Morning Chronicle*, May 14, 1864.

16   Bucke, *The Wound Dresser*, 178.

17 Bucke, *The Wound Dresser*, 37.

18 Bucke, *The Wound Dresser*, 194.

19 Bucke, *The Wound Dresser*, 44.

20 Walt Whitman, *The Complete Prose Works of Walt Whitman*, vol. 1 (New York: G.P. Putnam's Sons, 1902), 136.

21 "Letter to Ralph Waldo Emerson, January 17, 1863," *The Vault at Pfaff's*, https ://pfaffs.web.lehigh.edu/node/56380.

22 John Lidell, *Surgical Memoirs of the War of the Rebellion*, vol. 1 (Washington: U.S. Printing Office, 1870), 203.

23 Lidell, *Surgical Memoirs*, 201–202.

24 "Reeves file," *National Archives*.

25 Bucke, *The Wound Dresser*, 184.

THIRTEEN: THE BLOODY ANGLE

1 Nash, *A History of the Forty-Fourth*, 224; Rufus Wheelwright Clark, *The Heroes of Albany* (Albany, N.Y.: S. R. Gray, Publisher, 1867), 84.

2 O. W. Norton, *Army Letters, 1861–1865* (Chicago: O. L. Deming, 1903), 280.

3 Clark, *The Heroes*, 81.

4 Nash, *A History of the Forty-Fourth*, 224.

5 Clark, *The Heroes*, 69.

6 Clark, *The Heroes*, 71.

7 Clark, *The Heroes*, 74.

8 Miers, *Wash Roebling's War*, 26.

9 Nevins, *Diary of Battle*, 356.

10 *Warren Papers*.

11 Jordan, *Warren*, 142.

12 *OR*, I, 36, (2), 540–541.

13 See William Matter, "Chapter Six," *If It Takes All Summer: The Battle of Spotsylvania* (Chapel Hill: University of North Carolina Press, 1988); Rhea, *Spotsylvania*, 86–87.

14 *OR*, I, 36, (2), 542.

15 Jordan, *Warren*, 148.

16 Nevins, *Diary of Battle*, 364.

17 Grant, *Memoirs*, 413–414.

18 Grant, *Memoirs*, 414.

19 *OR*, I, 36, (2), 663.

20 *OR*, I, 36, (2), 663.

21 *OR*, I, 36, (2), 668.

22 *OR*, I, 36, (2), 654.

23 Porter, *Campaigning*, 108.

24 Meade to Rawlins, June 21, 1864, *Meade Papers*. Meade eventually decided not to send the letter, perhaps after talking with Grant about it.

25 *New York Times*, May 18, 1864.

26   Augustus Alexander, *Grant as a Soldier* (St. Louis: 1887), 213.

27   Rhea, *Spotsylvania*, 253.

28   Power, *Lee's Miserables*, 32.

29   Ruth Silliker, ed., *The Rebel Yell & The Yankee Hurrah* (Camden, Me.: Down East Books, 1985), 157.

30   Power, *Lee's Miserables*, 30.

31   Francis Barlow, "Capture of the Salient," *Papers of the Military Historical Society of Massachusetts*, vol. 4 (Boston: Historical Society of Massachusetts, 1905), 247.

32   Lyman, *Meade's Army*, 153.

33   Barlow, "Capture of the Salient," 256.

34   Gordon, *Reminiscences*, 281.

35   Rhea, *Spotsylvania*, 249.

36   Barlow, "Capture of the Salient," 258.

37   Barlow, "Capture of the Salient," 254.

38   Agassiz, *Meade's Headquarters*, 114.

39   *OR*, I, 36, (2), 652.

40   *Meade Papers.*

41   Mulholland, *The Story of the 116th*, 213.

42   Rhea, *Spotsylvania*, 308.

43   David Craft, *History of the One Hundred and Forty-First* (Towanda, Penn.: Reporter-Journal Printing Company, 1885), 196.

44   Lyman, *Meade's Army*, 156.

45   Robert Krick, "An Insurmountable Barrier between the Army and Ruin," *The Spotsylvania Campaign*, Gary Gallagher, ed. (Chapel Hill: University of North Carolina Press, 1998), 109.

46   Alistair Horne, *The Price of Glory: Verdun 1916* (New York: Penguin, 1993), 174.

47   Robert Dunkerly, Donald Pfanz, and David Ruth, *No Turning Back* (El Dorado Hills, Calif.: Sava Beatie, 2014), 49.

48   Power, *Lee's Miserables*, 38.

49   Taylor, *Warren*, 186.

50   Miers, *Wash Roebling's Civil War*, 24.

51   Uberto Burnham to Parents, May 14, 1864, *Burnham Papers.*

FOURTEEN: ARLINGTON

1   *New York Times*, May 13, 1864.

2   *OR*, I, 36, (2), 654.

3   "Pvt. William Reeves files," National Archives.

4   Gary Laderman, *The Sacred Remains: American Attitudes Toward Death, 1799–1883* (New Haven, Conn.: Yale University Press, 1996), 113.

5   "Arlington Estate," Box 49, RG 92: Records of the Office of the Quartermaster General, Consolidated Correspondence Files, National Archives.

6   "Arlington Estate," National Archives.

7   John Reeves, *The Lost Indictment of Robert E. Lee* (Lanham, Md.: Rowman & Littlefield, 2018), 174–175.

8   Robert O'Harrow, *The Quartermaster: Montgomery C. Meigs, Lincoln's General* (New York: Simon & Schuster, 2016), 207.

9   O'Harrow, *The Quartermaster*, 207.

10   Elizabeth Brown Pryor, *Reading the Man: A Portrait of Robert E. Lee Through His Private Letters* (New York: Viking, 2007), 312.

11   Karl Decker and Angus McSween, *Historic Arlington* (Washington: 1892), 62–67.

12   Drew Gilpin Faust, *This Republic of Suffering* (New York: Vintage Books, 2008), 4.

13   "Jim Parks," *National Park Service*, August 7, 2020, https://www.nps.gov/arho/learn /historyculture/parks.htm.

14   "Arlington Estate," National Archives.

15   "Arlington Estate," National Archives.

16   Details about Reeves's burial from correspondence with Roderick Gainer, Chief Curator, Arlington National Cemetery.

17   "The Rambler," *The Evening Star*, August 17, 1912.

18   Thucydides, *The Peloponnesian War*, Steven Latimore, tr. (Indianapolis: Hackett Publishing, 1998), 95–96.

19   "Unknown Loyal Dead," Frederick Douglass, *Autobiographies* (New York: Library of America, 1994), 850–851.

20   "A District of Columbia Freedmen's Cemetery in Virginia? African-American Civilians Interred in Section 27 of Arlington National Cemetery, 1864–1867" http://www.freedmenscemetery.org/resources/documents/arlington-section27.pdf.

FIFTEEN: GEN. WADSWORTH'S BODY

1   Z. Boylston Adams, "In the Wilderness," *Civil War Papers Read Before the Commandery of Massachusetts*, vol. 2 (Boston: 1900), 389.

2   Adams, "In the Wilderness," 384.

3   Adams, "In the Wilderness," 390.

4   Adams, "In the Wilderness," 391.

5   Adams, "In the Wilderness," 391.

6   Adams, "In the Wilderness," 396.

7   Patrick McCracken to Mrs. General Wadsworth, May 9, 1864, *Documents of the Assembly of the State of New York, 85th Session* (Albany, N.Y.: 1865), 76–77.

8   Adams, "In the Wilderness," 398.

9   McCracken to Mrs. General Wadsworth, *Documents*, 76–77.

10   *Wadsworth Papers*, Library of Congress.

11   Michael Burlingame and John Turner Ettlinger, eds, *Inside Lincoln's White House: The Complete Civil War Diary of John Hay* (Carbondale, Ill.: Southern Illinois University Press, 1997), 196.

12   Mahood, *Wadsworth*, 251.

13   Mahood, *Wadsworth*, 190.

14   For details on obtaining Wadsworth's body, see *Wadsworth Papers*, Library of Congress.

15   Mahood, *Wadsworth*, 275–276.

16   *New York Times*, May 19, 1864.

17   *New York Times*, May 21, 1864.

18   *Wadsworth Papers*, Library of Congress.

19   John Motley to Mrs. Wadsworth, *Wadsworth Papers*, Library of Congress.

20   *New York Times*, May 21, 1864.

21   Warren to Mrs. Wadsworth, December 31, 1864, *Wadsworth Papers*, Library of Congress.

SIXTEEN: FATHERS AND SONS

1   Charles Milliken, *A History of Ontario County, New York and Its People*, vol. 2 (New York: Lewis Historical Publishing Co.), 147.

2   F. Scott Fitzgerald, *The Great Gatsby* (New York: Broadview Editions, 2007), 50.

3   Mrs. T. B. Hurlbut to Clara Barton, September 26, 1865, *Clara Barton, Missing Soldiers Office Museum*.

4   "Clara Barton's Missing Soldiers Office: 1865–1868," *Clara Barton, Missing Soldiers Office Museum*.

5   Michael Burlingame, *The Inner World of Abraham Lincoln* (Urbana: University of Illinois Press, 1994), 103.

6   Elizabeth Keckley, *Behind the Scenes, or, Thirty Years a Slave and Four Years in the White House* (New York: G. W. Carleton & Co., Publishers, 1868), 103.

7   For information on Willie Lincoln's death and funeral, see "William Wallace Lincoln," *Files of the Lincoln Financial Files Collection*, 1862.

8   O'Harrow, *Meigs*, 216.

9   O'Harrow, *Meigs*, 217.

10   O'Harrow, *Meigs*, 217.

11   Jordan, *Warren*, 286.

12   Michael J. McCarthy, *Confederate Waterloo: The Battle of Five Forks, April 1, 1865* (El Dorado Hills, Calif.: Savas Beatie, 2017), 102–103.

13   "Last Stand of Pickett's Men: Battle of Five Forks," Library of Congress.

14   Joshua Lawrence Chamberlain, *The Passing of the Armies* (New York: G. P. Putnam's Sons, 1915), 157.

15   Young, *Around the World*, 290.

16   Chamberlain, *Armies*, 176.

17   Miers, *Wash Roebling's War*, 32.

18   Warren to Emily, *Warren Papers*, 1881.

19   Jordan, *Warren*, 307.

20   Carswell McClellan, *The Personal Memoirs and Military History of U. S. Grant versus The Record of the Army of the Potomac* (Boston: Houghton, Mifflin and Company, 1887), 219.

21 George Shrady, "General Grant's Last Days," *The Century Illustrated Monthly Magazine*, vol. LXXVI, 1908, 105.

22 Grant, *Memoirs*, 403–408.

23 McClellan, *Army of the Potomac*, 43.

24 Shrady, "Last Days," 424.

25 The Battle of Zama was fought in 212 BCE between Hannibal and Publius Cornelius Scipio; The Battle of Waterloo featured Napoleon against the Duke of Wellington in 1815.

INDEX

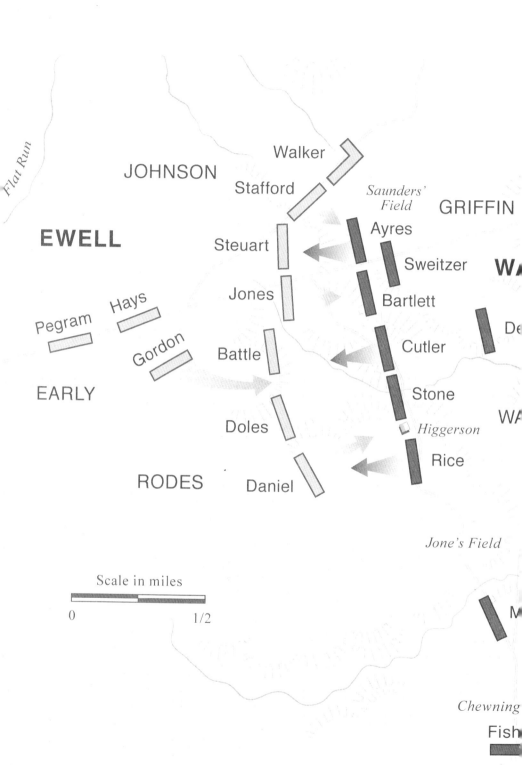

Flat Run

JOHNSON

Walker

Stafford

Saunders'
Field

GRIFFIN

EWELL

Ayres

Steuart

Sweitzer

WA

Hays

Jones

Bartlett

Pegram

Gordon

Cutler

De

EARLY

Battle

Stone

WA

Doles

Higgerson

Rice

RODES

Daniel

Jone's Field

Scale in miles

0   1/2

M

Chewning

Fish

George Skoch